Real South Pembrokeshire

Also in the Real Wales series
Editor: Peter Finch

Real Aberystwyth – Niall Griffiths
Real Bloomsbury – Nicholas Murray
Real Cardiff – Peter Finch
Real Cardiff Two – Peter Finch
Real Cardiff Three – Peter Finch
Real Liverpool – Niall Griffiths
Real Llanelli – Jon Gower
Real Merthyr – Mario Basini
Real Newport – Ann Drysdale
Real Swansea – Nigel Jenkins
Real Wales – Peter Finch
Real Wrexham – Grahame Davies

Real South Pembrokeshire

tony curtis

series editor: peter finch

SEREN

Seren is the book imprint of
Poetry Wales Press Ltd
Nolton Street, Bridgend, Wales

**Explore 30 years of good books at
www.serenbooks.com**

ISBN 978-1-85411-537-9

A CIP record for this title is available from the British Library

The publisher works with the financial assistance of the Welsh Books Council

Printed by Thomson Litho, Scotland

CONTENTS

SERIES EDITOR'S INTRODUCTION

Out west can time really be this slow? In this place where ufos still fly. Where the sky is full of light. Where the winds don't show on the national charts. Where the past still simmers. Where Wales begins and ends. The most beautiful place in the world.

I'm in the car again heading for Bosherston where the lily ponds look like Louisiana and saints stalk the cliff tops. The roads bend and turn, the fields roll like a billowing quilt, the blue sky runs to where Wales once went but is now drowned. Where the world ends. Sea flowing off the edge like it did when the earth was flat. That. Or if you don't believe then certainly flowing on unhindered until you get to America.

Down here at Stackpole where Haroldstones still stand the Normans came to establish a Barony. Stackpole Court, limestone hulk, the power behind the damned valleys that make the ponds. You can't see the great house, unless you hunt for it. It's hidden behind the rising trees.

Stackpole, named after the rock stack at the pwll, the mouth of Broadhaven, is not why I'm here. Nor is the jetty from which limestone was once shipped, nor the tourist café, which never seems to be open, hidden behind it. I'm here to walk the clifftop to Barafundle. A place that sounds like it comes straight from *Lord of the Rings*. I'm crossing the fields. Getting myself to one of Pembroke's most secret spots. So secret that this flawless spot was voted in 2004 the best beach in Britain. In 2006 it was designated *Country Life* magazine's UK top picnic spot. The Gorkys named one of their albums after it. Even the poet John Tripp, not known for his physical energy, got himself across two fields to gaze down at its perfectly formed sands.

Why come? Because it's there, amid the honey smell of the gorse and the pellucid light. A place at the end of the rainbow.

South Pembrokeshire, which is what this latest Real book is all about, has a reputation for being calmer that its wild counterpart, north of the Landsker. Easier to reach, civilised, places closer together, colonised earlier. The south, once Norman dominated, was the country Henry I turned into little England beyond Wales, land given to the Flemings, the process of Anglicisation begun, the Welsh tongue drained from the soil.

And it is calmer. The rain seems softer. The wind blows less.

There are more caravans. You meet kids with dogs and men with pipes far more often on the coastal path. Somehow the trails take less effort than they do around Solva or Dinas Head. At Barafundle, when I reach it, there's hardly anyone about. Winter. Sand cleaned by the pulling sea. Gulls whirling. It's a place just to gaze at. A total city antidote. A Pembrokeshire speciality.

In Haverfordwest, the only conurbation of any size in the entire county and even there feeling more like a village than a town and certainly never a city, I'd done the trail along the Cleddau, bought chips half way up the hill, trawled the market for second-hand CDs and checked in the Victoria Bookshop to see how *Real Wales* was doing. In the Bristol Trader the bar is full of men in Barbour jackets and dirty boots. Wales does not do cities. As a nation we have come to urbanity late, preferring the wind on the skin and the hand in the soil. These psychogeographies that track life in a built environment break new ground.

At the library where I am giving a poetry reading and talking to local creatives about the shape of the market and the way that culture is now changing like a demented traffic light there's a good crowd. Everyone sits in a circle like stones at the Gorsedd. No-one comes late, no one sleeps, there's only a single carrier bag fiddler and one woman with a flask. She drinks tea as I recite. You get the feeling that literature reaches here rarely but that's untrue. Giraldus Cambrensis came from Manorbier. The great Waldo Williams was born in Haverfordwest. The short-fictioneer Robert Nisbet lives here now.

But if anything it's the painters who have made the county. John Piper, Grahame Sutherland, John Knapp-Fisher, Brendan Burns, David Tress. Osi Rhys Osmond looking west from his home in Llanstephan. It's the light, they tell you. The shape of the cliff paths, the richness of the rocks, the way the landscape falls, the taste of the air.

In my youth I'd spent an age looking long at Sutherland's 'Entrance to a Lane' at the Tate in London. Sutherland painted this just before the Second World War. It 'paraphrases' a lane at Sandy Haven, west of Milford. I couldn't see it as more than an abstract swirl until eventually I visited the lane itself, or one very much like it, and saw the way that only Pembrokeshire has this combination of green and grey-green bent with gorse and infused with light.

Why wasn't this place filled with painters, I wondered. Go one hundred metres down any lane in the county today and you'll start to spot the signs. Gallery. Crafts. Exhibition. Artist's Studio Open Now. Admission Free. The painters have certainly now arrived.

My first Pembrokeshire visit was to Freshwater East, a place where my parents had taken me on holiday. It was my earliest memory of anything to do with the coast. I can just about recall being walked across sands, finding bladder wrack and pools and water draining in sheets into the sea. The county actually starts next door at Amroth, west of Carmarthenshire's land speed record beach at Pendine. The coast path heads west from here for 186 miles.

This is National Park territory. Designated because of its spectacular scenery in 1952, the park runs almost the entire length of the county's coast with only the industrialised sections around Milford and Pembroke Dock excluded. I didn't know this, of course, when I came here again in the sixties. This time it was on the back of a Vespa to stay at Saundersfoot, then a sort of Welsh Brighton where stand-offs threatened between mods and rockers and money was made by anyone selling drink. It's still the same today, in a way. Fewer stand offs. The warring factions morphed into Goths and Emos. More families. Same landscape pulling them in like a magnet.

Tony Curtis, himself Pembrokeshire bred and now again Pembrokeshire-based, has realised the same pull. He edited *The Poetry of Pembrokeshire* some twenty years ago and all his poetry collections have included poems set in the county. His *Real South Pembrokeshire* is filled with the recounted history, described landscape, quirk, reflection, joy and wonder that this place engenders. Its highly readable landscape described as only a poet can; the place perfectly celebrated.

What often amazes me on my trips around Wales is the number of people who have never been here. They imagine somehow that Pembrokeshire is somehow too far away to bother with, a land where things end, with little to recommend it bar basking seals. Site of the last invasion of Britain (by a raggle-taggle force of drunken French at Fishguard in 1797). The county where Dylan Thomas lost the manuscript to *Under Milk Wood.* Land of green and standing stone. Read on to discover how real south Pembrokeshire actually is. TC has done an excellent job.

Peter Finch

GOING BACK – GETTING THERE

"Look over there! See? The sky's clear already. Pembrokeshire." And then he'd stop the wipers as they scraped slowly over each half of the split screen, and I'd look across above the narrow road to the west up the hill at Llanteg past the garage on the left and the cross-roads and, yes, it had lighter clouds and the promise of blue. This is what you have done coming down from Carmarthen to Little England Beyond Wales and not bothering to cross the sea to Ireland, because why would you pass through this little heaven-haven and not stop?

And even if that blue were not 'enough to stitch a sailor's suit', it meant sun in the garden at 'Ashburnham', so I could escape the gloomy rooms of my Aunt Annie, who was a witch and didn't take to soft town boys that were spoilt and never knew what a day's work was or the right end of a spade and were squeamish of pecking hens and drowned water barrel rats floating like old socks in the wash. Or, more often and more anticipated, adventures over the fields at Pwllcrochan with my shotgun-toting cousins. Planting spuds or picking spuds. Hiding in the elderflower that sprawled at the side of the Old Rectory. Going down into the Rectory's cellar (pirates perhaps? Smugglers, more like) to watch my dad tinker with my Uncle Ivor's generator that ran the lights and the radio. Down the lane and into the rushes at the start of the little bridge to follow the stream to the pebbly beach with its crushed scallops and razor shells and squeaking bladder-wrack 'ooze of the sea' and the Haven clear and deep (the deepest natural harbour in Europe). And this was before the tankers and gas pipes and the Texaco refinery that would buy up Ivor's few acres and the Old Rectory and then bulldoze it for no earthly reason; so that there is nothing I can show you there. Except the little bridge at the end of the deep, dark musky-sweet lane, that little bridge to nowhere in particular but lakes of oil, and the rushes and the boot-crunching shells and the wide Haven with its tankers and the Irish ferry tall and off-white and the sheered edges of the fields with the Graham Sutherland roots and half-buried rocks.

You will have driven down west and over the western bridge, the new bridge over the Towy at Carmarthen, swinging west past the livestock mart in the fields to the left that was moved there some thirty years ago from the town, from behind the council house in

Pentrefelin Street where I was born, just, thanks to Nurse Evans who got me out feet first on Boxing Day 1946. Because the road misses Bancyfelyn where the boy who bought my second car died in it on a turn; missing St Clears where the blue boar rampaged and rampages still on Petersen's blue iron railings and Dylan drank, where the main street has two of the best butchers' shops in Wales (you choose) and where two years back Margaret turned and saw and pointed me to a magnificent heron priesting the Cynin, an unwitnessed river-lord, perched fish-watcher in the summer-shallows of the little river before lopping up and away toward Laugharne and the sea, spreading his black, grey and white surplice against the sky; always Dylan's heron, forever Dylan's Laugharne. And now, also, Margaret's heron. Wherever you travel, whenever you witness here and there and in Pembrokeshire, know that whatever the poets and singers and artists have recorded, these things are only preparations for your witness, your life. Travel on west and deeper go. Pack and fetch back such things, for there is enough for all of us.

But, this time, do not turn left at St Clears with its brown heritage sign for the Boat House. Drive on to Pembrokeshire through Llanddowror where my mother came to work in the Land Army in the war; where in the nineteenth century the Rev Williams took learning out into the hedgerows and started for the first recorded time 'education in the community'.

These twists of the woods are forty miles an hour slow, and slower when you are in a line of huge Irish lorries bound for Pembroke Dock and the Haven crossing to Rosslare. Resign yourself to the dank gloom and snaking double yellow lines, because you are almost there – out of the woods, straight over the Red Roses cross-roads, the sharp right bend and, no do not overtake, wait and then the straight that is never straight enough or long enough and anyway there is the county sign and you are into the next county, Pembrokeshire. Llanteg: something and nothing. And if you miss the sign you'll know it by the change of sky and the change of air. Now, whether this is to do with the western curve of the bay of Carmarthen away over the fields to your left and out of sight, the nudge and kiss of the Gulf Stream, or whether it is to do with the miles you have travelled and the needs you have brought with you, the weather and your mood will change and, as Dylan said in that over-milked wood ten miles behind you over your left shoulder, the weather 'turns around'. And though you may not know it, may not have known it when you set off, this is what will enfold you, insinuate itself, so that you will come back, time and time again. As I do now.

This book is my personal guide to south Pembrokeshire: it follows the series format in dealing with geographical areas and, within those, towns and villages with their castles and beaches, cliffs and industrial scars, inlets and islands, traders, artists and friends and characters from my past and present. For I came first to the western tip of our islands before I can remember, before the Coronation, before television, when we still had an Empire and when my mechanic father had to change the oil in our succession of cars every one thousand miles. Visits to my Aunt Annie the witch on Kingsmoor Common, Kilgetty, the Pembrokeshire Charmer, and my Uncle Ivor the school teacher and my cousins in Pwllcrochan. Pwllcrochan – a forgotten village and a forgotten inlet to the haven. Before the oil, before the tankers, before the power station and the destruction of farms and villages. Going down from Carmarthen I would sit or stand in the front seat with my mother and count the cars and salute the AA man on his motorcycle. Returning after these green and golden weekends I would fall asleep somewhere between Pembroke and St Clears until the Radio Luxembourg Top Ten Show arrived and would keep me awake the whole journey.

When I was thirteen we moved to live down there, near Kilgetty and Kingsmoor Common where Augustus John had first seen gypsies. I went to school at Greenhill in Tenby which a year later became a comprehensive school. I played rugby for Pembrokeshire Schoolboys and in my last year became deputy head boy. Now we live partly in Lydstep, three miles west of Tenby, in a bungalow and in the community in which my mother had been so happy in her last twenty years. Pembrokeshire has always been my county; my father insisted it be so. Our family, the Barrahs and Thomases, had lived in Rosemarket and Jeffreyston and other villages for centuries. They had worked the land and mined beneath it. As a poet and writer I have worked that land too.

SOUTH

TENBY

As you swing around the corner after New Hedges you get a glimpse and then a view of Caldey and the sea. And as you pass the town sign 'Tenby – Dinbych y Pysgod' that view will be a metallic-blue slice of the Tenby Roads and the promise of beaches, the finest and views across to Glamorgan, Lundy Island and the Atlantic. Remember, "You may travel the world over, but you will find nothing more beautiful."[1] Then it's down under the arches of the railway and up past the old Greenhill School and the town walls to the brutal concrete of the municipal car-park. This serves, with its stifling ugliness, only to heighten the pleasures of the town and beaches which await.

Or you may arrive at Tenby station on the line down from Carmarthen and the rest of the world. By this route you will have changed from the 125 at Swansea, given up notions of speed and enjoyed that spectacular coastal run around the eastern side of Carmarthen Bay; stopped at Ferryside and enjoyed the view of Llanstephan Castle across the estuary of the river Towy. The transition from Carmarthenshire to Pembrokeshire is lush and green, with glimpses and echoes of Fern Hill's poetry, though Dylan's Laugharne, Sir John's Hill and the racing sands of Pendine will have been seawards to the south and to your left.

The GWR – God's Wonderful Railway – conceived by Isambard Kingdom Brunel to run from Paddington to Neyland and the deep waters of Milford Haven, which gave access to Ireland – also opened up south Pembrokeshire as the railway had opened up Cornwall in the nineteenth century and introduced the Georgian splendours of Tenby to the greater British public. The amazingly successful coal-owner David Davies, later Lord Davies of Llandinam,[2] was responsible for the line which branches south from Whitland to Pembroke Dock; it was commerce and industry which incidentally brought holiday makers to the area. From the 1870s significant numbers of visitors arrived to stay at the newly established hotels – the Coburg, the Clarence and the Cawdor; Tenby as a popular resort was born. The station now has a faded presence, the frequency of trains and the volume of passengers hardy justifying the platform's size and length. But modern Tenby is here as it is because of the railways, not the motor car. Tenby doesn't welcome cars within its walls and the sooner you park yours in the aforementioned concrete bunker the better.

Take in the Gothicky station's character; then, turning immediately left out of the station yard you'll encounter the offices of the local newspaper *The Tenby Observer* and opposite those offices what remains of the garage of George Ace & Sons. What are now flats were, even in my time, still the premises of Ace the pioneer cyclist and car enthusiast. The Tenby cycling club is still called the Tenby Aces.

Following the railway line westwards you come to the steep lane which leads to the golf club, established in 1888 and the oldest in Wales.[3] On the corner is the unusually situated Quarry House, the sunken garden of which is the small limestone quarry, which its new owners have developed as a fine garden. The wall is low enough for you to look over and imagine a childhood afternoon in that magical spot. The main quarry remains are behind what is now the practice area of the golf club itself.

Further along Queen's Parade live two of the most notable[4] Welsh artists of their generation. Gwilym Pritchard and Claudia Williams have lived, off and on, in the town for a number of years following their return from living in France – Provence and Brittany – for almost two decades. Now in their eighties, they seem settled in that terraced late Victorian house with its three storeys of long, narrow rooms. While I am waiting for the tea to brew Gwilym takes me up

to his studio on the third floor; skylights give views directly in a line due west down over the golf club and the first and eighteen fairways to Black Rock and the headland beyond. He is working for an exhibition at the Martin Tinney Gallery in Cardiff where he and Claudia have shown for a number of years and there are four or five works in various stages of completion. There is a preponderance of yellow: "It brings out the blue so well when I paint over yellow," he explains. Certainly, since settling down here Gwilym has characterised the landscape, specifically the coastline of south Pembrokeshire and the aspects of the town and its sea at Tenby, as vibrant in its summer colours. It is as if he has brought a Brittany eye to appreciate the pastel colours of the Tenby townhouses and the same green sea which excited Monet off Finistere.

Claudia has invited me to see her new, her first, lithograph from the Curwen Press in Cambridgeshire. The Curwen has been the most significant art press of the second half of the twentieth century and she is excited by the work and the experience of working with the master printmaker Stanley Jones.[5] 'The Bather' is a two-colour litho, blue and green – in an edition of fifty. A bikini-wearing woman is towelling herself dry at the beach. A man swims and a surfer is glimpsed over the left shoulder. The curves of her body, the towel's flow and the sea's surge combine in a matrix of arabesques.

Claudia has made the Tenby beach scenes her own: parents and children at play and picnic. Tenby's four beaches, especially the South Beach and Castle Sands, feature strongly in her mature work. While Gwilym's landscapes are often battered by the vigour of the sea, Claudia's explore the coast as playground. People re-introduced to their bodies interact.

There are three main roads in Tenby itself: High Street, The Parade and Frog Street (Upper and Lower). High Street begins at the ruins of the Gate House Hotel and its flattened space. If you can pull your gaze away from the stunning North Beach and eastern coast views at the corner of White Lion Street, walk down High Street towards the shops, taking particular note of the County Clothes shop which is, in fact, the Prize House re-constructed from the Great Exhibition of 1851. It's worth going in, if only for the details of the building itself; there are fine rose-entwined plaster cornices and two curved stained-glass alcoves.

Mr Abbot who is fitting new curtains at our house in Lydstep contracts for T.P. Hughes, for whom he worked full time at one point. There's not the trade to give a full time employment, though T.P. Hughes has kept going as a tidy department store in a small town (they once had branches in both Carmarthen and Haverfordwest). Mr Abbot and his wife run two children's clothes shops in Saundersfoot and Tenby. I ask him what sort of season they have; it's pretty much the same as for everyone – six months and a long winter, though few ever admit to having had a good season down here – the tax man might get wind of it. One of his suppliers is a man at my tennis club in Barry. Wales is a small country.

T.P. Hughes, which fronts on to High Street and stretches back to both sides of Upper Frog Street, is an institution in Tenby and was opened in 1903. As you come down the stairs from the curtain and bedding section there's a fascinating selection of historical photographs of the Hughes family and their staff. This is a family firm proud of its trading history.

Further down High Street, opposite St Mary's church is a small record shop with basket stands of knock down CDs – 'Jazz', 'Blues', 'Rhythm and Blues'. Not your usual music store, then. I go in to ask about a Julie London CD I'd requested some three weeks back. It's in and I'm remembered: because this is Laurie Dale's shop, one of last small independents left in the country.

I'd been reminded of Julie London by a BBC Four programme in the winter. Laurie knew her work. Of course. Her remarkable voice had given her a recording career that stretched almost twenty years from the mid-1950s. And then she'd walked away from music to star in a medical soap opera. But 'Cry Me a River' was hers and hers alone. Oh, and she looked as devastatingly gorgeous as Sophia Loren. But Laurie Dale knows all this before I do. He is Australian-born and tanned like a career beach boy. While we talk about Tenby he plays his own self-cut CD of the Great American Songbook – like Michelle Pfeiffer in *The Fabulous Baker Boys*, he can 'carry a tune'. Laurie and his shop are a Tenby fixture. Laurie's son, Charles, is the third outstanding actor to come from Greenhill School, after Kenneth Griffith and Clive Merrison. A remarkably early drama training followed by the RSC touring the world and the West End before *Coronation Street*, *The Bill* and other tv series that mean he has several houses in addition to the one in Tenby and a soap-cult following. Above Laurie's head behind the counter is a poster advertising Laurie himself in a one-man play about Augustus John, written by the former curator of Tenby Museum, John Beynon. The acting gene is passed on, clearly. It's for one Friday evening performance, and I realise that we are not going to be down that day. But there will be others, just as one cannot imagine Tenby High Street without those baskets of bargain blues and Laurie's beard behind the counter. After all, he's a mere eighty-one.

The church of St Mary's is one of the finest in the country. Richly endowed and well maintained, it is the town's focal point, especially the fifteenth century spire – the most striking landmark for miles, and its jewel – and until the 1830s it was set in, fixed to rows of cottages. In 2010 it celebrated the appointment of Gerald of Wales as its priest in 1210. John Harrison, son of Wilfred Harrison my history master at Greenhill and the curator of the town's museum, is the organist, fully supported by St Mary's. Under its wagon roof light streams into this stunning church, over the 1634 pulpit and the bleached pews. There are notable memorials, including the wonderful polychrome Jacobean commemoration (opposite) of Margaret Mercer, who died in childbirth in 1610. Her husband kneels above her in prayer with her seven surviving children below her.

Others range from Robert Recorde (1510-1558)[6], the famous Elizabethan scholar who invented the equals sign, to Peggy Davies who was 'seized with apoplexy' whilst bathing in 1809. And Roger Lort, whose larger memorial in the church of St James and Elidyr at Stackpole, 1613, rivals the Mercer memorial in its artistry, but is a little stiffer in its portraiture.

Of the stained glass windows I am drawn to that by Karl Parsons, an Arts and Crafts style memorial to the fallen of the Great War. As you enter and leave you pass the damaged but poignant tomb with cadaver: St Mary's is a cool, quiet refuge from the bustle of the seaside town's crowded streets; both in the church and its memorial gardens to the rear, there is a salutary depth.

Spot Tenby's Blue Plaques: George Eliot overlooking the harbour; Nelson and the Hamiltons in St Julian Street; Augustus John, on the Esplanade, Beatrix Potter (who visited Tenby in 1900 and stayed in Croft Terrace where she sketched the pond and incorporated it in *The Tale of Peter Rabbit*). There's also the strange and child-scaring skull on the wall to the right of Crackwell Street just up the hill from the George Eliot plaque. This is over the left of two green circular metal doors set in to the side of the cliff at the rear of the Father Thomas garden. It is the site of the town's mortuary, though it was used as an artist's studio in the 1960s.

FRESHWEST SURFER DUDES IN DESIGN

Tenby can be taken for a sleepy backwater out of season, but as well as artists like Gwilym Pritchard, Claudia Williams and Naomi Tydeman, there are two new, young artist-designers in the town who are literally making waves all year round. Their workspace is centred at Wallsfield Lane and their inspired designs, in furniture, lamps and plates, are travelling the world to growing acclaim.

Marcus Beck and Simon Macro are self-styled surfer dudes whose designs are, appropriately labelled as 'Freshwest'. You'll find their work marketed by MOOOi, the Dutch design from with a strong Milan base. Their exhibitions have included the Milan Furniture Fair, Moooi Gallery, Amsterdam, London Design Week and Liberty's in London. Commissions include Oriel Myrddin Gallery in Carmarthen, where their strong yet apparently delicate wooden bench won an open competition. They have private clients in New York, Milan, Dubai, Hong Kong and London and won an *Elle* Decoration Design Award in 2007. Marcus and Simon were featured in an exhibition at the Glynn Vivian Gallery in 2009 alongside two sculptors. It's that sort of work, functional but, like the best of contemporary design, visually provocative and witty.

For example, 'Contemplates' is a set of eight white dinner plates on sale through Liberty's on each of which is a figure and shadow of a person on a beach. These are taken from over two hundred random photographs from a year in Pembrokeshire. Each plate has the beach location, date and time on the reverse. You eat off the event.

Their 'For Two Hours Only Fruit Bowl' was cast from Tenby's north beach and is a fruit bowl which has been moulded out fibre glass resin and sand from a sand formation left by waves. Again, the date and time are printed underneath, together with a map reference. These everyday utile objects are referencing land art – think Richard Long and Andy Goldsworthy – and are beautiful forms in themselves. In a sophisticated, high-street wise fashion, Marcus and Simon are taking Pembrokeshire to the world. Making waves.

Their inside-out bathroom and drinks cabinets in an aluminium composite are simple and so obvious you wonder why no-one's done it before – Patrick Caulfield inspired, apparently simplistic designs of what those pieces contain.

The flat-pack dining table is from locally sourced fallen oak and is assembled using a mallet and pegs; the mallet fitting underneath the completed table for future use. As with 'The Duke' table there are clear Pembrokeshire inspirations. The Duke is a surf-board topped occasional table named after the legendary surfer Duke Kahanamoku, made from Pembrokeshire ash and cherry in combination with a darker wood found washed up on Freshwater West. It's a surfer dude's dream piece of furniture.

'Pool Table' is an acrylic piece, 122 x 90 cms, with a diving board at one end. It shimmers like water, is playful and a talking point. As with their 'Brave New World Coffee Table', Marcus and Simon want tables to be both utile and the expression of a room which pulls visitors out of the ordinary.

So where does this genius come from? And why Tenby? Well Simon is a graduate of Brighton and Marcus from MMU. They were boyhood friends and set up their design and production unit in Tenby in 2005. I visited them on a dull September day: their wall chart was full of scribbles and ideas which lifted the spirit.

WALKING FROG STREET

The oddly named Frog Street (so good they named it twice) is in fact two streets that cross St Georges Street and are distinguished by being named Lower Frog Street and Upper Frog Street. Most people will begin at the north end and enter from White Lion Street. On the left is the rear of the White Lion Hotel and on the right, just after Fecci's café is the De Valence Hall. This is named after one of the Norman power brokers of thirteenth century Pembrokeshire; William De Valence was half-brother to King Henry III and became, among other things, the Earl of Pembroke. He and his wife Joan bestowed upon the town of Tenby much generosity: its "first charter of liberties, free common yearly upon all his grounds and meadows...and, the report goes, he gave the glebe, until now is pertaining to the parsonage, out of his lands there... and Joan, his wife, built the hospital of St John near Tenby."[7] On her death in 1307 it was recorded that she "held *in capite* in that town twenty acres of land worth one shilling per acre, a windmill and a water mill, six burgages, twenty quit rents, prise of ale toll and perquisities of court."[8]

The De Valence has undergone several manifestations as a public resource.[9] In Edwardian times it was developed as an enclosed

garden for walking, with shelters and the security of the ancient town walls. In the last decade it has been revamped by the council, being now the building housing the council's chambers, but also a dance hall and performance venue for music and theatre.[10]

The Parade/St Florence Parade, the main road that passes outside the walls leading to the Esplanade and the multi-storey car park would have been a moat protecting the earthwork defences of the town. There were originally seven towers; of course, Five Arches is the iconic monument to this. The arch next to the Imperial Hotel at the sea end of the South Parade was cut through in the nineteenth century and the hotel grafted on to the ancient walls at the height of the railway tourist boom of the second half of the century with a gusto which would have caused a major political controversy in our time.[11] Lower Frog Street ends just past Frogmore Villas at this point and you can walk to the right through the Imperial arch towards the Torquay-esque Esplanade and its large hotels.

In White Lion Street you will find the White Lion Street Gallery, an eclectic gallery run by two painters and former teachers, Margaret Welsh and John Faulkner. They also run an annual art competition and attract some serious artists. The gallery has two floors with a selection of work by some notable and collectable artists – the potters Simon Rich of Narberth and Barbara Lock and Mick Morgan of Cardiff, sculptor Perrin Butler and painters Elizabeth Haines and Andrew Douglas Forbes, for example. Andrew is a remarkable man. At the Tenby Festival[12] in 2008 we attended a concert of tenor arias in St John's Methodist Church followed by an exhibition of new works at the gallery – both by Andrew Duncan Forbes. He lives in Llandeilo and in Italy and paints and performs in both. We bought his 'Manorbier, Pink Bag' from that show and it hangs in our front room in Lydstep. The works featuring couples or groups on the beach, houses in the country, catch suggestive moments at Tenby, on the Gower and in Ceredigion with titles that direct you to what you may not have seen at first: 'Saundersfoot Dog Walkers', 'Lime Green Coat', 'Shadowy Fisherman'.

Of course the ancient walls of the town curve from White Lion Street to the Parade and on to the Five Arches. As I write, at the end of White Lion Street, just past the Tenby Playhouse cinema is a building site of regrettable ugliness. This was the site of one of the oldest and grandest of Tenby hotels, The Royal Gate House. This fifty-nine room hotel was set alight in March 2008 and two men were subsequently charged with arson. In truth, it was a place of faded glory and will in due course, no doubt be replaced by flats and, perhaps, a newer cinema. Both properties are owned by the Fry family for whom I worked one school summer holiday collecting the money from visitors to the St Catherine's Island zoo. The 'zoo' was a pathetic affair consisting of, as far as I can remember, a couple of monkeys, a parrot and any mice who could swim. The job had less purpose and a shorter life than most vacation jobs. The Pembrokeshire National Park Authority have rejected several plans for redevelopment and there is perhaps a back story to the whole sorry saga. This could be as costly as *Titanic* and run for longer than *The Sound Of Music...*

In truth, I can only remember going in The Royal Gatehouse a couple of times: both involved meetings with actors. I had a drink with Clive Merrison around 1989 when I was launching my anthology *The Poetry of Pembrokeshire.*[13]

Back at the start of Upper Frog Street the Coach and Horses, on the right, claims to be the oldest public house within the town walls. And there certainly seems to have been some hostelry thereabouts for hundreds of years. It also claims to be the pub where Dylan Thomas left a manuscript of *Under Milk Wood*, rushing back to retrieve it before flying off to the States and its first performance in the USA in 1953. This claim is blazoned outside on the signs and features on the bar menu, but when I questioned the barman, he seemed to know little, "I've only been here two years." I recall that my old Maths teacher, Bill Davies told me of the occasion when Dylan did read or 'perform' the play to the Tenby Arts Club, possibly a world premiere, but the Coach and Horses's claim that Dylan was holed up there for days drinking, was unconfirmed. I have read my work for the Club several times in the years following my leaving university and establishing myself as a poet and on each occasion the Dylan story was told. What I am certain of is that Dylan would not have stayed for any length of time in the present establishment with its loud piped music (some sort of rap crap) and a video of a Lily Allen festival gig which had no soundtrack and was bizarrely out of synch with the unrelated piped music. Coach and Horses? More like the Rap and Carrot. In common with most pubs: to be avoided.

The estate agent's office a little way further down was a coffee haunt of my teenage and undergraduate days in the late Sixties, called The Koolibah. It had an Australian theme before themes had been invented – white-washed walls decorated with Aboriginal-ish painting and wicker chairs and tables. Then there is Brychan Court (see p.22). Go in and look to the left and see on the wall a horse plaque; attractive, but much later than the arch of 1807, the mews itself and even later than the association with significant twentieth century winners at the races. This court and several other double doors in Lower Frog Street are the clearest reminder that this was for most of its existence a horse powered town with houses and inns needing stables. Brychan Court has particularly important horse associations, for the family had two Grand National winners in the 1920s. The Shaun Spadah Tearooms is named after them.

A few yards further down, just past the Air Wales Ambulance charity shop there's the only direct lane cutting through to the walls and the Parade. To the left is the Audrey Bull antique(ish) shop and then (thank goodness) the only Oirish bar in Tenby. Across from that arch, on the Parade, notice the nineteenth century fire insurance plaque. Did that mean that the fire crew went to you faster? Or, if you did not have a plaque, did they bother to come at all?[14]

Back on Frog Street, across to the left is the rear entrance to the Market Hall, which was built in 1829 on the site of an outdoor market. Originally comprising an open space with protecting walls, the market acquired its first floor in 1861 and this held the court

room and town hall. The first thing that will strike you is the thirty-two foot by eight foot mural across the south side of the space. It depicts notable aspects of the town's history and is by the artist Eric Bradforth who was born in 1920 and who worked as an artist for the Royal Artillery for many years. The mural includes the arrival of the railway, the maritime trade and the swimming of cattle over to Caldey Island. Here are Augustus John and Gwen John and Nelson and Harry Truman wearing his international rugby cap. We see *The Tenby Observer* and its role in winning the freedom of the press; Bradforth's 'Tenby 1856' painting is in the Tenby Museum collection and is a useful imaginative tool in assessing the development of the town.[15]

Recommended are the fish counter and Braun the butcher (you couldn't make it up). Herr Braun first came to Pembrokeshire as a cook with the German Army – known always locally as 'the Panzers' – in the 1980s. Under a NATO agreement the German tanks used the Castlemartin Range for firing practice.[16] Mr Braun stayed on and now sells excellent meat, some of it sourced from an organic farm near St Florence.

In the summer of 2009, after an absence of many years, I visited the clubhouse of Tenby Rugby Club, situated opposite Church House in Frog Street. I wanted to watch an early evening mid-week match from the British Lions tour of South Africa. It was a high-scoring romp which in no way prepared the Lions for the brutal, gloves-off first test in Durban. The club is dark and rather seedy. There's the standard line of photographs of capped Tenby men on the walls – including several I knew and played with – Jim Shanklin, Barrie Llewellyn and my friend Mervyn 'Jim' John – and numerous photographs going back to the 1890s. In the 1924/5 season Tenby United won the Llanelly Rugby Football League. There's Harry Truman, the first Tenby player to play for Wales, his jersey in a glass case and that of his grandson who played for the Welsh Students in 1990. I check the list of captains and see that my teacher Arthur Booker had that honour in 1949, not long after being de-mobbed.[17] But the clubhouse seems to mirror the state of the team itself. Tenby Rugby Club plays on Heywood Lane, just past the comprehensive school on the west side of town. You pass it through a squeezed part of the lane, a rat run via the Serpentine Road, avoiding the Arches of the Green, as you head west towards Penally and Pembroke.

I played a few games for the club in the middle Sixties between sixth form and university: some for the seconds and once only for a 'first' mid-week team against the Pembrokeshire Police. And I did turn out a couple of times for the 'Exiles' against Tenby United in the run-off-the-turkey-and-pud Boxing Day game. I remember a regular full back called Owen Morse who seemed like an Ancient Mariner of the game – he played into his forties apparently – and my friend Jim John propping me ("the 'ooker from Carmarthen") in the front row. The ooze of mud, dubbin leather grease being worked into the boots and their stitching and the high perfume of Wintergreen in the dank and dark changing room.[18] We played one of the seven county matches in the year I represented Pembrokeshire at Schoolboy level at Heywood Lane, and lost, as we did all but one of our fixtures that season. Pembrokeshire is a small county in terms of population and we were usually well outgunned by districts like Carmarthen and the Swansea Schools. Jim hadn't touched a rugby ball until the summer of 1961 and yet had a Schoolboys Welsh trial before that Christmas. He was still learning the rules, but was built like a young ox and would enter the shambles that were mauls in those days and emerge the other side with the ball, leaving a splatter of opposing forwards in his wake. In due course he graduated into the back row and I flirted with the notion that I might be a centre. He went on to London Welsh, then a county cup with one of the teams in Surrey. I discovered that I needed glasses and contacts had not been invented, so finished my career with a couple of games for Winnington Park VI (or was it VIII?) in Cheshire and a game for the staff v pupils at Maltby Grammar in 1973.

Sport is an education though, and without that county cap I would not have been encouraged to throw myself into school completely and eventually pass some exams.[19] My first experience of a coal mine came about through Tenby United Seconds, though. We had a fixture against one of the Rhondda Valley teams, probably an early morning game before going on up to Cardiff for an international. We changed and showered in the pit-head baths at that site. For that game I had wangled my way out of the front row and into the centre. "The bloke you're marking played once for Wales", they warned me. I weighed him up at the kick-off – old, very old, probably thirty-something – I had his measure. Probably no more than a social run out in the twilight of his playing years. About ten minutes in they won a scrum just inside our half and the ball reached him. I lined him up and closed for the tackle. It was like a large intake of air, and that's about all I clutched at. He left me for dead and gave a scoring pass to the wing. I never saw him or laid a hand on him for the next hour. The muscles get tired and slack, real life takes over from games, but class doesn't really go away, does it?[20]

The photo of the Welsh international Jim Shanklin with whom I played in my last year in Greenhill in the 1964/5 season takes me back. I was in the third year sixth and a regular first team player. He was a rangy, blonde runner of a centre, all hair and legs, difficult to stop. Jim went up to London for work and played for London Welsh before being capped four times, between 1970 and 1973, in the golden era of Welsh rugby – Phil, Gerald, Gareth and JPR. There were no tactical substitutes allowed in those days and he was picked when Gerald Davies or one of the others was injured. He scored a try against Ireland in a victory at Cardiff. Of course, his son Tom has been a regular centre for Wales in recent years.

We were taught by Denzil Thomas whose own single cap had been against Ireland in 1954 when he'd dropped the winning goal at Lansdowne Road.[21] It was said that when Denzil came down as head of games at Greenhill he was approached by Tenby United to dust off his boots and play for them. When he asked "What's to be in the boot?" he was met with a blank stare. Amateurs for top clubs like Neath and Llanelli, for whom Denzil had played, were always left a five pound note or two in a player's boots after the game. Tenby had to do without the former international.

That was the problem with Tenby United at the beginning of the professional era; they became over ambitious and though that they could attract on-the-cusp-of-past-it players to pull them into a premier division. It all went pear-shaped and Tenby, as I write, are languishing in a lowly Division Four West in the Welsh league system. So, a team formed in 1901 when the Swifts and Harlequins joined forces has sunk to a level when, at the end of the 2007/8 season they could not raise fifteen players for an away game. Next time I go to the clubhouse perhaps I should take my boots. And the Wintergreen for my dodgy knees.

Just below the United pitch on the back road to Penally on Clickett's Field is Tenby AFC, the soccer club, which seems to be more thriving. There has always been a vibrant, well-supported network and league system for both soccer and cricket: small villages such as Monkton, Lamphey and Manorbier have soccer teams, while Cresselly is a cricketing village which has hosted a Glamorgan county game.[22] Heywood Lane now has rugby pitches for Greenhill

School and the junior school, but in the years before and just after the war there were also tennis courts there and top players from Wimbledon would appear. When I first moved to the area there were courts in what is now a caravan park on the road leading to the Green from the Norton. Later, in my last year in school I persuaded the games mistress, Penny Hilling, to let us run a boys team alongside the girls. We played a handful of matches, including one against my old school in Carmarthen on what had been the Queen Elizabeth Grammar School site. I don't think it lasted long after our year had left and the town seems bereft of tennis since the hotel court on the Parade has been turned into a car park. Tenby is strong in golf and bowls, but if you arrive with your tennis racquets, than you'd have to hire a court at Lydstep's Celtic Haven, or perhaps one of the other hotels. It's a long wait for the next winner at Wimbledon; and he or she will come via some hothouse coaching academy in Spain or Florida, certainly not from Tenby.

Most people who enter Lower Frog Street are lured by the smell of fish and chips from Fecci's chippy, one of the oldest and still the best in Tenby. I have crossed St George's Street which is notable for the entrance to St Mary's Church garden of remembrance at one end and the pokey Five Arches tavern at the other.[23] This latter had been part of the medieval town hall and in the Second World War opposite a brothel.

Fecci's have several ice cream outlets and cafes in town and first came to do business there in 1935. They claim to source all their fish from Milford Haven and offer the unusual choice of local mackerel and chips. I can confirm that this is very good. Also, that Charles Fecci knows a few things about Frog Street. He lives above the business but his father occupies one of the oldest houses (in the sense of being continuously inhabited) in the whole of Wales. Just across the road from the chippy is a low red-roofed building, the former coal-yard and stable block, which the Feccis also own; and behind that in a courtyard is Tower Cottage in which Charles's father now lives. That is actually built into one of the town wall's towers that butts into the Florence Parade just before the Imperial Hotel arch. The Feccis are among those many Italians who came over to south Wales in the years of the coal boom at the end of the nineteenth century and prospered in the ice cream and café business. He says they came on the cusp of the new century on a boat from Bardi in northern Italy.[24]

The British Legion Club is next on the left after Fecci's and has the sort of run-down air that I felt characterised the Rugby Club. I went in there a week after Armistice Day in 2009 and not long after the last Great War veteran, Harry Patch died. A desultory group of afternoon losers huddled around a table. The young girl serving behind the bar didn't know whether I should be signed in or not. They all viewed with suspicion my notebook and pen. Perhaps they thought I was from the council, or that I was some other sort of official. Along from the dart board there's a case holding a Ghurka knife (2nd Bt. Parachute Reg.), several medals and gloomy photos; some bad reproductions of paintings of warships in dusty frames. The only reward for me was a large photograph of sappers digging trenches at Penally in 1914; proper trenches with strong wooden sides and defensive zig-zag angles. How many of these men got far enough and lived long enough to perfect such skills in Flanders?[25]

Across Lower Frog Street are Frogmore House, 1856, with its 1910 original shop front, Frogmore Villas (four of them) and Frogmore Terrace (of three three-storey Regency houses – 1830s – with the original wooden porches): surely here we have a clue to the oddly named streets? A family of builders or architects called Frogmore? Charles Fecci tells me later, with total conviction, that the name derives from mediaeval Tenby when further up the hill and still within the walls of the town wells had fallen into disrepair and numerous frogs made their way down the hill which became this street. Who knows?

The former Presbyterian Chapel on the left is now The Ocean Commotion Adventure Play Centre for Tot to Ten: caged-net-safe climbing levels and soft-play padding and balls. Its Romanesque facade of 1894 (originally 1837) must surely seem forbidding for some of the Tots to Tens. But at least this building has some young life to it. Unfortunately, the Crown Inn at the end of the street, one of the older and smaller pubs in Tenby has little character and the usual loud video filling its vacuous space.

At the end of Lower Frog Street I look right at the entrance of the Imperial Hotel and the arch through to the Florence Parade and the Esplanade curving to the west. To your left there is a view of St Catherine's Island and two sympathetic developments of flats at Paragon House and Paragon Court. Turning up either St Mary's Street or Cresswell Street will bring you back up to St George's Street and then to Tudor Square.

TUDOR SQUARE

The square is too often a circus with traffic jammed tight and angling for a parking place; often there will be two rows of vehicles double-parked. All the locals seem to know when there's a traffic warden on duty in the town. In season, of course, you will not be allowed to drive into the walled town between eleven in the morning and four in the afternoon. Don't feel miffed; the locals aren't allowed either. It would have been a lot worse when the fountain was positioned in the middle of the square, and there are moves afoot to replace it. Potentially the finest house on the Tudor Square is Tenby House at the bottom right, though now only the façade has character. Inside it's the usual gloomy noisy pub, but they have some decent photographs reproduced – the Hunt in 1914 taking their medicine before attempting to give the fox his; Edwardian royal wedding celebrations; the horse-drawn charabanc for the visitors' tour of the town, just as in season you can still catch the horse and carriage tour outside the church.

There's a reasonably discreet Tesco's Express where Woolworth's was for decades, a formidable frontage on the Nat West bank, but at the bottom end only the Equinox shop has the accessible residue of period mouldings on doors and ceilings. You have to edit out the tat and incense to enjoy those. The bookshop is okay and just around the corner of that lane is Naomi Tydeman's Gallery of her accomplished watercolours: check her out.[26]

At the bottom of St Julian's Street is the Ocean restaurant, formerly St Julian's House, decent coffee and wi-fi, with views of the harbour. It's run by Viti from Bucharest and the evening meals are fine.[27] So Crackwell Street has at each end a source of good coffee. Ahead of you is the harbour and to your right the old east gate of the town which leads to Castle Beach. Down past the touting booths of the fishing and Caldey boats is the remarkable white cube of Paxton's bathing house with its Greek inscription and the path around Castle Hill past both lifeboat houses.[28] And next to that, in the same whitewashed finish, and with a similar, low classical facade, is Harriet's House, a charity property set up in memory of an eleven year old girl who died from a rare degenerative metabolic disease. This is one of four properties in the area which provide respite and holiday breaks for seriously ill children and their families and carers.[29]

To the right is the incline to the west side of the Hill and the Museum. This is a treasure, a little jewel of a place; perhaps the most attractive small museum in the country. Or the world. At its front door you have views past Lexden Terrace[30] and the South

Beach, at its rear wall Pendine and the Gower, and a delightful band stand. Above stands the upright statue of Prince Albert, the main commemoration to Victoria's love in Wales. It's Sicilian marble, by J. Evan Thomas, erected in 1865. Set just below this is one of the most desirable properties in this town or any other. The former coast-guard house, white and proud above all the town was a council house that the occupants bought under the scheme of the Blessed Margaret (Thatcher). Eat your heart out with envy.[31]

One *must* enter Tenby Museum, which is open all the year round. It's better to simply join as an annual member than pay the single entrance fee. You are surely not just going to come to this wonderful county once in a year are you? And it is well worth supporting, anyway. The works they hold by Augustus and Gwen John are the obvious attraction, but there are other treasures in this unique place. For example, Romano-British brooches, bowls and coins from Trelissey Farm, near Amroth. 'The Tenby Gun' is an early sixteenth century cannon retrieved from the sea off Tenby in the nineteenth century. There are also cases of fossils and stone age remains.

There is probably the earliest surviving painting by Gwen – 'Landscape at Tenby with Figures', 1896, a view of the harbour with two girls in the foreground, and an early self-portrait. There are prints, drawings and paintings by Augustus, including a 1902 portrait of Ida and a 1937 portrait of David John. Views of the area include 'A Drawnet at Tenby' from 1795 by Julius Caesar Ibbetson which shows the South Beach and the 'Bay of Caldey' watercolour by David Jones from 1925. That indefatigable and notorious Nina Hamnett[32] is represented by pen and ink and pencil drawings and John Piper by prints and a gouache 'Robeston West with smoke from refineries'.

In the centre of the permanent gallery collection is the large bronze bust of Dorelia by Augustus John and a bust of the old artist himself by the equally remarkable Italian sculptor Fiore De Henriquez (1921-2004).[33]

There is a fine gallery extension for touring exhibitions and upstairs a local museum of 'Tenby at War', 'The Tills of the Town' and a collection of memorabilia concerned with the actor Kenneth Griffith. On the outside, back wall of the Museum, facing the band-stand, is a mosaic designed by Jonah Jones (see page 33), whose small polished bronze 'Icarus' is in the collection. Jonah won the commission to install the mural in an open competition. It is, however, in need of restoration as gales and inquisitive fingers have

taken their toll. Castle Hill's prospects, its Albert memorial statue and the remains of the castle make this one of the most memorable of walks in Tenby.

MANORBIER

Manorbier, just four miles along the coast from Tenby, is "curiously recessed, a very sequestered vale ending in a little creek of the sea below it."[34] This village has a remarkable history of creativity: Augustus and Gwen John and their brother and sister would escape from Tenby to stay with the MacKenzie family, school teacher and philosopher; "Here in the castle, Giraldus Cambrensis... was born. He described the place as the most delectable spot in all Wales: we thought so too. We lodged with a homely German lady whose husband, immersed in philosophy, kept his room. These departures from the routine of home life were hailed with joy, for at Manorbier we did as we pleased... We weren't so silent at Manorbier: the recluse upstairs used to complain of 'those turbulent Johns'".

Lewis's *A Topographical Dictionary of Wales* in 1833 describes the area thus:

> The parish is situated on the small bay to which it gives name, in the Bristol channel, and within two miles to the south of the turnpike road leading from Tenby to Pembroke: it contains a moderate portion of good arable and pasture land in good cultivation, and a small tract of hilly and barren waste; and, with the exception of such as are employed in the limestone quarries, which are worked only to a small extent, the population is wholly engaged in agriculture. The stone obtained from these quarries is shipped in small vessels, and sent into Cardiganshire: at Lydstep Haven vessels of one hundred and thirty tons' burden can ride in security.... The sands on this part of the coast are fine, specially at Lydstep Haven, where they are well adapted for sea-bathing; and the beauty of its situation, and its convenient distance from Tenby, render this a favourite excursion from that watering-place. Within the limits of the parish are two small villages, called Jamestown and Manorbier Newton.... The church, dedicated to St. James, is an ancient and spacious structure, in the early style of English architecture, with a lofty square embattled tower, and is in a rather dilapidated condition.[35]

Manorbier's name may derive from the manor of Pyr, or Pirhus, as Geraldus calls him, Prior of Caldey Island. Almost opposite the post office and village stores, there is a 'bier house' which, it is claimed, may be involved in the name of the village. The present small building dates only from 1900, however, and not only housed the man or horse-drawn bier to and from the church, but was also a resting place for bodies washed up on the coast. The metal-framed bier itself was donated to the National Folk Museum of Wales at St Fagan's in 1958.

Manorbier Castle probably owed its foundation to William de Barri, one of the Norman lords who accompanied Arnulph de Montgomery into Britain, and who married the granddaughter of Rhys ap Tewdwr, Prince of South West Wales. The castle and manor remained in the possession of that family until the time of Henry IV, when they were bestowed upon John de Windsor, but afterwards reverting to the crown, then to Thomas ab Owain of Trellwyn, from whose family they passed by marriage into the Philipps family of Picton. You may visit it for a small entrance fee and the remains of some state apartments and the possibility of commanding views from some of the walls are worthwhile. Below there would have been fish ponds right up to the position of the present car park and to the west there is still the remains of a dovecote, which may be

accessed from the main road between the castle and the beach. Fowl and fish were staple diets of the Normans in their castle and would, of course, have been supplemented by rabbits and other game from the chase. It is for the views of the castle from across the valley and from the beach that these remains are most notable. John Piper's paintings and a late screen print, published by the Curwen Press, are especially fine. In 2009 the beach featured in the filming of a feature-length movie *Round Ireland with a Fridge*, written by the comedian Tony Hawkes, and re-telling his 1997 story of hitchhiking around Ireland with a fridge in order to win a bet. He was, apparently, drunk when the challenge was accepted. See Manorbier and think Ireland. The beach has some of the best pebbles anywhere; the result of the fault lines of two types of stone – Old Sandstone and Carboniferous Limestone. There was, unsurprisingly, a limestone quarry here as with so many other coastal villages in the county. Beach kids of all ages will find green, red, purple and blue-black stones which acquire a gem-like beauty as the tide covers them.

If you take the Coastal Path in either direction from the village there are stunning views. Going up on to the path from the beach to the left and eastwards you climb gently up to the King's Quoit. This is a burial chamber thought to date from c.3000 BC. Looking back from this point gives you a fine view between church and castle and there's often a request from other walkers to take their photo against that landscape. The path grows steep and narrow as you bear left around the cliffs and the point called Priest's Nose. This spot is characterised by a series of dramatic cuts vertically into the sandstone, the deepest of which is called 'Fisherman's Cave', though you'd be hard pressed to land anything there. Virginia Woolf described this feature as, "...a little ridge just at the edge of a red fissure. I did not remember that they came so near the path. I have no wish to perish. I can imagine sticking out one's arms on the way down, and feeling them tear, and finally whirling over, and cracking one's head. I think I should feel as though I saw a china vase fall from the table, a useless thing to happen..."[36]

You can follow the Coastal Path right round past Precipe Bay and Old Castle Head to Skrinkle and its 'Church Doors' shaped by the sea, but it may well be that you'll cut back up the hill and short-cut to the church or car park. If you follow the Path westwards you walk through the garden of the Daks. I remember when this was a cafe, but it has been a private house for decades now. This is a more demanding walk and especially the climb up and around Moor Cliff. To your right there may well be a farmer ploughing on the most precipitous slope of a field. In autumn one can feast on banks of blackberries. The cliffs here are dramatic limestone sculptures with views across to Stackpole and Barafundle to the west. From a point down on the edge of Swanlake Bay you may bear left and inland to East Moor Farm where there is a camp site or a little further on you can turn to West Moor Farm, a Georgian farmhouse that has accommodation and which does tea and cakes.[37]

The village of Manorbier itself has had a distinguished succession of writers and artists living there or staying at the castle and elsewhere since Gerald of Wales, one of the first travel writers in these islands.[38] Virginia Woolf may have stayed at the Tarr Farm estate but, certainly, she did stay in the village twice, once at 'Sea View' with a second rented room in which to write: once in March 1904, a few days after her father's death, together with her siblings and her eventual publisher George Duckworth, and again in August 1908, when she was alone.

Her 1904 letters from here bear no address other than Manorbier R.S.O., Pembrokeshire (the post office). The first letter is dated 28 February, addressed to Violet Dickinson, and enthuses about Manorbier: "We have come to the right place. Never were people so lucky as we are in practical things. The house holds us perfectly, and is warm and comfortable, and I haven't seen such splendid wild country since St Ives – indeed one thinks of St Ives in many ways. We have already spent an astonishing amount of time walking about on the cliffs. Even lying in the sun. We live almost under the shadow of a great feudal castle, which stands on a cliff over the sea.... / There are about 3 houses here, and a wild queer Church on the hill. It is cold, but very clear and bright, and no sound but wind and sea."[39]

On 4 March she tells Lady Robert Cecil: "This is a very strange wild place, something like the Cornish Coast. We live like barbarians, and never see anyone...' On a later unspecified date [but before 31 March] she tells Violet Dickinson: 'We saw Choughs and Ravens the other day, climbing up rocks to get at them, and rolling about in the maddest way. /Our only excitement has been the death of the washerwoman! ...The first 6 rows of mourners held black edged handkerchiefs to their eyes, or mouths: they weren't crying; and the rest look fairly cheerful. Aint it barbaric? As you can imagine the whole village turned out to watch, and last night the young men who have nice soft voices sang a hymn under our windows." The charms of Manorbier were not lost on her family and friends either: her sister Vanessa and Clive Bell honeymooned in Manorbier in February 1907.[40]

She refers to the second visit in a diary entry – 3 September 1922 – "[At the age of sixteen] ...I was for knowing all that was to be known, for writing a book – a book – but what book? That vision came to me more clearly at Manorbier aged 21, walking the down on the edge of the sea." That book was the novel first called 'Melymbrosia' and then much revised, to be published as *The Voyage Out*.[41] This was certainly re-drafted and worked on at Manorbier when she stayed in 1908.[42] The quietude of the village and coast must have been a welcome time for someone who was under considerable stress and who would attempt suicide just after the novel was published in 1915. Though she could find little solace in the church: "I have tried to walk myself into a philosophical mood, in the churchyard, but I can't help feeling melancholy. It rains and blows..."

The notable author and war poet Siegfried Sassoon visited the older poet Walter de la Mare in Manorbier in 1924. The de la Mares stayed at Skrinkle on several occasions for family holidays and Sassoon was much taken with their son, Colin. He judged the local eisteddfod at the castle that summer.[43] The great playwright George Bernard Shaw was a visitor to the castle too. More recently, Leslie

Kenton the novelist, broadcaster and life-style guru[44] was resident at Vigilant House at Tarr Farm for two decades.

John Piper, the Byng Stampers and writers and artists who were their guests all enjoyed Manorbier. Mrs Rees of Withy Hay who I knew in her last years was one of the founding supporters of *Dock Leaves* and *The Anglo-Welsh Review*. James Campbell, the potter, until recently lived here and Philip Sutton R.A. has been living and painting in the village for some years. Philip and his wife, Heather, live in two Victorian houses in Morfa Terrace. One of these was owned by Heather's family for many years and the next-door neighbour is now given over to Philip's studio and storage spaces. And what storage spaces! Visiting Philip is a bewildering delight: his canvases and drawings are hung from or propped against every wall, including the corridors. For two decades he has lived in Manorbier and been inspired by the castle and the coastline. His reputation was made by his exuberant paintings of Fiji and prestigious commissions from the RSC and the Labour Party (it is his design that was adopted by New Labour as their up-to-date rose symbol). Philip was eighty in 2008 and a hard-back book was published to celebrate his life and work.[45] His paintings burst with the life-force and the paint escapes from the rectangle of the canvas to spill over the frame. With regular exhibitions in London galleries

and further afield, Philip's work has taken the essence of Manorbier, its rook and crow-filled trees, castle, coast walks and hugs skies, to the wider world.

The wonderfully-named Byng Stampers were two sisters who were importantly involved in the arts in the middle of the twentieth century helping to found, with Lord Howard de Waldon and Augustus John, the Contemporary Art Society for Wales and setting up the remarkable Miller's gallery in Lewes in Sussex during and after the war. They were the granddaughters of the first recipient of the Victoria Cross, awarded by the Queen herself in 1857.They rented Manorbier Castle after Frances had married Edwin Stamper, a lieutenant in the Royal Welsh Fusiliers and son of a Pembrokeshire doctor. Caroline painted in Pembrokeshire and exhibited widely. The sisters were important supporters of original print making and later commissioned new work by Piper, Sutherland and Ceri Richards. In 1957 they curated an exhibition *The Importance of Wales in Painting* at the Brighton Pavilion Gallery: their time in Wales was clearly formative and abiding.

The castle which they rented[46] was, of course, the birthplace in the twelfth century of Gerald. Giraldus Cambrensis was of Norman stock, but also the grandson of Nest, the daughter of Rhys ap Tewdwr; he was trained in church law in Paris and made his aim to secure the elevation of St David's to that of a bishopric. Between 1199 and 1204 he made no fewer than four journeys to petition the Pope in Rome, all to no avail. A passionate if non-Welsh-speaking Welshman, he wished to promote his county (and, no doubt, himself). He wrote in Latin, of course. It may not be too much of an exaggeration to claim that Gerald of Manorbier and Wales was a proto-nationalist, protesting that this small country had distinctive features of landscape, language and culture which argued for its recognition as a distinct entity.

Just at the entrance to the castle path there is a small war memorial at which, each Armistice Day wreaths are laid (the church and the local chapel take it in turns) and the names are read out, usually by Reg Smith who was born in Lydstep, but who lives in the village and served in the Royal Welsh Fusiliers in the Second World War. He's probably the oldest survivor now in this area. There are thirty-one names in all, twenty-eight from the Great War and three from the 1939-45. From the Great War four pairs of brothers are listed from this small village. They include the sons of the Viscount St. David, who owned Lydstep House: the Hon. Arnold who died in 1915 and is buried at Aveluy on the Somme and the Hon. Roland who died in 1916 and whose name is on the Menin Gate and whose body, therefore, must have remained undiscovered. The upper classes went over the top first and died first. One can surmise that they would all be perhaps surprised, certainly consoled by the fact that in the year of writing this book there were fifty or sixty people attending the short ceremony. We do remember them.

The Church of St James the Great, Apostle and Martyr across the valley is ancient, having been mentioned by Gerald who saw it as a place of refuge in 1153; the nave is certainly Norman with the tower, in recent years a distinctive white-washed landmark, dates from the time of William de Valence in the second half of the thirteenth century. The oldest of its three bells was cast in 1639. It had originally been part of the properties of the Fellows of Christ's College, Oxford, given to them by Margaret, mother of Henry VII. Though Lewis in 1833 described it thus: "The church, dedicated to St. James, is an ancient and spacious structure, in the early style of English architecture, with a lofty square embattled tower, and is in a rather dilapidated condition." He would be pleased to see it now: well-tended graves, its fresh bright tower and a healthy congregation.

A little later in a paper given to the British Archeological Association in 1884 the Rev. Wratislav seemed equally critical:

> From whichever side we approach this extraordinary church, we cannot but be struck by its remarkable irregularity. It does not seem to have been built upon a plan at all; or, if so, the parties carrying it out must have quarrelled, and gone each their own way in the execution of it, so that the results of their work were not very consistent with one another. Take away the north aisle, and you have an ordinary cruciform church; and, indeed, the north aisle with its separate compass-roof and separate bell-turret, appears to have actually been a separate church.
>
> Entering at the south door, and observing the remains of painting on the ceiling of the porch, the first thing that now strikes one is the irregularity of the arches of the nave, which are not of the same size, and are not built as such arches usually are, but springing straight from the floor of the church. Proceeding a little further up the centre of the nave, you find the key to this otherwise extraordinary problem. The remains of a little Norman window meet the eye on the right hand side; and this, taken together with the singularity of the arches, appears to indicate that we have in the nave the original Norman church, out of the thick and solid walls of which

> the present arches were cut, just enough of one window being left to betray the secret."

This poor church, Woolf's "wild, queer church on the hill", has survived despite these strictures and is one of the more notable landmarks on the south Pembrokeshire coastline.

On the way back from Manorbier shop where I buy the papers, I pop in to Springfields nursery for some more aparagus. Springfields is a left turn about half a mile past the main Manorbier sign on the Pembroke road from Tenby; or from the village you can wind your way past the castle entrance and turn right at their sign just short of that main road to Pembroke again. This is a farm shop: no, really. It is a farm. And it is a shop. There is now a fine house where once was a caravan; and there is an L shape of work sheds; lines of plastic hothouses and hidden acres of produce – cauliflowers, beans, whatever is in season. There is a van from the Four Seasons shops ('Farm Shops', two of them – Tenby, near the war memorial and near Wooden on the road back to Carmarthen), for

Springfields supplies wholesale to shops and many of the hotels in the Tenby area and beyond. If you have stayed in the area for a day or so and had proper food, you will have eaten the Beans' produce. The Beans' signs are hand painted and hung only to indicate what they have picked and what is in season. One season. Today, at the beginning of June, it is Asparagus and Strawberries. That's it. Nick and Pat Bean have a thriving business built on imaginative horticulture. They brought idealism to green issues before everyone nodded to those issues, and unrelentingly hard work. Oh, and Nick has a background as a research fellow at the University of Aberystwyth, where they have a renowned agricultural centre.

Pat has no time for talk, but I am invited into the packing shed and have a conversation punctuated by her large helper's large knife tailing this morning's asparagus and her continuous weighing and bundling of the spears; just the plump, full spears (do the spindly ones go for soup?) I tell her that I remember calling here as far back as my parents began renting a flat at Croft House. Pat says that today is one of her son's birthday; he's twenty-seven and was a week old when they started at Springfields. I imagine her toiling in the field with the baby swaddled her like some archetypal head-scarfed peasant from a Josef Herman painting. Mittel Europe, middle everywhere. But that's fanciful poetry and the Beans' pragmatism would, no doubt, reject that. Nick had been involved with research into the methodology of potato production and development at Aber. At one point that group of academics had been doing field work at Trefloyne estate and he'd got to know this area.

He tells me that Trefloyne had been owned by Dr Thomas, a crystal scientist and member of the University of Wales senate. Trefloyne, where Tenby's second golf course is now situated, was a large estate incorporating, historically, a limestone quarry. In the second half of the twentieth century the quarry was a significant supplier of stone to the developers of the oil refineries on the Haven. Dr Thomas and his wife lost both their sons, one in the war and one in an accident, and bequeathed the estate to the University for agricultural research purposes. At some point, and for some reason, late in the last century it was sold and the golf course was developed. I remember playing it in its second week. Tough: on one hole you have to drive over the edge of part of the quarry. It had been formally opened a week before by Tony Lewis, the broadcaster, cricketer and chair at that time of the Wales Tourist Board.

The asparagus I've bought is steamed at dinner time for starters with seasoned butter: they are crisp and succulent. They couldn't be fresher: 'Merlys/Manobier/Asparagus' the label reads, with a colour photograph of Nick clutching a bouquet of green spears to his chested apron. Of course, your pee smells of asparagus for hours, like green ghosts.

Across the main Pembroke road from Springfields is Penuel Chapel, a Baptist congregation which my mother attended, and where she wished to be buried, until one of those unchristian, unprofound disagreements between an overbearing deacon and other members more than halved the attendance and threatened its survival. It staggers on, just about, but the single storey building next to it is noisy and vibrant with an evangelist crew who advertise miracles in the local paper. It pays to advertise.

Just along that stretch of road I call on a remarkable young artist, Ivan Black, at New House Farm. Ivan is in his late thirties and trained at Middlesex. He makes kinetic sculpture and, like the Freshwest lads, is clearly inspired by the landscape here. His workshop has finished and partly-made constructions which hang or swirl in the wind. Some are geometric and some play on wave forms. His most notable public commission has been for a large construction at Addenbroke's Hospital in Cambridge. This a ceiling-hung swirling and twisting column made of metal. There is a clean purpose to what Ivan does, and in an ultra-modern way, his pieces imply more spirituality than the stodgy chapel and dodgy ejaculations back down the road. I've seen his work as far afield as the Yorkshire Sculpture Park.

"It is now thundering out at sea, and some silly women, out for a holiday, are bathing. It is too fantastic of them – but they won't drown."[47] You will come to Manorbier for the castle and its history, for the WI market on a Wedneday in season, for the King's Quoit and the coastal path, but most of all for the sea, its power and its solace. And the air, the inspiring air.

LYDSTEP

Most visitors to Lydstep will think of it only as that very large caravan site, Lydstep Haven. The village itself has an entirely different atmosphere. This is where my mother lived for the last twenty years of her long life and where my family and I are based in Pembrokeshire. Thanks again to the Blessed Margaret, who sold the family assets back to the family. That's why there are so few opportunities for social housing now.

After dinner one evening I walk down the back lane from Lydstep village past Windy Ridge and South Lodge to the car park and the Headland; wild garlic flowering with its sweet stink. Bright, bright gorse in banks and the worn, rusty foundations of the wartime gun emplacements as I walk on the south, sea side of the Headland. Across to the west is Skrinkle and Manorbier camp and firing range. The sea is calm and the deepest green. 'Church Doors', the wave-worn sculpted natural arches, are clear. There's the edge of Skrinkle Haven with its pristine sands, reached only by a steep climb of steps (and steeper coming back). The circular walk around the Headland is National Trust property, and sometimes you come upon ponies and cattle, so the land must be rented for farm use too. At the very tip is where our son Gareth stood to shake out the ashes of my mother; and our daughter-in-law Madeleine threw some flowers of lavender and wild garlic. It was almost impromptu and, we think, fitting. Back along the sea-edge path was where my mother and I had scattered my father's ashes. I had looked up into "a sky that goes on for ever."[48]

That was in 1978. My parents were renting a flat in Croft House in Manorbier, a tarted-up and developed Victorian house first on the left after you pass the soccer pitches. My father had been suffering from lung cancer for more than a year and died there. The previous night he had spent working at Lydstep Haven. I turn anticlockwise on the Headland and follow the path back to the car park. Behind me the sheer limestone faces – Mother Carey's Kitchen and the White Tower, rock climbers' challenges – and to my right the sheer drops into two abandoned lime quarries facing the haven. Lydstep Haven is now a large, sprawling caravan site run by Bourne Leisure. For six or seven years my parents worked there – cleaning at first and then my mother in the office and my father as a general mechanic in the workshop. They had fallen on hard times and the owners, the Thomas family, had given them a break.

Lydstep estate had been the quarry owner John Adams's property in the 1830s. By the twentieth century it was one of the homes of Lord and Lady St David's whose gardeners and workers greatly enhanced the grounds.[49] Viscount St Davids was created in 1918 and Lydstep was just one of the family's houses; Picton Castle is the most illustrious in Pembrokeshire and the seat of the Philipps family since the seventeenth century.

Lydstep House had been a fine private residence with twenty bedrooms, billiard room, servants' quarters and substantial living rooms; the tracks up and around that estate had hosted hunting and motor car sprint and hill climbing, including an appearance by the famous racing driver Stirling Moss. Large crowds were attracted by these competitions. The Pembrokeshire Motor Club ceased these events at Lydstep when the property changed hands in the 1950s. It was bought by H.V. Thomas and run as a guest house and then developed as a caravan park by his son David and grandson Graham. It was for this family that my parents came to work in 1970 when their village shop in Begelly failed. The Thomas family were supportive and generous and, when my father died his funeral took place in Lydstep House and was paid for by the Thomases.[50] My father so enjoyed driving David Thomas's pink Rolls Royce back from Heathrow for him.

David Thomas had sold the site as a going concern to Pontins in the 1970s, who in turn sold to Bourne Leisure, a large holiday and entertainment company who also have Kiln Park at Tenby and Lydstep Court caravan park. It is clear that the place has now been developed about as fully as it could. From the headland you can see most of the sites and the expanding boat park with its leisure boats and water jet skis. What infernal, yobbish things they are – water motor cycles with the attendant roar and danger to riders and others: an intrusion which should be banned from the National Park.

In the Lydstep Tavern there is a drawing taken from a nineteenth century photograph of a brigantine at anchor in the haven to take on limestone from the quarry bitten into the side of the headland. The pub was originally named The Quarry Inn, though 'Lordy' and Lady Philipps insisted that it close in the 1930s because their workers were dissipating their wages there. John Lewis writing in 1849 observed: "There are excellent limestone-quarries in Lydstep bay, where a very considerable number of hands are employed, the stone being shipped during the summer months in great quantities by vessels belonging to other parts of Wales, and to North Devon: vessels of 130 tons' burthen can ride in security..." From here, St Margaret's Island off Caldey and several other sites in south Pembrokeshire there was, clearly, a substantial trade in limestone to Devon and the West Country and to other ports in Wales. Holiday makers will, quite understandably, enjoy the sun and sand, the escape from urban life. But, as we have seen, the presence of industry and trade and warfare is evident and widespread. Lydstep

Headland has its quarries, gun emplacements, the ashes of both my parents and one of the most spectacular views in Wales: both the end-on length of Caldey and St Margaret's, or the seemingly endless ocean with its occasional glimpse of Lundy Island. And those skies.

Lydstep Headland[51]

I start with the visible and am startled by the visible
– Dannie Abse

This balmy evening on the Headland
it is enough to be startled by the visible:
behind me six Welsh Blacks snuffling at what grass
they can find between the clumps of gorse.

An August moon three-quarters silver
set above the south horizon that is rusty-rose,
magenta and grey in layers
holding the charcoal smudge of Lundy Island.

The Headland's sloping cliff edge falls sheer from my feet.
This is where I scattered my father.
The sea is a wide, flat lake stirred only by currents
and the surface creases of a fitful breeze.

Then one, two, three birds
which rise from nothing –
black-backed gulls that soar and dip
for fish only they can see.

I know that Somerset and Devon,
lights and lives, are over the southern edge;
and to the west sailing for days
nothing until America.

In the fragile focus of my field glasses
that tightening O-O of sharpened vision,
the black tipped span of the gull becomes immense:
my Pembrokeshire albatross.

The landlord in the Lystep Tavern is as gloomy as most of his colleagues in the pub business: "The locals don't appreciate the pub. We need support." Still, if you choose the home-made items on the menu here it's a good meal and we don't always want to come back from a day on the beach or exploring the county to face the kitchen, do we?

"And the Celtic Haven development must have made a difference?" I ask. But he says that he's welcomed that. There are as many beds in the former turkey farm as in the rest of the small village. And they do patronise him. Celtic Haven has been well developed, with taste and style. The farmhouse itself, the outbuildings and a cluster of new houses to the rear must give hundreds of people a sense of the coastline's beauty. The new houses and the restaurant, pool and spa building have a wonderful view of Caldey and the sea. There must be few villages in Britain of less than a hundred buildings with such amenities, and tennis courts and a nine-hole pitch-and-putt. Though the shop that occupied the building across from the Lydstep Tavern, which had been run as a general stores by my old school friend Stephen Sutcliffe[52], is now a rented property.

My friend Reg Smith, the war veteran, was born in Lydstep in 1922. He agrees to walk me through the village one day in late July. Reg was born in Lydstep Court, a small, house at the rear of the

Tavern, which now has a renovated Flemish chimney. We begin at our house 12, The Green and Reg says that he remembers when what is now a development of sixteen bungalows and semis was the village green, though, in truth it was not some calendar's rustic scene, but rather an open space and a waste tip. We walk down the back lane to the Haven through what were, at West Lodge a set of gates. Reg points out the rusty hinge on one of the 'jombs'. West Lodge was an extremity of the Lydstep estate; Reg remembers that it had a hand-pumped water closet which drained waste down the slope to the copse below. Rose Cottage to our left was a cow shed and to our right there were 'pig cots' where Fieldhouse has been built.

At Manor Farm there was a horse-driven mill for grinding corn. In Sea View Cottage Lady St Davids established a small public reading room; it was there that Reg remembers the men and boys of Lydstep gathering on the 30th of August, 1938 to share the headphones of the wireless set to listen to Tommy Farr[53] fighting Joe Louis in Madison Square Gardens, New York, the first ever live sporting event to be broadcast across the Atlantic. Thirty-two thousand in Madison Square Gardens were joined by that huddle in Lydstep as the Brown Bomber pummelled the brave Tonypandy Terror. Of course, Farr was heroically beaten, as is the British way, a result which dimly crackled through to Pembrokeshire. He said later, "My face looked like a dug up road." "Lady St Davids also had her own small reading room and study on Lydstep Headland, or 'Spion Kop' as it was known. Her family had lost a son in the Boer War and, as we have seen, two more in the Great War.[54]

The stone wall of the Meyricks' house is topped in the fashion of 'cocks and hens', one small stone alternating with a larger one. The Meyricks have been land owners in the village for centuries and the name resonates back to Tudor times. Pantiles, across the lane, was originally The Gables. Here was the first car in the village, an Austin Seven with a 'dickie seat' in the rear which Reg had rides in. The owner, Miss Vaughan-Summers, had an orchard and a tennis court. There was a public hand pump at this point in the lane which was fed from a small reservoir in the village which was, in turn fed by a windmill at Whitewell in the Ruins half a mile way opposite the Lydstep Haven entrance on the road to Tenby. Apart from those booked into the Celtic Haven, most visitors to Lydstep village will come on one particular day – the Easter Monday point to point races. Reg recalls them beginning here in 1947, but originating near

Flemyngston near St Florence. He and his friends would take the path behind Lydstep Palace, past the ancient stone (a cromlech?) across the present point to point fields over the Ridgeway and through St Florence, a walk of over five miles to the races.

Reg left school in Manorbier at the age of fourteen and began work as a trainee gardener at the Lydstep Estate. He would have passed a barn structure halfway down which was used seasonally as a slaughter house by butchers coming over from Tenby. Reg and the other boys would get pigs' bladders from the slaughter men for use as footballs. And the house called Windy Ridge was another 'haggard' which Reg's father would have to use for cattle. We turn left into what is now the Celtic Haven holiday centre. Reg, in common with the Tavern owner and most of the residents sees this as an enhancement. What was Home Farm has been tastefully developed into holiday residences and a free standing house. The barns, the granary and the 'haggards'[55] have been transformed into a restaurant, spa and swimming pool. There is a golf tutoring set-up with video projections and a small conference centre. Where Reg and his school mates ran wild and free before the war there are the tennis courts and child-safe play area with rubber matting. The view is still one of best in Wales, in Britain, anywhere: the surf-splashed cliff running to Giltar Point and beyond the end-on prospect of St Margaret's Island and Caldey. Reg left this heavenly place to join up in Pembroke and go with the Royal Welsh Fusiliers to Brecon, Burma, Singapore and Java.

Reg points out that 'Goose Cottage' was originally stables; 'Atrato's Stables' were, in fact, the engine house for the sawing of timber. 'Rafters' was the granary and Reg remembers a little ratting dog brought in to the clear the place killing "upwards of fifty rats" in an evening: necks snapped and thrown over his shoulder.

At the Conference Centre we are met by a manager who immediately contradicts almost everything that Reg remembers about the farm buildings and their original use. I shrug my shoulders a lot and manoeuvre him away from the place. She may be right and Reg may be right, for to which period are we referring? How else is a narrative constructed except by a mix of memory and imagination?

Lydstep Palace is, of course, no such thing. It is undoubtedly medieval, but at best a hunting lodge or small residence with Church connections. Reg says that Mrs Cater who was in the WI with my mother was the step granddaughter of the last occupant of the Palace. The front part of the building, now administered by

CADW, was an occupied residence up to the middle of the nineteenth century, apparently. The Lydstep Tavern was two buildings in Reg's early years: the left half was a house called Hillsides and the right was a Post Office, stores and, in Reg's war, a canteen frequented to his delight by ATS girls.

Reg and his friends played cricket on what is now the sharp right-hander coming from Tenby to Pembroke, using the new telegraph pole as a wicket. The blue house opposite is a post-war construction which served for many years as the village police station. The wall to the right of the pub had a notice board advertising the films showing at the cinema in Tenby and a water pump fed from the reservoir on the Ridgeway to the north. The courtyard at the back of the Tavern was Nicholls Yard, a lawn and then a path leading back to Lydstep Court and two outhouses, one of which was where Reg's family had their pony and trap and one which was owned by Stanley Thomas who kept the village's second car, an Austin Eight. Motor transport was also rare in Manorbier village before the war and Reg remembers that when the former Home Secretary Sir John Simon visited his mother at Tenby House he had to be fetched from the station in the local grocery lorry.[56]

You can still make it down to the caverns at Lydstep, though the

bay at Skrinkle is, effectively, unreachable owing to the very dangerous clamber down the steep cliffs. From the village it is a twenty minute walk and scramble down to the narrow delights of Lydstep caverns where

> A child might play where late the embattled deep
> Hurled serried squadrons on the rock-fanged shore,
> Where now the screaming filmy shallows creep
> White-horsed battalions dashed with ceaseless roar...[57]

On an August day we make our way down. The steps cut into the path are safe, though quite steep, and you are faced by a rock and boulder scramble for the last twenty yards or so. The tide has to be out, for there is precious little sand except for low tide. The rocks stand tall and are like templates for Gaudi's cathedral in Barcelona – strange, naturally-carved mountains of almost animated or humanoid energy. It is only when the tide is out that the sand is revealed and access is possible for some of the caves. The Victorians and Edwardians would have travelled by boat to this coast from their hotels in Tenby. They would not have seen the plastic and wood flotsam which mars most of our coastline; Bear Cave is magnificent, despite the rope, bottles and a green frog bucket which

the tide has left. The difficulty of access and the small scale of this little haven mean that one is rewarded by the effort of clambering down at low tide. The rock-pools with their mussels and anemones, the promise of kestrels and choughs and the window of pure sea that standing at Lydstep caverns offers are very special.

PENALLY

Penally is Alun's hill: possibly, 'pennalun', a name that pre-dates the Normans and refers to the stream that is all but invisible in the village now. There is also a well named after St Deiniol, on the path past the Abbey Hotel (and its Abbey ruins). Mick Jagger and Peter O'Toole (for Kenneth Griffith's funeral in 2006) have been guests. But the earliest evidence of habitation are the finds from the Hoyle's Mouth Cave and Little Hoyle Cave: Stone Age tools and Bronze Age finds confirm very ancient dwellings from Penally through to Giltar Point. You are not allowed to enter Hoyle's Mouth as it is designated an SSSI.

Over the last fifty years in particular, the archaeological importance of Penally has been established with especial interest being given to the Longbury Bank settlement on the Trefloyne estate.

Finds that include Mediterranean pottery show that there was a degree of wealth and that south Pembrokeshire was linked by sea travel to the rest of Europe by the navigable Ritec river, which is now little but a stream. In fact much of the area of the present Tenby golf course and burrows would have been a tidal inlet, giving access right up to the church and village of Gumfreston; meaning that the Trefloyne estate and the Longbury Bank settlement was ideally placed for trade and communications: "an undefended high-status secular site", in fact; rather like present-day Penally.[58] Trefloyne witnessed skirmishes in the Civil War and little remains of the original house of that period. Now the Trefloyne Manor estate and golf course is based around a nineteenth century farmhouse, with recent developments of large chalet-style holiday accommodation.

Penally is now a cluster of houses around the church of St Nicholas and St Teilo which has spread up and across the hillside, sometimes to splendid effect and sometimes (those awful sixties and seventies again) to no great effect at all. It has a little post office and shop and the inevitable caravan park which is owned by the Kiln Park firm and which fronts the passing Tenby-Pembroke road. Just along that road is Court Farm which dates back to the sixteenth century at least. One of the village's main claims to fame is the legend that St Teilo, a contemporary of St David, was born here. The church has a tenth century Celtic cross as well as the obligatory Norman font.

More recently the village has become associated with the larger-than-life actor Kenneth Griffith who is buried in the churchyard close to his paternal grandparents, Emily and Ernest, who brought him up. Griffith is the most celebrated of old Greenhillians and it was his headmaster J.T. Griffith in Tenby who persuaded him to drop the 's' from his name as an English aberration. Griffith spend much of his career as a film producer and director taking the English and the British Empire to task for their arrogance and cruelties. Griffith left the area in 1937 for Cambridge, where he worked at an iron monger's but wangled his way into the Cambridge Festival Theatre and life as a repertory actor. A year later he made his West End debut and within four years his film career began; this amounted to nearly a hundred films, including his role as the slimy Jenkins in *Only Two Can Play*, with Peter Sellers, Boulting Brothers comedies and a succession of later television roles gave him more security than many an actor. Griffith never 'rested' and his production of a series of provocative television films

– on the South African runner Zola Budd, on the Boer War and on Irish Republicanism – made him one of the most outspoken and controversial of commentators.[59] In fact, when Margaret and I attended a Greenhill School anniversary evening some twenty years ago at the ill-fated Royal Gate House Hotel Griffith was the guest speaker. After a very ordinary dinner, he began an apparently ordinary old boy's speech which quickly and alarmingly descended into a rant about the IRA and his sympathies for both their cause and their methods. "If some of my friends asked me to carry a suitcase on to an aeroplane, I would not hesitate to do so…" Years later I spent a pre-International lunch with him in Cardiff. I raised the Gatehouse incident and he conceded that it had been inappropriate. Several people had walked out and the local MP and MEP had been pinned to their seats in evident anger and pain. Kenneth, the wild-boyo actor and director was frail and near the end that rugby afternoon: I helped him at lunch by cutting his meat for him and he went slowly to the Wales-England match on my arm; and that was the last I saw of him. I could not make it to his funeral in Penally.

One of our favourite walks is to park at the station car park at Penally and cross the railway line (there is a clear and safe crossing

with pedestrian swing gates – just a handful of trains each day) taking the path to the edge of the golf course at the eighth tee. This path has spring and early summer bright yellow marsh irises and rushes which have been conserved by a new fence; though there will often be cattle grazing there too.

To the right is the stretch of the army's rifle range going towards the large butts against the slope of Giltar's headland. You will see a stone-mounted illustration of the headland and its wartime significance and wild life. You have the choice at this point of turning right and following the fenced path (Pembrokeshire Coast Path) up the slope alongside of the range; this rises quite steeply all the way around the eighth green and the ninth tee to the top of the headland with its spectacular views across to the west end of Caldey and St Margaret's Island – that "calf and whale,/greys and greens set in sparkling water."[60] That route will take you to the "handful of softened foxholes" which were used for trench training in the First World War. They are quite difficult to spot now and are at the far end of the headland walk before you turn right and back down to the beach level. I always imagine those young men being barked at by drill sergeants, lobbing their dummy bombs over the parapets, then taking a breather in one of the most heavenly spots in this country; at their backs and below them the tents and drilling and khaki comradeship; and out before them the holy mix of prayer and farm and limestone of the islands, and further beyond to the south west the Atlantic's new worlds.

Bearing left at the golf tee the path takes one through the course some three hundred yards to the dunes where a set of steps and a seating spot open out the western end of that stunning length of the South Beach. Crumbly sand gives way to firm sand and pebbles and shells. And the view – from Caldey and St Margaret's round to the squat ugly defence of St Catherine's Napoleonic fort. Your long gaze taking in on most days the clear outline of the Gower peninsula with its three end peaks of Worm's Head where Dylan rode to play and escape the stuffiness of Swansea Uplands. And then the less clear edge of Carmarthen Bay, that six mile long racing beach of Pendine and Sir John's Hill over which lies Dylan's Laugharne. One can walk, always except for high tides, the length of South Beach to the Esplanade, or round past those St Julien's town houses and Nina Hamnett's Lexden Terrace to Castle Beach and climb up to Tenby's harbour and town centre. Stop for a coffee or an ice cream. You will tell yourself that you deserve it, but the exhilaration of the walk and the views will have been ample reward. Then descend to the beach again and walk back.[61] Or, and getting the timing right is a challenge, catch the little pull-push Arriva train that one stop back to Penally.

It's an evening in the last week of the autumn. I visit Mike Argent the architect in his house and planning studio in the village.[62] We remember each other from the Sixties and golf at Tenby and our paths cross on occasions when I am walking to the golf course from Penally. Mike and his brother John were not at Greenhill school with me, but went away to Clifton College in Bristol; both studied architecture at Cambridge under, amongst others, Colin St John Wilson, worked in London and then returned to the county to establish a successful and innovative business in Pembrokeshire. They set up their firm following on their father's business as a builder based in Pembroke. Argents have been responsible for a number of projects in Pembrokeshire and Mike tells me that he secured the contract for the new doctors' surgery in Tenby shortly after his return and hasn't looked back. Other work has included the art gallery at Tenby Museum, the Farms for City Children School at St David's and the Haverfordwest Community Hall. Their website proclaims a laudable philosophy: "We aim to produce sustainable life enhancing environments for happy clients (who tend to be fully involved in the design process). Our approach is

strongly contextual, and we take great trouble to blend the old with the new. The reduction of perceived bulk to achieve a comfortable human scale is a particularly important preoccupation."

Mike shows me the plans for the conversion of the old lifeboat house and slipway in Tenby, a controversial residence but sufficiently dramatic and radical to warrant a feature on the upcoming *Grand Designs* television series. There are photographs of the work progressing and I begin to believe that what seemed to me to be a crazy scheme might actually work. The Irishman who has bought the place and commissioned Mike has obviously fallen in love with the notion: I hope that neither he nor any of his family is a sleepwalker. The mackerel off the slipway are said to be very fine.

Mike and his wife Olivia offer a glass of wine and we look at some of Olivia's paintings. She was at Chelsea School of Art just after the time of Ceri Richards and also trained as a ballet dancer. For over a decade she has kept a studio above the courtyard in Brychan Court in Upper Frog Street. She is explains that she is currently working on a series of paintings of the Bolshoi Ballet backstage based on a friend's photographs. These are two energetic productive people, working through their seventh decade, who have the vision and commitment to still make changes to Pembrokeshire, Wales and beyond. At the porch of their (predictably) beautifully-designed house at Penally we pause to take in the view. It is the third week in October; the full moon and Venus extend the day and offer evening views over the tower of St Nicholas and St Teilo to Caldey and the lights on the Gower; St Mary's at Tenby has its spire illuminated for its 900th birthday and the sea is moon-silver. I cannot imagine even that old rebel Kenneth Griffith restless under such a sky, under such a pleasant land.

ST FLORENCE

The narrow lane to Trefloyne, past the execrable Nitespot disco place leads on after a couple of tightly cornered miles to St Florence, though this is more easily reached off the Ridgeway. St Florence is the 'Flemish' village with some notable Flemish chimney-ed houses, especially Old Chimneys, encircling the well-restored church of St Florentius.[63] This has a square Norman font and a simple and fine stained glass Annunciation of 1873 in the north transept. One of several interesting memorials records that Harold Berkeley Beynon, an only son, died in Penally in 1919 after contracting malaria in Salonica 'while serving with his Majesty's forces'. Standing before that marble plaque I bring to mind Stanley

Spencer's Sandham Chapel mural on canvas of the trapoys of wounded lit by the operating lights of the surgeon's tent. Harold Beynon was twenty-one. There is also a memorial to Bishop Ferrar, one of the Protestant martyrs burned by order of Queen Mary at Carmarthen.

St Florence is a highly-desirable village with some fine modern houses near the delightfully situated mid-Victorian Elm Grove, as well as the usual sixties and seventies unfortunates. Its attractive inland isolation is because in 1811 Sir John Owen of Orielton began the Penally embankment, which follows what is now the railway line. This was designed to enable more pasture land at Penally, but another effect was that the Ritec river silted up and St Florence was effectively cut off from the sea. The place would be closer to the sea and heaven if it were not for the necessary one-way system and a couple of seasonally noisy pubs.

CALDEY

Caldey can be visited by taking one of the small fleet of boats which ply their trade in a long season from the harbour and depart from that harbour or from a landing stage off the Castle Sands, depending upon the tide. It is inexpensive, shouldn't take longer than half an hour, and is usually not too bumpy a ride: look at the sea and judge for yourself. There is little swell until you pass Sker Rock behind St Catherine's Island and you may see seals. It is always exciting to approach Caldey as it fills the horizon "like some cretaceous monster at ease/in an ancient ocean."[64]

It is called by Giraldus Cambrensis Ynys Pyr, which George Owen of Henllys, the Elizabethan writer takes to mean the island of Pyrrhus.[65] He goes on to praise its corn yield and to note that the ploughs are horse-drawn, the use of oxen being threatened by the landing of pirates who, presumably, would have slaughtered the beasts for provisions. The straits between island and town are "a good and safe road for shipping, from twelve to six fathoms deep in good ooze, safe for all winds, those of the east points excepted." These Roads will take "200 ships, as has been certified by upon a late survey, all in safe riding and a good anchor hold." St Margaret's Island, which he calls 'Little Caldey' "bears good grass for sheep and conies, and a store of gulls, and is the Queen Majesty's land." It is good to be reminded of Tenby's significant role as a trading

port for some centuries. And also of the abundance of conies, for rabbits were transported in great numbers to London after the coming of the railway.[66]

The boatmen land you on a jetty at the west end of Priory Bay (at low tide they may use the ugly but effective DUKW which dates from Communist East Germany to transfer you to the jetty); and it is a short walk to the tea-rooms and, then further up to the Monastery. The white landmark you have seen from Tenby is, of course, the lighthouse. This is at the south side and may also be walked to. On a summer's day you may be tempted to simply stay on Priory Beach, which is pristine and quiet at its eastern end. Apart from the boats plying their trade, and you would not be there without them; swimming and sunbathing on Priory is a wonderful escape from commerce and traffic. You'll have a marvellous view of Tenby and the coast to Lydstep.[67] The ocean side of these islands has a seal colony and there are boat trips from Tenby harbour to view these. Note, the ocean is not the Roads and there is more than "twelve fathoms deep in good ooze": it can be rougher.

The tea rooms are good enough and there are plenty of chairs

and tables for use on the grass. It's worth spending a half hour here to take your bearings and to look at the monastery itself. This is a 1920s building unique in Wales and of European architecture. It was begun in 1906 by the Anglican Benedictines who set up the abbey and changed their allegiance top the Roman Catholic church in 1913. They were forced through financial constraints to sell up in 1925 and were succeeded by Cistercians from Scourmont Abbey in Belgium in 1929. It was these Cistercians who developed a financial independence through their products and the tourism which has flourished since the second world war. Monks have used the island as a retreat and their home since the sixth century with Benedictines from St Dogmaels establishing a priory in the twelfth century.

Caldey would once have been another peninsula, a headland like Giltar and Lystep, but thank goodness for the rising of the sea at the end of the Ice Age, for we now have one of the most beautiful prospects in Britain. Of course, you have to take a boat ride, which can be a bit bumpy in the Tenby Roads that separate Ynys Pyr from the mainland, but that's an important part of the Caldey experience: "monarch, bird, monk, bursting flower/we are all visitors to this island planet."[68]

This is not a big place – about one and a half kilometres by one – but there are fine walks, great views and the intrigue of a functioning monastery. There have been monks here at various times since the sixth century, the place being particularly significant between the twelfth century and the dissolution of such establishments by Henry the Eighth. What you see today is a building by the Anglican Benedictine order, dating from 1906. It was re-dedicated as the Abbey of Our Lady and St Samson (the sixth century Celtic monk and second Abbot of Caldey) in 1929.[69] This order is based on principles of contemplation and silence; women visitors are not encouraged in the monastery. Having said that, the brothers have a steady trade in the production of perfumes and other cosmetics.[70] You can buy these in the island shops and in the Caldey shop next to the Ship Tavern at the bottom of Tudor Square in Tenby. There is also a chocolate shop on Caldey where you may see the vats of brown stuff swirling and paddling for your delectation: the pleasures of the flesh are, in a way, catered for by the monks.[71]

One occasion when I came over was during the days when Pope John Paul II was on his death bed. The monks were at constant prayer and one was not allowed near the monastery: it would be facile to see such prayers as unanswered by the old man's death – prayer being an end in itself and requiring no further validation. On Sundays and through the long out-of-season months, who is to say that an island such as this, isolated and quiet, would not be the place to get closer to an understanding of god?

The clean white garb of the monks and their clean white church underline the simplicity of their approach, but there is evidence of art and colour too. The glass windows by Dom Theodore Bailey bring colour into St David's Church, built on the site of a pre-Christian Celtic burial place; his Tree of Life in particular, seems to reference the very earthly delights of Tiffany's and the Art Nouveau movement of the early twentieth century. The simple, substantial font has lettering by Eric Gill,[72] founder of a Catholic lay brotherhood of makers and artists who set up their community in Capel-y-Ffin near Brecon and later in the Sussex village of Ditchling. Gill attracted talents to his cause, notably David Jones, that wonderful poet-painter. Jones drew, painted and engraved images of Caldey during his visits in the 1920s. There are examples in Tenby Museum but, sadly, nothing on Caldey and little mention of him in the island's small museum collection held in the post office (another building by the architect John Coates Carter). Jones's bay of Brobdingnag in his illustrated *Gulliver's Travels* is surely based on views from Caldey. David Jones admired Caldey's "garden of small trees and winding paths... I have been nearly demented trying to capture its beauty even but vaguely." He spent two weeks again painting on the island in the autumn of 1931 in the company of two friends, Burns and Grisewood. They boarded at Ty Gwyn, the large cottage, a half-mile north-east of the island monastery. From the balcony, they could see the Pembrokeshire coast from Tenby to Giltar Point. Each morning they attended Mass in the monastery and occasionally the singing of the Divine Office, which Jones found not too pleasing: "the Trappists sing the Liturgy very badly indeed." Still, he thought the island 'adorable' in autumn "an ideal place to paint in every way" on "the best kind of autumn day with the sun warm & the day quite still & everything a pleasant slightly golden tone."[73]

He may also have been influenced by the ancient stone with its combination of Ogham script and Latin text: calligraphy played an important role in Jones's art and he delighted in connections between Wales and the Romans.[74] Though David Jones did "an immense amount of tearing up at Caldey", the paintings and prints which his stays on the island inspired were significant works – "in a curious way the best things I have done so far." Certainly, the art and writings of David Jones are of a different order to the slim volumes of clumsy verse which monks have published over the years: avoid these.

Of course, the boats to Caldey should also do a thriving trade with visiting Rastafarians; they believe Haile Sellasie to have been Jesus in his second coming and so, in a sense, god came to Tenby and the holy island at the end of the 1930s and the beginning of the war. Certainly, my old school chum Stephen Beasley, a retired solicitor, judges the evidence to be convincing. A series of letters and claims and counter-claims by Stephen and the writer Roscoe Howells and others fuelled the letters columns of the *Tenby & District Observer* in the winter of 2008. It is said that the Lion of Zion stayed at the Atlantic Hotel on the Esplanade; more certainly that the children of his family stayed for a period on Caldey.

Rastafarians, including family members of Bob Marley, mobbed the Emperor's plane when he visited Jamaica in 1966 and he had to negotiate a more dignified entry to the airport which was wreathed in ganja smoke. How would that go down in the Caldey tea rooms? He never actually disabused these people of their bizarre beliefs, so perhaps the Tourist Board could run adverts in the Caribbean: "Leave the predictability of those palm trees, that reggae, sun and

rum – come to Georgian Tenby, follow your Emperor, man". Consternayshon through the Cistershons...

Caldey should be on the timetables of anyone spending more than a few days in the Tenby area. The beach, the sense of history, the walks (the one straight up to the 1829 lighthouse is an obvious one, as well as the cliff walk which offers spectacular views of the mainland and the ocean) and the absence of traffic are all highly rewarding. There is too the option of taking the Calvary route back to your boat. This brings you to a large crucifix and the Oratory, a dovecote-shaped building for meditation and prayer – white-washed and circular with that view of Tenby and the coast. And, of course, whichever way you choose, the humour of the boatmen again.

Notes

1. Augustus John: though he rarely returned after his Slade days. He received the Freedom of Tenby in October 1959. He looked "deeply moved and at times somewhat overcome...", *The Tenby Observer*, quoted by Michael Holroyd in his *Augustus John: a Biography* (Heinemann, 1975).
2. There are two versions of an upstanding statue to David Davies, at Llandinam in mid-Wales and in front of the Dock offices in Barry where, with the Earl of Plymouth, he built one of the largest coal ports in the world. His money eventually passed to his granddaughters, Margaret and Gwendolyn, who used it to develop Gregynog Hall in Powys, several idealistic garden suburbs – Newtown and Rhiwbina – and bought many remarkable and important works of art by Turner and the French Post-Impressionists which now are the core of the National Museum of Wales in Cardiff; among them Rodin's 'The Kiss' and Renoir's 'La Parisienne'.
3. See my whole section Festivites, based on the course and history.
4. See Robert Meyrick's books on these two artists: *John Elwyn* (Scolar Press/Lund Humphries, 2000) and *Claudia Williams: A Retrospective* (National Library of Wales, 2000).
5. Other important artists from Wales have produced work with the Curwen: Sir Kyffin Williams, Ceri Richards, John Elwyn and Josef Herman.
6. This eminent native of Tenby is celebrated in the local museum as one of the significant figures from the town.
7. *The Description of Pembrokeshire by George Owen of Henllys*, ed. Dillwyn Miles (Gomer, 1994). Written by Owen in the sixteenth century. Laws says this was "in St John's Court near the town well, just to the east of the railway viaduct."
8. See Edward Laws: *The History of Little England beyond Wales and the non-Kymric colony settled in Pembrokeshire*, 1888, p. 181.
9. During the writing of this book, in 2010, the De Valence lurched into serious financial difficulties and had to close.
10. We went to an excellent concert by Jacqui Dankworth in the Tenby Festival a couple of years back. An annual event in the third week in September, the festival is an enjoyable cultural bridge between the end of the tourist season and the shorter, darker days of winter. They have had significant names such as Julian Lloyd Webber and the harpist Catrin Finch.
11. Some aspects of the architecture of the town have been pointed out to me by Rob Scourfield, Buildings, Officer at the National Parks. He admits that his family of builders were responsible for the Imperial arch and hotel desecration. The Imperial has a stable clientele of coach parties now but has hosted regular conferences and business events. I attended Welsh Academi of Writers conference there in the 1993 which had the great poet Miroslav Holub as its main guest. The dining room offers the usual spectacular views of Caldey and the Gower.
12. The Arts Festival at Tenby is held every September and brings a number of significant artists and musicians to the town. Check the gallery at its website: artmatters.org.uk
13. Published by Seren and including poets from the early Welsh to contemporary voices in English.
14. Such insurances were introduced in the late seventeenth century following the Great Fire of London. In that city and later in larger towns insurance companies would employ their own fire services – buckets and ladders – to be deployed when one of their policy holders was stricken.
15. The Museum staged an exhibition by him in 1996.
16. See my visits to Arthur and Bim Giardelli at Warren for first-hand experiences of their fire power.
17. Jim John, Arthur Booker and others appear elsewhere in this book.
18. Is Wintergreen still used? When I Googled it I got the assurance that "Wintergreen is excellent when used as a winter warmer in the colder months by massaging into hands before venturing out or working outdoors. Use for aching, tired feet by massaging in each morning

or evening. Is also widely used as a pre-sport rub on muscles especially in winter." I'd rather hoped that it had disappeared, like, Garrad record changers, or collar studs; something so tied into its era that you had to have been there to know the reference.

19. Thanks to Arthur Booker, who ran the Under 15s. He was a hero of mine. See the Playing the Course section.

20. Other brushes with the greatness of Welsh rugby for me included marking the exceptionally gifted and impossibly arrogant Terry Price when we played Llanelli Grammar at Greenhill in 1964. Price played for Wales and the British Lions before turning pro with Bradford Northern Rugby League club for £8,000. He also tried out as a kicker for the Buffalo Bills in American Football. A year later he closed the bar at Swansea University where I was a fresher by his post-match antics. My only appearance at a first class ground was in a warm-up match for Tenby Youth against Llanelli Youth at Stradey Park, now a housing estate.

21. See also our encounter on Tenby Golf course. Denzil's time at Greenhill School was blighted by a tragic incident. One of his sons was left badly crippled under a collapsed ruck when Denzil was refereeing a school match. Remarkably that paraplegic son went on to father a child. He died in 2009.

22. South Conference versus Surrey in 2007.

23. Also for the establishment of the Pembrokeshire Pasty firm in 2010. Types of pasty include 'The Caldey Island', 'Tenby Treat' and 'Friendly Dragon'.

24. cf the painter Ernest Zobole who I interviewed in *Welsh Painters Talking*.

25. See the golf club section and the Giltar Point trench system.

26. As with all artists, avoid giclee prints and save up for an original.

27. We ate here in 2010 with the sculptor David Nash and his wife Claire Langdown whose exhibition of paintings had been shown at the Museum: a series of sunsets seen from their chapel in Blaenau Ffestiniog which chimed remarkably with the sun falling over Giltar; in both cases our used light sinking into Ireland.

28. See the Festivities section.

29. The other properties are in Tenby's Southcliffe Street, Narberth and Penally. To contact the charity to discover more and to make a donation go to www.harriet-davis-trust.brecon.co.uk

30. This terrace was built by John Rees, one of three brothers, with the proceeds of their involvement with the opium trade with China in the nineteenth century. See *A Legacy of Opium* by Douglas Fraser (Tenby Heritage Publications, 2010). See note below regarding Nina Hamnett whose blue plaque is on the wall of the Terrace.

31. Thatcher's desire to sell off council houses was a dubious and mixed blessing. We own our bungalow in Lydstep as a result of this. As do most of our neighbours there.

32. Nina Hamnett was born in Lexden Terrace in 1890 and died in London in 1956. She was a talented artist, also the lover of Henri Gaudier-Brzeska, the major sculptor, who died in the First World War. His bust of her is in the Tate. She lived in Montparnasse, Paris before the war and knew Satie, Picasso, Modigliani, Poulenc and many other musicians and artists. She worked in the Roger Fry Omega Workshops in the Great War (Fry painted her) and between the wars and up to her death she became one of the notorious characters in the Colony Club in Fitzrovia. See *Nina Hamnett: Queen of Bohemia* by Denise Hooker, 1986 .There are two autobiographies by Hamnett which achieved a certain success: *The Laughing Torso* and *Is she a Lady?*

33. Fiore was a remarkably talented person who sculpted JFK, the Queen Mother, Olivier, Shirley Bassey and Peter Ustinov. She had a studio in Chelsea at one stage and a Bentley. She featured on USA tv programmes shaping a clay likeness of other guests in the duration of the show. She was, despite this, a serious artist; her life was complicated by her indeterminate sexuality. This was not resolved until later in her life when surgery was more sophisticated. Augustus John made a pass at her, he always did, but discovered that all was not straightforward. See *Art and Androgyny The Life of the Sculptor Fiore de Henriquez* by Jan Marsh. Also www.fioredocumentary.com

34. Fenton pp. 238-240.
35. See the website for 'Manorbier Fish Ponds'.
36. *The Letters of Virginia Woolf Vol. I 1888-1912* (Harcourt Brace, 1975).
37. 'Four Circular Walks around Manorbier' by Brian John (PCNPA) appeared in 1993, but is still a good guide.
38. Richard Fenton calls him, "our earliest tourist", in *A Historical Tour Through Pembrokeshire*, 1903.
39. *Ibid.*
40. *Ibid.*
41. There is an entry in her early journals making account of her 1908 stay (*A Passionate Apprentice: The Early Journals*, Hogarth Press 1990, pp. 380-1) – when she took a room in a cottage called 'Sea View', in Manorbier. The house was owned by a Mr Barclay. A number of letters from Sea View – nos 438-446 are collected in *The Flight of the Mind. The Letters of Virginia Woolf vol. I:1882-1912.*
42. This despite the dark concerns of the man from whom she was renting her rooms: "I lodge in one cottage, but have my sitting room in another. The room belongs to a young farmer, Mr Barclay, who let it me on condition that I would write neither fiction nor poetry at his table." By contrast the Beach Break Café is a welcome wifi spot when the present writer wants to work.
43 *Siegfried Sassoon – The Journey from the Trenches* ed. Jean Moorcroft Wilson (Routledge). Sassoon was one of the outstanding poets of the Great War.
44. Leslie Kenton is the daughter of the jazz musician Stan Kenton. A woman of huge energy and invention, she lists among her achievements the design of a range products for the Estée Lauder cosmetics group and an ITV cookery programme. Her claim to be able to "reverse the aging process" (http://www.lesliekenton.com/to_age.html) may, however, need a sprinkling of Manorbier sea salt. Leslie is, undoubtedly, the most influential of recent Manorbier residents.
45. 'Philip Sutton: Life and Work' is available from the Royal Academy website. Heather Sutton has just published a book of their time with peter Peers and Benjamin Britten – *Phillip Sutton: Peter Peers, His Patron.*
46. A more recent house in the castle grounds is still available for rent.
47. Virginia Woolf, 1908. *Letters.*
48. My poem 'Return to the Headland' was first published in *Preparations* (Gomer, 1980).
49. 'Lordy', as he was nicknamed by the locals, and both his wives were generous to the villagers and held children's parties in the great library in the 20-bedroomed Lydstep Houuse, often clothing the children for these occasions too. Lord Philipps had his main residence at Roch and another at Newmarket too.
50. See my poems 'Last Things' and 'The Last Night At Lydstep' in *Heaven's Gate* (Seren, 2001).
51. This poem was published in the landscape anthology *Countourlines* (Salt/Magdalen College Cambridge, 2009).
52. Stephen is one of the more remarkable characters in the area. A useful golfer and financial manager of the local Ford garage, he undertook a change of life and style, becoming the warden of Skomer Island and a leading authority on bird life.
53. Tommy Farr (1913-1986) fought 126 bouts, despite a ten year lay-off. Like so many boxers his riches faded and he was bankrupt at one time. Joe Louis held the world heavyweight belt from 1937-49 and was an important figure in the move to win respect for black Americans.
54. Both commemorated on the war memorial in front of the Manorbier Castle entrance. I refer to this in the introduction of my anthology *After the First Death* (Seren, 2009). Reg Smith died as this book was going to press.
55. Stone structures with arches rather than solid walls for storing hay etc.
56. Sir John (1873-1954) was a long serving member of parliament and Home Secretary in

Asquith's coalition government in 1915. He served as Foreign Secretary, Chancellor of the Exchequer and Lord Chancellor under later governments. When elevated to a peerage he took the title Viscount Simon of Stackpole Elidor in the County of Pembrokeshire. His grandson, Jan David Simon (b.1940), the third viscount, sits in the House of Lords as a Labour peer.

57. From 'Lydstep Caverns' by Sir Lewis Morris (1833-1907) in *The Poetry of Pembrokeshire*.

58. There is a very detailed and academic study of this by Cambell and Lane at ads.ahds.ac.uk/catalogue/adsdata. Campbell, E. & Lane, A. 'Excavations at Longbury Bank, Dyfed', *Medieval Archaeology* 37: 15-77.

59. He even named his house in Islington 'Michael Collins House' after the executed Irish rebel. Griffith's film about Collins was banned by ITV.

60. 'The Trenches at Giltar' in *Crossing Over* by Tony Curtis (Seren, 2007).

61. In the summer of 2009 a group of 36 schoolchildren and four adults from the Valleys got into serious trouble when as a 'character-forming activity' they were encouraged to walk backwards en masse into the sea. This was about halfway along the South Beach and beyond the regulated flag-defined safe bathing zone. The large sand bank to which they had paddled and on which they stood suddenly collapsed under the incoming tide and they were left, some of them, up to their necks in the sea. The Tenby lifeguards, the Air Wales Ambulance and other services rushed to save them. It was close thing. Some of those children had never been on a beach before, apparently: we always have to respect the sea and our coastline, both for its preservation, and our own.

62. John Argent is also a consultant for the Chevron oil company and has been based in Houston. Adam Chandler is their associate partner and specialises in sustainability.

63. By CADW and others in the last twenty years.

64. As described by Raymond Garlick in 'The Elate Island' in *The Poetry of Pembrokeshire*.

65. *George Owen The Description of Pembrokeshire* which existed only in ms until Fenton's extracts appeared in 1796. There was an edition in 1892 and most usefully the 1994 Gomer edition edited by the indefatigable Dillwyn Miles.

66. The 'Conies' is the name of the rabbits section (handicap 18 and over) at Tenby Golf Club. The actual rabbits are entertaining, but a nuisance on the burrows course.

67. Be sure not to miss the David Jones wood engraving of this view. He shows the cattle and a dirty British coaster in the Tenby Roads.

68. Alison Bielski's 'Visit to an Island' in *The Poetry of Pembrokeshire*.

69. The Belgian connection is evidenced in the fact that the monks' choir stalls are made from hardwood from the Congo, the territory notoriously and brutally administered by the Belgians in their nineteenth century 'heart of darkness'.

70. Though these are based on Caldey plants, they are made elsewhere.

71. They have also introduced commercial meat supplies from their Hereford-cross-Friesian cattle.

72. Gill was a genius of design, but also incestuous and domineering. David Jones was engaged to Gill's daughter Petra for some eight years and she became the woman depicted in much of his early art. They never married, however, and it is likely that her father was her lover. See *David Jones: The Maker Unmade* by Jonathan Miles and Derek Shiel (Seren, 1995). Gill, in fact, leased the Anglican monks' buildings from them when they experienced financial difficulties in the late twenties.

73. David Jones to Petra Tegetmeier on the 3rd of November 1931, as quoted in Professor Thomas Dilworth's article in the *T.L.S.* Feb 4th, 2011.

74. Jones's *In Parenthesis* is arguably the most extraordinary work to have come out of a soldier's experiences in the 1914-18 war. His means of dealing with the senseless horrors which he witnessed was rooted in a sense of the continuity of man's wars from Celtic through Roman times to the twentieth century. His fine etching of the view from Caldey, as well as an interesting watercolour are in the Tenby Museum collection.

CENTRAL

FOLLY FARM AND BEGELLY

Five giraffes teeter out of their house and take the air at their altitude. I take a photograph and realise that in the shot in the edge of the frame is the roof of the shop on the Narbeth road at Begelly where my parents tried and failed to run a village petrol pump and stores in the late 1960s. This is at the Williams's farm which has over the last twenty years morphed into Folly Farm, one of the leading visitor attractions in Pembrokeshire. The giraffes have been trailed on tv ads and on the sides of buses throughout south Wales for months now and are, in the taut flesh on their wiry frames, truly strange and impressive. Their necks are endless and they walk with a circumspect delicacy on impossibly thin legs. There are poles with pulleys from which branches are hung for them to feed, but they are also happy to take the July-wet grass; this they do by means of spaying their front legs quite alarmingly and reaching down, nose bisecting the stance, to graze. They are housed in a new, million pound building at the west end of Folly Farm and to the south of the African section. This has zebras and a secure gate system which means that sheep may roam and be petted by the children. This is just what Megan, our granddaughter wants and what every big girl or boy of five or six or ten will be pleased to do. This is the age group which Folly Farm best suits, though the fairground rides will

keep older children (and adults) going quite nicely, especially when rain falls.[1]

Folly Farm is a remarkable success story, though Begelly must have hardly registered in the second half of the last century when the motor car became common and the coal was long forgotten. This small village en route to Narberth and points north in Pembrokeshire and on to Ceredigion had nothing more than a scattering of B&B places, a church you'd miss as you took that sharp right-hander up from the main Pembroke road and the tiny, tinny shack of a village shop which my parents tried to make a go of. I remember that when they moved in it had a hand-pumped petrol pump which would have fetched a pretty price now on eBay bid for by someone big on motoring nostalgia. I was an undergraduate filling my head with history and literature, but even I could see that this was a big challenge. The whole enterprise was sunk by a combination of bad luck and poor judgement. Exactly the opposite of the Folly Farm story.

Begelly, even then in the 1960s, had had a rich history of which I was unaware and about which no-one informed me. It had been part of the Kilgetty and district coal workings, owned largely by the Philipps family of Picton Castle, including mines at Kingsmoor and Thomas Chapel;[2] fine anthracite was carted down to the coast at Wiseman's Bridge and Saundersfoot, later by a railway. In its heyday the Tenby and Begelly Coal Company had two vessels shipping from Saundersfoot and its own wharf. The church was served by a parsonage which, according to a report in 1844, was so situated on a coal seam that it would have collapsed had any more digging of coal taken place. There was evidence of a cromlech close by. As early as the sixteenth century the intensity of the coal workings had alarmed Tenby council and travellers were warned of subsidence as their carriages used the road north.[3]

The nineteenth century surgeon, Thomas George Noote who lived in Begelly noted the dangers of employing children in the pits. "Were it possible to be done, I would not allow a child to be taken into the pits before the age of fifteen, but in consequence of the depth of ore they are frequently taken at a much earlier age." He goes on to deplore the living conditions in the area and notes that typhus is not uncommon.[4] Where children enjoy the adventure playgrounds and widen their eyes at giraffes, other children would have toiled and died, or died before they could be asked to toil. The Williams at Folly Farm may well open the drift mine on their land; they are serious and responsible people in the tourist business, but it may be a tough tale to tell in its entirety.

Begelly has a moral and religious tradition of course. The Calvinistic Methodist Chapel Zion was established in 1828 and is still in use. The church of St Mary's, is the site of a motte and bailey castle; it was restored in 1887. One of the bells, dating from 1760 is inscribed "My sound is good, my shape is neat – Twas Bailey made me so complete"; it had been cast by Bayley of Bridgewater in the west country.

Begelly House was the only residence of gentry proportions and its owner Captain James Child (1825-1877) was greatly involved in the local coal industry and its transportation in the zenith of its importance.[5] It was to Begelly House that my parents wintered in 1969 when Begelly Stores proved too cold. I remember Margaret and I spending a chilly Christmas in the high-roomed flat they rented. Unaware of the village's history I also didn't know that Augustus and Gwen John were frequent visitors as children, escaping the Victorian strictures of their home in Tenby. "Left to ourselves in the big house overlooking a wide infertile common, distained by the land-grabbers, and populated only by a few cattle, geese and gypsies, we ran happily wild."[6] Had I known that I would have spent no doubt fruitless hours prising open old cupboards for scraps of genius. On that journey from Tenby to Begelly House they would have seen and met members of the Romany community camped at Kingsmoor. Those gypsies and their nomadic lifestyle, or John's romantic notion of that lifestyle, would feed his imagination and surface again when he met John Sampson, the Romany enthusiast in Liverpool where he was university librarian, and Augustus taught.[7] The John family – wife, children, lover and ostler would later tramp their way around Wales and England in an enactment of the Romany ideal. The drawings, paintings etchings of this period would help to make John's reputation in the art world internationally and that must have its roots in those Begelly visits and holidays. Certainly, when my father worked at his cousins' garage at Kilgetty and at Stepaside in the early 1960s he would also do repairs on gypsy vehicles as a side-line. The Proberts and the Mochans always paid. In cash.

My Aunt Annie, who had left us her house 'Ashburnham', one of two on the sharp bend at the top of the common, was my Gran's sister and had experienced the same trauma of being, effectively, cast off from the family farm in Jeffeyston.[8] She'd married a man called Bowen who had fought and survived the Great War and whose service medal I'd kept until someone relieved me of it on a schools visiting poet session. My memories of Annie were confused and almost completely negative. She smelled of chicken meal and had wooden clogs; her dog smelled of dog, only worse. She haunted 'Ashburnham' for a year or so until we redecorated and added a kitchen and cleaned the place up, and let air in. On our visits to Uncle Ivor's in Pwllcrochan we would sometimes swing over to her old cottage called Leverocks ('Levereux' on the OS map), down a winding, narrow lane that turns to the right just after the Saundersfoot left turn and the Fountain Inn on the A478 at Pentlepoir. One afternoon we arrived to see her hanging out something on her washing line. It was the skin of an adder she'd killed: "as if we had discovered some lurking thing/the gypsy moor and woods held secret." I was convinced that she was a witch, but, in fact, she was a 'charmer' and had the traditional folk medicine skills to 'charm' warts and tend other minor ailments. I unfairly characterised her as an insensitive woman in an early poem, then much later tried to make amends in 'Annie' –

> The Bible verses, wild garlic, thyme,
> chicken's feet, whatever she practised,
> tricks or gift, vanished with her last pinched breath.

If that was witchcraft it was small thing,
a bunched grasp of herbs and words and a wishing
that now I begin to understand, and could learn to take,
like a child reading an S, seeing a snake.[9]

For years I'd blamed her for the fact that Ginnie, her daughter had been locked away in the St David's asylum up the hill from our house in Carmarthen. That unseen and barely-talked-about woman was another constituent of my Annie nightmares. Oh those good old days, the Fifties. When no-one called a spade a spade and cancer was 'trouble downstairs' or 'a lump'. We had no language for a range of feelings and the generation who brought up my generation were, for the most part, emotionally crippled by the war and that lack of honesty. In truth, as I found out many years later, Aunt Annie was making the long bus journey up to Carmarthen to visit her damaged niece, when the girl's mother and others in the family had, in effect, abandoned her. Annie was a good woman, a good, rough-and-ready country woman to whose charms I was deaf and blind. She had become wrapped up in a childhood pattern of the gypsies on Kingsmoor Common – Hairy Mary and dull Davy who'd disappeared (kidnapped? murdered?), folk tales, prejudice and dark dreams; soon to be replaced by Duane Eddy, the Everly Brothers and our moving house to Valley Road the other side of Pentlepoir hill.

JEFFREYSTON

I have in my study a photograph of my grandmother's brother, Matthew Barrah (1883-1953) posing in his Pembrokeshire Yeomanry uniform with swagger stick and the style of field hat they wore in the Boer War. He's gone up to Carmarthen to the studio of George Weakes of Lammas Street, so that journey and his involvement with the Yeomanry[10] must have been of some significance and pride. Matthew was the man who, in 1909 had to make the immense journey from his sheep farm in Manitoba to Jeffreyston to settle the Jeffreyston Farm estate. That would leave my grandmother and her sisters effectively disinherited and forced to move from the property. That is why I am here and why I am writing this book.[11]

And the man who set all those events and actions in motion was

Stephen Thomas Barrah, my great grandfather whose grave is at the rear of St Jeffrey and St Oswald at the heart of the village. 1856 – 1908: Stephen was the head of our family and ran the farm adjacent to the church. The farm was lost when he was killed in a pony and trap accident when returning home from the pub. It is a family legend, which my grandmother denied, that he was racing another pub goer for a wager down one of those winding narrow lanes. Whatever: the result was that his only son had to return from Canada to settle the estate, leaving his five sisters to make their own way, presumably with some of the money.

That's why I was born in Carmarthen; my Gran married James Charles Curtis from Berkshire who had been sent down by the GWR to what was then a large terminus and engine centre. He worked as a guard on trains in west Wales and they settled in No 50 Pentrefelin Street where I was born. In the year before she died I sent Gran a list of typed questions about her childhood in Pembrokeshire. I learned something of the narrow world of farm tasks and markets and fairs in the Jeffreyston/Cresselly area, but there was no mention of coal, nor did I think to ask. In his detailed and fascinating book *Pembrokeshire: the Forgotten Coalfield*, Martin Connop-Price develops what was a doctoral thesis at Aber. into a seemingly exhaustive explication of the history of mining in the county, from Amroth to Newgale. Jeffreyston, Kilgetty, Saundersfoot and Begelly, all places which were part of my family background and my early years in Pembrokeshire, figure importantly. As coal mining can be traced back to the thirteenth century in the Jeffreyston area, it seems obvious that my family must have worked in coal as well as in farming and this was confirmed to me by a letter from a distant cousin in the 1990s: members of my extended family were heavily involved in mines around Freystrop. Driver's aerial photograph of the village shows quite clearly the depressions of former pits, drift and bell pits, in the field immediately behind Jeffreyston Farm. Connop-Price points out that the taking of coal from Jeffreyston began in the thirteenth century, long before the south Wales valleys were dreamt of as the coal-house of the industrial revolution. My ancestors were miners of sorts when the two Rhondda valleys were relatively inaccessible sheep lands. The nineteenth century's astonishing expansion of the south Wales coalfield has come to be iconic, a metonym for the whole of Wales. But the green, green grass of home was lifted for black treasure first of all in such areas of south Pembrokeshire. It was the riches of the villages of Jeffreyston, Loveston and Broadmoor which led to the building of more formal quaysides at Cresswell Quay, probably early in the fourteenth century. As Connop-Price says, "it is reasonable to suggest that Cresswell Quay may well have been the site of Wales' first purpose-built coal shipping quay."[12] Certainly, Jeffreyston was a substantial village because of the coal industry rather than simply for its farming activities. In 1784 when John Wesley brought Methodism to Tenby he found the place depressed and relatively unpopulated. Three year previously he had preached to "a large congregation of honest colliers at Jeffreyston". By the beginning of the nineteenth century the coal industry in many of these villages had declined. The seams were not profitable in the context of increased industrial demand and the necessary investment for deep mining and the attention of the Victorians shifted south to Kilgetty and Saundersfoot and, much more significantly, away from Pembrokeshire to Glamorganshire. Now the village is neat and sleepy.

A couple of miles from Jeffreyston is the smaller hamlet of Loveston, which had its own mining industry and its own, more recent, mining narrative. In 1931 in the last flush of optimism in the Pembrokeshire coal industry a pit was dug and a slope developed by five men of the Wallace family. Over the next two years the enterprise expanded and up to thirty men were employed. The workings became more difficult, however, and they came across the workings of older pits as they mined further away from the village. In the spring of 1936 water broke through into the pit and seven men were drowned or crushed. It is difficult to imagine the impact of such a tragedy on such a small community and there is little evidence of the pit now. Loveston is another tiny village which attracts few except the passing-through strangers.

OAKWOOD AND BLUESTONE

These two developments have not been without their detractors and controversy. While the apparently uncontrolled housing developments of the 1960s and 1970s have been a blight on the county (had no-one been to Brittany and seen how development need not compromise the character of an area?) Pembrokeshire does need a variety of accommodation and entertainment for a range of people and rainy days. Oakwood brings something of Alton Towers and

Bluestone something of Center Parcs to the county. Neither is a serious blot on the landscape and you are less likely to be aware of their presence than that of the refineries that dominate the Haven.

Oakwood's attractions include Skyleap, Megafobia and Vertigo – you get the drift – but at over sixty quid for a family of four ticket you need to be sure that you want to leave the beach and the beauties of Pembrokeshire for a whole day of screaming. The place had a serious setback following the death of a teenage girl on the (now closed) Water Coaster ride in 2004. It is closed in the winter months.

Bluestone is a self-catering site with cottages, 'executive lodges' and studio flats. There is a sports hall and spa with extensive bike tracks, but the attraction which will bring in day visitors is the Blue Lagoon 'swimming park' with its Wild River ride and wave machine. But, I wonder, how long might you spend in the place and at what cost are you missing the rest of the county? At Freshwater West and all along the coast you have god's own wave machine and the "sky that goes on forever."[13]

NARBERTH AND TEMPLETON

Narberth, that boring village of my childhood, has recreated itself as a trendy town, the Cowbridge of Pembrokeshire. Crafts and arts and pricey frocks; bric-a-brac, dried flowers, jewellery and deli food. It's mainly one winding main street, High Street, like Cowbridge in the Vale of Glamorgan, and it's got a buzz. A few years back I attended the funeral of the painter John Addyman. The service was held in the church of St. Andrew (high wagon roof and some nice Arts and Crafts details) and the procession made its way through the town some two miles to the crematorium pacing behind a New Orleans style jazz band. John's coffin was in a horse-drawn hearse. The traffic was stopped, the town closed for any other movement. It rained steadily to complete the heady mix of grief and celebration. Narberth, where the ruined remnants of the castle of the Mortimers can be easily passed and missed as you drive in from the south, is also the place of modern death, where most of the region's deceased are cremated; both my father, in 1978 and my mother more recently, were transmuted by the municipal facility. There are worse ways to end it all and far worse places to say goodbye to loved ones.

What remains of the castle, and that's not a lot, is on the right just as you turn the town's first corner on the road north from Tenby. Originally recorded in the twelfth century, what is left is probably almost two hundred years later. Three of its towers still stand with one wall of its hall, though it was inhabited until the late seventeenth century. It does command a position overlooking one of the obvious approaches to the town, though whether it is the Arberth referred to in the *Mabinogion* and the base of Pwll, may be disputed. 'Arberth' is a Norman name, not Welsh, though the town and its castle mark a point on what is generally agreed on as the Landsker Line of cultural and linguistic delineation in the county. The name would have originally covered a large area of rule, rather than simply the town. The apparently undistinguished village of Templeton, a few miles south on the Tenby road may, in fact, be the site of an older and original fort. The Pesvner guide calls it, "a good example of Norman linear planning".[14] Sentence Castle in woods to the west of the present village, it is argued, was an earlier defensive position and the village itself is named after associations with the Knights Templar.

Taking the B4315 from Templeton on the way marked to the crematorium brings you to Princes Gate and the farm which produces the bottled water which carries that name and which is stocked by Tescos and other large retailers. Eira and Glyn Jones run a four hundred acre dairy farm, but probably now do better by bottling water from the secret spring on their land. They have been in that business for over twenty years. They have a sterile, automated, state-of-the-art bottling plant behind the farm. It's water, but Pembrokeshire water. Funny old world, isn't it?[15]

Off the A4115 at the south end of the village lies the site of the disused airfield from the Second World War. It's here and at Carew where any new 'affordable housing' could be located, not in some of the green pasture sites which greedy landowners have been encouraged to propose. Planning or 'planning' has been a curse in the county since the war. That war was won because such sites were effective. From 1943-1945 Templeton was used as a training base for light bombers and fighter planes. Some Nissen huts and other buildings can still be seen alongside the ghosts of the criss-crossed runways. There have been more recent exercises involving helicopters at the site. The Knights Templar may not rest easily.

In Narberth, turning left after the castle sign you enter Market Street and are confronted by an old hotel with the intriguing inscription 'Baron de Rutzen'; built in 1833 and named after the landowner from Slebech, this building had behind it a covered market originally. De Rutzen was a Latvian who secured the Slebech estate by marriage in 1822. He was ambitious and bombastic, being involved in disputes with the Anglican Church over the re-siting of the principal local church and the neglect and eventual demolition of two other medieval churches.[16]

Just a few yards along from the de Rutzen at 2, Market Street, is the pottery and shop of Simon Rich, his wife and daughter. Simon trained with Alan Caiger-Smith of the Aldermaston Pottery and has been based here for nearly forty years. The Rich family send their work, including Raku and zinc crystal glazed pieces, to many outlets and galleries through the UK. Worth a visit.

Opposite is the little museum which is in process of development. The most striking building at the beginning of High Street from the south is the town hall, built in 1835 and looking strangely continental and out of place in Pembrokeshire. High Street is narrow, one-way and almost impossible to park on unless you have a disabled sticker. (On a fine day you might be better coming by train and alighting at the child's story book 1896 station. Though it's a long walk to town.) High Street is doing its best to be an upmarket country town – there are decent butchers, and one of those Barbour and shooting stick places for real country types, or pseuds.

At the end of High Street is Oriel Q. The Queen's Hall in Narberth is an oasis in the middle of the county. That is not for the passable café and the public hall (tribute bands, flower shows) downstairs, but for the gallery/oriel on the top floor. The idealistic and energetic Lynne Crompton keeps the place going, and has done for nearly twenty years, though it takes constant applications to the Arts Council of Wales, lottery grants and an annual auction of donated art works to stay afloat.

One evening in May we arrive a little late at the opening of an exhibition of the paintings of Osi Rhys Osmond, with prints by Peter Blincow. Osi is sounding out in his best public manner, explaining that the images of Palestinian men and women are related to his sunsets looking Pembrokeshire-wards from his home at Llanstephan, just over the Carmarthenshire border. He has been shaken by the sound and sight of gunfire from the military ranges whilst walking his grandchildren on the beach and the hills. This, combined with visits he has made to Gaza have led to these new works. Surprisingly, two of the political paintings sell that night, not the Turner-esque sunsets. Chris Kinsey the artist is there and two people from the Zip tv company who have used Osi for a several programmes on S4C. Also, the larger-than-life David Petersen, artist-blacksmith, son of the famous boxer Jack, who won the British and Empire titles and held the Lonsdale Belt. David's public works include the fine blue bridge over the river in St Clears (a village now just off the A40, worth stopping at on the drive down to Pembrokeshire) and the memorial to the Welsh dead at Mametz Wood on the Western Front which I once described as "Petersen's brash memorial dragon."[17] He is enthused by Osi's paintings and tells me at great length about his scheme to work on assembling a 'White Book of Carmarthen', to be a pacifism declaration by writers and artists. The 'Black Book of Carmarthen (*Llyfr Du Caerfyrddin*) is a thirteenth century manuscript held in the National Library in Aberystwyth, probably by the hand of a solitary scribe from the Priory of St. John the Evangelist and Teulyddog in Carmarthen. It records and celebrates Madawg ap Maredudd, Taliesin, Arthur and Urien; this is warrior praise, of course. Not sure that Petersen's simplistic idealism will work and, despite the persuasive context of Osi's show, I tell him so. I doubt whether his White Book will sing the praises of Tenby – "There is a fair fort

upon the sea; a splendid rise, joyful on holiday… where cupping fosters pleasure, And praise and the cry of birds". Perhaps you need the threat of violence to sing the joys of nature's peace and beauty with real depth.

We move on to the excellent deli and Spanish restaurant Ultracomida across from Oriel Q. Strongly recommended, though you may need to book.

One of the best meals we've enjoyed in Narberth was lunch with the artist Geoffrey Yeomans (image, page 83) in his semi on the road to the station: a rich soup made from vegetables from his garden. Geoff was born in Birkenhead in 1934, but after a teaching career in the Midlands he has settled in Pembrokeshire for the last two decades and his paintings and prints have memorably focussed on wrecked boats and their detritus. The blue, orange, green and black sides of abandoned ships become almost Rothko-esque meditations in his most powerful paintings. In his studio he shows us the large triptych 'M72', which is a tour de force. He says, "Painting is a love affair with a surface." Found objects, metal bolts and angles assume sculptural significance on his hearths and shelves. Recent exhibitions have included the Torch Theatre in Milford, the Ceri Richards Gallery in Swansea and he won first prize in the Mall galleries, London, Marine Artists Exhibition in 2008.[18]

CAREW AND CRESSELLY

The reason for visiting Carew, rather than passing through on your way north/south between Haverfordwest or Narberth to Tenby and the coast is, of course, the castle. I usually first glimpse it between the high hedges of the Milton road, Stephen's Green Lane, off the Ridgeway on our way north from Lydstep to Haverfordwest, but it's more common to come upon it off the Pembroke road or, most dramatically and surpisingly, from the north. As you drive south on the A4075, a few miles past Cresselly you twist down a wooded hill called Carew Lane and come to a halt at the north end of the single-track road over the river and old tidal mill pond. The castle sits proud at the edge of the river. Park your car a few hundred yards past the Carew Inn, a solid nineteenth century house on the left, near the eleventh century Celtic cross and walk back to the entrance. The cross is a memorial to Maredudd, a ruler of the

ancient lands of Deheubarth, one of the three divisions of Wales, at the beginning of the eleventh century.[19] It was moved to its present position in 1923. Behind that wall is the site of a deer park which figured in the great 1507 tournament and banquet.

As you walk to the entrance note four raised humps of grass; these have been recently confirmed by aerial photography to be part of the defensive ditch system of an Iron Age promontory fort. Certainly, there is evidence for this site to have be occupied for over two thousand years. It is well worth walking onto the mill, one of the few tidal mills still to be seen in the UK.[20] It has been active from the middle of the sixteenth century and was further developed by Sir John Carew. Although the milling operation was based on the tides, it was also possible to run the mill more predictably from water stored in the mill-pond. What remains now is nineteenth century and was active until 1937. The restoration and running of the site is now the responsibility of the Pembrokeshire National Park Authority. There is an audio-visual display and plenty of information about the history of milling:

> The noble edifice of Carew Castle is situated on a neck of land washed by the tide of two estuaries with a gentle fall towards the water, and consists of a superb range of apartments round a

> quadrangle, with an immense bastion at each corner, containing handsome chambers.[21]

The castle itself is Norman in origin and was built by Gerald de Windsor, an Anglo-Norman baron who was constable of Pembroke Castle. He was given the land at Carew as part of the dowry of Princess Nest, an ap Tewdwr, and a great beauty whose charms encouraged Owain ap Cadwgan to attack the castle at Carew in 1109 and take it and her. At the end of the thirteenth century Nicholas de Carew, a successful soldier under Edward I, greatly developed the place in terms of its fortifications and accommodation. Sir Rhys ap Thomas who owned the castle in the fifteenth century was apparently loyal to King Richard III and promised that Henry Tudor would only land in Pembrokeshire "over my belly". Secreting himself under Mullock Bridge, Sir Rhys was beneath the future Henry VII's horse as he rode through the county to his victory at Bosworth. His support for the Tudor king led him to the Governorship of Wales and in 1507 Sir Rhys hosted the most extravagant celebrations ever seen in the county when for five days a tournament was held attended by some six hundred nobles and followers "most of them of goode ranke and qualitie, to be spectators of those rare solemnities never before known in those partes...".[22] It was, evidently, a vigorous and enthusiastic occasion, "and sound knockes you may be sure were received and returned on both sides, butt noe harme at all done, for Sir Rice had taken order with the stickes to parte them, and prevent all cause of jar, if anie the least occasion of it in that kind were offered."

The royal connection continued when Sir John Perrot, allegedly the illegitimate son of Henry VIII, took over as governor of the castle and modernised the north side in the Elizabethan manner. He became the governor of Ireland in 1572 and spent little time in Carew thereafter; despite the fact that he was one of four bearers of the canopy of state over Queen Elizabeth at her coronation, he died in prison, accused of high treason in 1592.[23] While the castle was in his possession it was lavishly furnished with tapestries from Arras and Turkish rugs. He had a fine collection of musical instruments including sackbuts, cornets, Irish harp, flute, violin and two virginals; the library also held books in French and Spanish.[24] Clearly, the fine houses of Pembrokeshire were as impressive in their culture and taste and extravagance as those in England.

During the Civil War the castle was defended by Sir George

Carew who sided with the King. He survived the vagaries of that conflict and died in Carew in 1685. He is buried at Carew Cheriton, whose church is well worth visiting and is sign-posted off the roundabout on the main Pembroke road, the A477 to the south of the castle. The family chapel in this small church has the memorial to Sir John Carew who died in 1637.

Just across the road is a fortified rectory and remarkably a military cemetery which reminds us of the importance of this tiny village to two world wars. On what is now used as the biggest Sunday car boot sale in the county, was built Carew Aerodrome. Originally known as RNAS Pembroke or RNAS Milton it saw early, pre-RAF activity as an air base being used by air-ships. In 1938, with war again threatened it was re-commissioned, as Carew-Cheriton, and by 1941 there were three concrete runways to replace the original grass strips. It served as a support operation for the Sunderland flying boats based at Pembroke Dock and the Haven which flew sorties against U-boats in the Irish Sea and the eastern Atlantic, and later as a radio training base, closing at the end of the war. The airfield may still be discerned between the car boot stalls and some newer industrial units. The control tower has been restored to its camouflage paint by the Carew Cheriton Control Tower Group, which encourages visitors. The original watch tower is close by and, according to local historian Derek Brock, was constructed from the wheel-house of the steamer *Montrose* from which was sent the radio message that led to the arrest of the infamous murderer Dr Crippen in 1910 when the ship docked in Canada. It is also the site of some tragedy for in 1941 an air raid claimed a direct hit on the sick bay and twelve airmen were killed. There was also loss of life when in 1943 two Airspeed Oxfords collided on the runway and five men were killed

More fortunate was the pilot who was forced to try for an emergency landing at Carew Chertion in 1943. His account written decades later captures the spirit of daring that was key to our survival as a nation in that war.

> During the next 20 minutes or so I was able to climb the aircraft very carefully to about 1000ft, with the starboard engine roaring flat out and becoming somewhat overheated by dint of our slow forward speed. Fearing that this engine might fail, I decided to attempt a straight in approach to the north/south runway at Carew Cheriton as it slowly came into view. I selected 'undercarriage

down', but needed to lose height rapidly in order to maintain speed above the stall. Increased drag from the lowering undercarriage, also began rapidly to 'consume' all remaining height and, to avoid crashing short of the runway, I selected 'undercarriage up' and attempted to 'go round again'.

We must have passed along the entire runway about 100ft up but, as the undercarriage was slow to retract – driven only by the starboard engine's hydraulic pump – the aircraft suddenly became inexorably committed landwards. I aimed towards a field straight ahead and the aircraft landed on its belly and slithered along the ground. Unfortunately, a rural electricity distribution line was in its path and a collision of the port wing with one of the line's wooden poles, caused the aircraft to swing sharply left and go sideways through a hedge, over a minor road and through its far hedge into another field, where it came to rest – on fire.

My unfortunate passenger was quickly out of the top hatch, going on to extricate the navigator who had been rendered temporarily dazed in the crash. I found that my headset leads had become trapped in cockpit wreckage and, in all the dense smoke which quickly surrounded me, I failed to think of freeing myself by slipping my helmet off! A third attempt to snap the leads succeeded – fear lent me brute force – and I leaped from the aircraft urging the other two to run clear as quickly as possible. When we had got about 100 yards away, there was a tremendous explosion as the fuel tanks exploded and the aircraft was subsequently almost completely destroyed.

I had meanwhile suffered a slight laceration of my right eyebrow in the crash and, unable to see out of the eye through a mass of dirt and congealed blood, I feared having lost it – a fact which my passenger quickly confirmed, fortunately wrongly as it subsequently turned out.

Almost immediately, however, we were met by three beautiful young Welsh maidens – blue-eyed blondes – the eldest of whom was probably only in her early twenties. Surprisingly barefooted, they escorted us to their nearby farmhouse and, after bathing my eye and thereby restoring its sight, they poured us each a tot of whisky, having debated whether or not they should do so, in the absence of their parents who were away at the local market.[25]

The appearance of those 'maidens' is like some vision from the Mabinogion. The local troops as well as the visiting American and European troops and airmen were, if they but knew it, re-enacting ancient conflicts and the carrying of arms in Pembrokeshire. My father "scraping field potatoes for the searchlight crew's supper" my mother in the Land Army "in ankle-up, corduroys, with long woollen socks/- the uniform completed by a khaki shirt and tie,"[26] the Sunderland flying boats crossing like white swans and the brutal, necessary concrete gun emplacements that still stand sentry along the coast – all those images are woven for me into a Pembrokeshire tapestry of war. Standing before the graves in the military cemetery at Carew Cheriton – or walking the Coast Path on a sunny summer's day, the reminders are there. So, the Poles Zenon Jerwicz and Jerzey Kontz, the Canadians Howard Dobbs, Charles Jackson, Morris Ezra Shaw, Robert Smith and Robert Middleton, the Dutchmen Marius van Kooij, Jan Michels, Franciscus Overdijk and Jacobus Rademaker, the New Zealander Francis McCaffry join the RAF men Anthony Barnes, Archibold Wills and Richard Wilson in the annex to the churchyard at Carew Cheriton. Take the trouble to cross over to this tiny village when you visit Carew's Castle and mill. The transatlantic jets chalk their paths overhead and there is the faint sound of traffic on the Pembroke road. As our troops work on in foreign countries it is salutary to note that Sergeant Richard Edmund Wilson who was killed when his Hawker Henley crashed in April 1940 had served for three years before the war in Basra where so many of our generation's young men have died. His daughter was born in September of that year.

On a fine day in May Margaret and I are in the Carew Inn having a decent pub fish and chips and mushy peas with Tom Lloyd.[27] Thomas Lloyd O.B.E. of Freestone Hall is the brother-in-law of Hugh Harrison Allen who lives in the fine eighteenth century Cresselly House, which his family have always occupied. Tom is one of the authors of the Pevsner guide to the county on which any writer rests heavily. His house is a fine large farmhouse, eighteenth century with nineteenth century alterations. It's about a mile as the crow flies from the even more remarkable Harrison Allen residence which he has been kind enough to show us around. Cresselly House is open to the public on limited occasions but there will be many local residents who have not seen its stunning rooms. We have been welcomed by Hugh himself, a bluff, genial master of the hunt who opens the car door for Margaret and is quite relaxed to have us nose around.[28]

We learn that the dining room is where one's family portraits hang – there are titles, a master of Dulwich College (always named Allen, by tradition, apparently), Lord Lieutenants of Pembrokeshire

and a marriage connection to the Wedgwoods. This last is manifested astonishingly in the drawing room which is Wedgwood blue and white with the ceilings scroll work picked out in blue. The prospects from all the rooms to the west, away from the main road, are impressive and stretch beyond Lawrenny on the Cleddau. The old drawing room has a late Rococo ceiling whose trailing vines decoration includes a cartouche with a military drum and an open music score. Tom Lloyd tells us that he has had a musician transcribe the notes, which are a playable melody.

The central staircase is lit by a glass canopy and the top floor has a large protruding metal hook from which one of the Allens' batchelor ancestors used to attach a rope by which means he climbed to his bedroom each evening for exercise. The central corridor, dark as always in old houses has, high on its walls, a line of twenty or so foxes on plaques which commemorate their ends. Each has been stuffed with its fangs showing, head somewhat to the side, giving them a shifty, predatory character. Many are the trophies of Hugh's mother who was a keen fox-hunting lady. Tom tells us that an au pair from Australia when being introduced to the house for the first time exclaimed, "Streuth! Look at all that vermin!"

Back at the central staircase on the first landing two walls have large portraits of young men in uniforms of the First World War. Both died. At Carew Castle they may have memorably played their war games, shooting and jousting, but from Carew Cheriton to Cresselly, from Polish and colonial airmen to privileged young gentlemen, there are memorials to the defence of a tired Empire and the more lasting principles of freedom.

WEST WILLIAMSTON

There are a number of small villages which you will probably never visit unless your B&B directs you there or your satnav goes really wobbly. Such is West Williamson which is a hamlet on the south side of the Cleddau, reached by the A4075, turning right before the bridge at Carew. It's on the south side of the river because the river has been man-directed to the place. West Williamston, like almost everywhere else in the world is on the map and inhabited for a very good reason; though that reason may often be hidden or buried. Fingers of the Cleddau reach inland at this point because gullies were blasted and shaped; this is the Cresswell River branch with West Williamston being situated on a promontory which divides the Cresswell from the Carew rivers. There was good limestone at West Williamson – blue limestone and freestone which is excellent for working into shapes and corner stones was quarried here and shipped out. Coal from the neighbouring pits was brought in, probably from Cresswell Quay, just to the north; quite possibly from the pits worked in the Jeffreyston by members of my family.[29] In fact Cresswell Quay was one of the more significant coal-handling villages. Richard Fenton in 1803 described it thus: "a scene remarkably pleasing and lively from the small craft perpetually on the wing, either coming or going down to and from Cresswell." West Williamston was not as remote then as it appears now. It was situated at the meeting point of two active rivers coming into the Cleddau itself.

We have come to visit the artist Susan Sands and her husband Martin who live down one of the winding lanes that constitute West Willamston.[30] Theirs is a modern house with lots of light for painting and printmaking, with an old walled garden that has a swimming pool much loved by their grandchildren and a large lawn that passes substantial outbuildings – more storage and studio space – going down to their inlet that is muddy and waterless. We walk down to the muddy inlet at the end of their lawn; Martin tells me that the two large mooring poles are marked in feet and that at high tides the water rises to well over the eight foot mark. They have a 32-foot yacht at Lawrenny which can be brought up to the end of their lawn and on which they have sailed to the Bay of Biscay. Mind you, he was in Dartmouth College at thirteen and in the Royal Navy for thirty-two years, rising to captain. Pembrokeshire has always been linked to the world and the world comes to Pembrokeshire.[31]

On the same elbow of estuary is a National Trust nature reserve and nearer to Carew where the oyster farm was in the 1990s there is now a naturists centre at Tything Barn; a cluster of caravans and no clothes allowed. Here the Cleddau tide reaches up past the castle and under the road bridge to salt the marsh grasses. Martin says that the tides bring in curlew, shelduck and egrets.

This is a different Pembrokeshire to that which I have known. There are successful people who fall for the county and come down to spend their mature years here; they bring skills, knowledge of the wide world and money to the place. Susan and Martin were both born into the last days of the British Empire, she in India and he in Malaysia; commerce rather than the military or the Foreign Office – his father was in rubber and hers as the man in India for bathroom ceramics by Shanks. They moved to the county in 1990. Each autumn they go to support two Indian schools at Tamil Nadu through the Mettupalayam Trust and have made significant changes to the lives of women and children in that place: education and cows. Susan shows us the work she is to exhibit at the Oriel Q gallery in Narberth later that month: a series of prints based on Hindu gods; paintings on canvas and paper of village life in India. I have been reading Lloyd Jones's novel *Mr Pip* this week and the character of Popeye the teacher in Papua New Guinea seems to be echoed in one of Susan's small paintings of a teacher in India in a crumpled white suit walking down a dusty track under the shade of his umbrella: I decide to buy it and put it on a wall in Lydstep – India in Pembrokeshire.[32]

Martin takes us across a rickety bridge by his quay to cross the rough marsh meadows and explore the inlets which were called 'gullums' by the locals. We pick our way over and through springy tussocks of marsh grass with scatterings of small whitened crabs deposited by the tides. There is a herby smell and he tells us to pick some leaves of the plant and rub it in our hands; it is sea lavender and has a musky man-balm character.

In two of the inlets are the skeletal remains of barges, one with some rusting engine parts, though Martin thinks that few used

engines. These flat-bottomed barges were the only way to reach parts of the tidal Cleddau and they were powered by a single square sail or by long oars called 'sweeps'.[33] In common with the grassy depressions of former small pits, the huge gouges in the faces of the limestone cliffs, the ribcages of mooring posts along the coast, these collapsed barges are the industrial interventions in the landscape that are becoming found objects of art. This is the hidden Pembrokeshire, the semiotics of who we were in this place.

We cross two more inlets with further remains of old barges, and see some of the sheer walls of the limestone quarrying.[34] A few years ago they were visited by a researcher from the University of Aberystwyth who was tracing the industry's rise and fall. She found examples of this West Williamston stone as far afield as London. Certainly, there was a regular trade with the West Country. West Williamston had six pubs and dozens of families working the stone. This was a small but thriving quarry and trading post in the heart of greenness.

COSHESTON AND UPTON CASTLE

Jim John and I are sitting awkwardly through an evensong service conducted by the Rev. Jones. Those present: the Rev Jones, Jim, me and Marilyn Jones, the vicar's daughter. It the winter of 1965, the year in which we will all go to university. Leaving Pembrokeshire. And Marilyn. Jim and I are in love with Marilyn, though no-one says anything and no-one ever does anything other than look. And pray.

Jim is the Head Boy at Greenhill School, and I am the Deputy Head Boy and Marilyn is the Head Girl.[35] We are clumsy rugby-confident nearly men, in our third year Sixth. We have come in Jim's father's car, because I haven't passed my test and, in any case, my dad had an old Rover 105 built like a First World War tank which is too heavy and cumbersome for me or Jim. Marilyn is still stapled in the centre-fold of *The Greenhillian* from 1963 on the shelf in my study above my desk. She's standing next to Clive Merrison.[36] He is Scrooge in *A Christmas Carol.* The lead, of course. I was in the rugby XV and the second eleven for cricket. I was not in the school play, having walked into a wardrobe in the house competition one-acters three pages before I should have. Available, but not selected. And the Dickens cast has Stephen Beasley in top hat (looking like the solicitor he would become) as the Spirit of Christmas Present and the beautiful Judith Larsen as the Spirit of Christmas Past, as blonde and light and Scandinavian as Marilyn was dark and deep and Celtic. Oh where are you now, my lovely girls?

Cosheston itself is more than desirable now, a secluded village just a click off the A477 Pembroke Dock road, still retaining its mediaeval field system and still predicated around its small church, St Michael and All Angels on the hill. On its bell tower swings St Michael, trumpet sounding to the four winds and playing their tune as the weather turns around. This village was noted for its boat building and was linked to Lawrenny and West Williamston by a ferry. Now it's quiet and secure, its houses developed into v. desirable. It situation has always been remarked upon: the topographer Lewis, in 1833 said, "The village is beautifully situated on the southern declivity of a hill, the base of which is washed by an estuary of Milford Haven, navigable for barges." And the captains of ships being constructed from the local oaks in the village would stay in Cosheston to oversee the final fittings.

"Would you like to buy a castle?" Well, if you'd moved back to your wife's area after making a success of a haulage business; and if you'd done with the farming in the north of the county, why not?

Two miles away from Cosheston is Upton Castle and its gardens, which the owner is pleased to show me round. The castle, built by the Malefant family in the thirteenth century, is evidenced now principally because of its towers which are part of the later house, developed in parts over three centuries to the present. There are substantial outbuildings and a Victorian walled garden and small mediaeval chapel. Richard Fenton described it thus: "There is but little of the castle remaining, besides the entrance between two bastions finely overgrown with ivy, giving it a picturesque appearance." And so it is.

The Malefants worshipped god and celebrated themselves in this tiny family chapel which now has plain whitewashed walls. It is distinguished now by its original thirteenth century font and by its effigies, a lady and a knight, as well as the monument commemorating William Malefant who died in 1362. From the wall nearby a clenched hand offers the possibility of lighting a devotional candle. As Fenton noted, Upton and Cosheston are "heightened by the accompaniment of wood and water.... There is still a great deal of wood remaining, something more than ornamental proportion." The shipbuilding and river trade may have made these places, but now it is the ornamental gardens with their huge magnolias, rhododendrons, acers and the handkerchief tree, which bring us to the place. It is a delightful, quiet and hidden spot, just two miles off the Pembroke road and the current owners are welcoming.

Notes

1. A fascinating short history of the funfair is given in *Fairground Fun at Folly Farm* (Folly Farm, 2001) by Brian Steptoe, which is sold in the souvenir and book store at the Farm. I have incorporated much of his research in this section.
2. The Miners' Walk now follows part of this rail route and goes on to the coast.
3. Chris Ebsworth told me that they had the old workings and entrance of a drift mine on the Folly Farm land, just beyond the zebras' compound and that he was looking into the possibility of using that to feature the coal history of the village and their farm.
4. Quoted by Roscoe Howells in *From Amroth to Utah*.
5. This gentlemen was one of the last masters of the hunt to rely on a 'trencher-fed' pack of

hounds, dogs kept by individual farmers in the area which would be called together to form the pack. Child could, apparently call all the dogs by blowing his horn from the steps of Begelly House. See *The South Wales Squires*, Herbert M. Vaughan (Golden Grove Press, 1988).
6. *Chiaroscuro* (Jonathan Cape, 1952).
7. Sampson's *The Dialect of the Gypsies of Wales* was his great academic work, though he also translated the Bible into Romany. 'The majestic Sampson' was Augustus John's description of his new friend. Their relationship and the importance of John's Romany adventures is described with great erudition and humour by Michael Holroyd in his biography *Augustus John*, one of the finest biographies and one of the funniest books I have ever read.
8. See the section on Jeffeyston.
9. In the collection *The Last Candles* (Seren, 1989).
10. See the note 32 in the North Section.
11. See my poem 'The New Settlement' in *The Last Candles* (Seren, 1993). A fictionalised account of this family disaster, one my grandmother never fully discussed even seventy years later.
12. Connop-Price pp.192-3
13. From Tony Curtis *Selected Poems*, *Preparations* and other anthologies.
14. *Pevsner's The Building of Wales: Pembrokeshire*, ed. Lloyd, Orbach & Scourfield (Yale University Press, 2004) is a formal, dry, academic and invaluable source.
15. The regional marketing manager of Tesco was quoted in the *Tenby Observer*, 16/7/2010, thus: "We are extremely pleased to be working with Princes Gate Spring Water. Their quality products will go down a storm with our customers across Wales." You couldn't make it up.
16. See the piece on Slebech in the North section of this book.
17. The poem is 'Mametz' from *Heaven's Gate* (Seren, 2001).
18. I had the pleasure of opening his Tenby Museum gallery show in 2011.
19. See the night-lit photograph of this in the Toby Driver book p53.
20. The mill is open from Easter to October.
21. As described by Richard Fenton in 1811.
22. Quoted by Fenton from "a manuscript life of Sir Rhys ap Thomas, already communicated to the public through the channel of the Cambrian Register."
23. Not the later owner Sir James Perrott who Fenton calls "this charlatan baronet" and who held the castle in 1650. See also Edward Laws p275.
24. See *Elizabethan Wales*, G. Dyfnallt Owen (University of Wales Press, 1964).
25. See the 'Beauprang' website www.mossie.org/stories/Frederick_Lacy_2.htm
26. See the poem 'Land Army Photographs' in *War Voices*, Tony Curtis (Seren, 1995).
27. Tom Lloyd has served on many of the national committees of Wales and is the author of *Lost Houses of Wales* (1986). This pub is where Robin Hood and his Merry Men sat down to eat in 2009. Russell Crowe and other actors in the Ridley Scott film are reputed to have left a tip of £300. See also the Festivities section. Though they did not use too many of the local hostelries: the National Parks head warden reported that "Russell bought generous quantities of steak from the local farmers and barbequed with his entourage every night..." (*Tenby Observer* 14th May 2010). From the rich to the poor, eh?
28. In hand-written memoirs prompted by a list of questions my Gran (Barrah, Curtis) told of how she and her siblings would walk across the fields and through the lanes from Jeffreyston to Cresselly for marts and fairs. Born in 1891, she would have seen the young Allen boys with their nannies in their prams or driven in their carriages. The Allens owned much land and made some of their fortune from the mines worked by my ancestors the Barrahs and Thomases. The Allens were instrumental in developing the coal exports from nearby Cresswell Quay. Incidentally, Hugh has been in dispute with Tenby council over the traditional South Pembrokeshire Hunt meeting in Tudor Square. There were protests in 2010 and in 2011 the taking of a glass in the square before heading out will not happen. A pity: it is a colourful,

horsey, impressive spectacle and as the nearest fox or fox-substitute must be miles from the centre of Tenby they probably need a drink.

29. See the section of Jeffreyston and, of course, the Connop-Price book.

30. They are both in their seventies: Susan was trained at Reading and shows her paintings and prints internationally.

31. Note also the evidence of shipping in the now land-locked villages of St Florence and Gumfreston.

32. This novel won the Commonwealth Writers Prize and was published in 2007 by John Murray. Lloyd Jones is an Australian writer.

33. Connop-Price (p.155) points out that they also often had a crude cabin for the two man crew to shelter and, on occasions, sleep. The dangers of drowning or of fires is underlined by the report in *The Cambrian* newspaper in 1840 of the death in a fire of one such crewman near Landshipping.

34. See p.155 in Connop-Price: "a flat-bottomed barge-like river craft with a shallow draft and bluff, rounded bows. They were able to move at most states of the tide..."

35. See the East section for details of Jim John's life and death.

36. Clive Merrison has enjoyed a long and successful career, notably on Radio 4's *Sherlock Holmes* series and also in *The History Boys* at the National Theatre.

EAST

KILGETTY

Like so many smaller villages Kilgetty, once a thriving coal centre, is now by-passed by the main road which takes you on to Tenby, Saundersfoot and Pembroke; my friend Mervyn James John is partly to blame for this.

Jim and I first met when his family moved up from Stepaside to live a few hundred yards down the road from me at the top of Kingsmoor Common. We played rugby in the front row together, for Pembrokeshire Schoolboys (and Jim, later for Wales Schools against France at the old Cardiff Arms Park). My father ran the service section of the local garage there and at Stepaside. But the fortunes of the business slumped and so did those of my parents for years afterwards. Two decades later Jim returned from engineering contracts in the Middle East and became a county engineer, supervising the building and improvement of many of the roads you'll drive on in the county; including that huge slice through the hills above Stepaside and Kilgetty which give you welcome bypass relief from those Irish lorries and tedious caravans you've dragged behind since Llanddowror and the edge of Carmarthenshire. Should you stop at Kilgetty, there's a useful Visitor Information Centre just off the Kingsmoor roundabout, but no significant remains of the mansion and deer park of the Canon family,[1] and little reason to stop at this village unless you want to trace the Miner's Walk that links the coast to the collieries of the areas, through Begelly, Kilgetty and Stepaside to Wiseman's Bridge; this is recommended not just for industrial archaeologists, but because the seasons lend the old lines and workings a poignant beauty.[2]

We visit Mervyn James John at the nearby hamlet of Wooden most times when we come down to Lydstep. Jim is fighting illness, but is still a bear of man with huge shoulders and a great barrel chest; a wounded, saddened bear. He has been building and re-building their house for two decades and more. There is a kind of man who will not let brick and plaster settle; they must be 'improving'. The work will not be finished before Jim is; such projects have no end, are meant to have no end. He has discovered at the rear of his house a metal capping plate that covers one of the ventilation shafts from the Moreton colliery which was situated at the bottom of his land and which, like some of the pits my relatives worked at Jeffreyston, were owned by the Pryses of Cardiganshire.

One day we were talking at the front of his property when from the other side of a low hedge came a screech and squawk from his gaggle of hens. We went round the hedge and found the hens scattered to four corners of his patch, all except for a flurry of feathers settled into the grass and the neat head of a chicken. These are the fields of old coal mines and the wildnesses of nature. Men and coal move on; the fox remains, and must eat.[3]

SAUNDERSFOOT

One of the most popular holiday and tripper destinations in the county is, in fact, a much more recent creation than Tenby or Pembroke. This small fishing village did not expand to the size of a town until the coal industry in the middle of the nineteenth century sought better means of transport. In common with many of the inland villages of south Pembrokeshire, Saundersfoot owes its existence to coal and quarrying, and dates back to the fourteenth

century.[4] Small pits and drift mines in the area produced quantities of some of the finest anthracite in the world, and this was brought in wagons pulled by horses or oxen to the sandy beaches between Saundersfoot and Amroth, especially at Coppet Hall and Swallow Tree Bay; this would have been laboriously loaded onto small coastal boats and ships for other ports along the south Wales coast and as far as London.[5] Anthracite from this area was said to have an oily sheen and miners often referred to it as 'peacock' coal.[6] It was the finest coal and it is reported that Queen Victoria favoured its use above all others for her steam yacht. In common with the rest of the Pembrokeshire coal field, the conditions for mining and the need to greatly expand production at the height of the industrial revolution, meant that the local industry could not complete with larger fields in Carmarthenshire and the Valleys.

When you walk down The Strand you are walking along the route of the railway that linked Saundersfoot and Wiseman's Bridge to the mines.[7] Those dark, dank, spooky tunnels so attractive to young children were cut through the cliffs for profit, not pleasure.

The Strand was called Railway Street and was re-branded when the coal disappeared and the tourism that sustains Saundersfoot developed new shops and houses on the beach side of the road. When you reach the car park at Coppet Hall the Coastal Path guide on the wall reminds you of the vigorous trade that the valley and beach witnessed. Mining at Coppet Hall was recorded by the middle of the eighteenth century. There was, too, iron digging along the cliffs of this stretch of coast. This was exported to Pembrey in Carmarthen Bay and later to the Grove ironworks at Kilgetty where there were lime kilns, blast furnaces and a foundry, served by a coal mine between Stepaside and Kilgetty village. Starting at either end of Pleasant Valley there is an enjoyable walk between the coast and the iron works.[8]

Of course, these small concern mining operations and iron works used women and children as manual workers and accidents were not uncommon. In the 1840s a mine report noted that, for example, in Kilgetty there were thirty-six women employed, some seventy men and youths, with a further six females under eighteen and four below the age of thirteen. The development of mining as far north as Begelly and Jeffreyston led to the building of the Saundersfoot Railway which by the 1940s also linked Thomas Chapel and the larger concern at Bonville's Court just to the north of Saundersfoot. In fact, by the 1860s one man controlled that railway, the Kilgetty and Bonville's Court mines and the iron works at Stepaside.[9] Charles Ranken Vickerman was a solicitor from London and Essex who bought and rebuilt Hean Castle in Saundersfoot with his considerable wealth.[10] 'Hean Castle' may be derived from the Welsh 'Yr Hen Gastell', the old castle, and there was probably a very ancient fort on that position. The level of that man's wealth may be judged by the 1898 photograph of Hean Castle in its late Victorian splendour.[11] He was not the most loved man in the district, as few men of great power are. In 1894 when the miners at Kilgetty and Bonville's Court petitioned for a rise he gave the latter two weeks' notice. Four years later, the men at Bonville's Court were to be the smallest branch of the South Wales Miners' Federation.

When I moved down to live in the Kilgetty area in 1960 Bonville's Court was still in existence, though it had ceased working in 1930. My parents lived in one of the two houses at the top of Kingsmoor Common left by my Aunt Annie, though I never realised then that there had been a railway line up through the west side of the common and that the Miners' Walk which links

Saundersfoot with Kilgetty via Pleasant Valley passed just behind our house and the main railway line. Certainly in the garden of that house and again in the bungalow in Valley Road, Pentlepoir to which we moved there was a coaly shale in the earth which yielded less produce than one would have expected in this richly agricultural county. The coal industry was there, was fading fast and no-one wanted to see it.[12]

The actual railway which passed a field or two behind our house was a single line track, as it is now through from Tenby on to Pembroke. Lacking the sophisticated communications of today, there was enacted the serious safety precaution of the stationmaster having a key token passed from driver to driver at Saundersfoot to prevent a collision. I remember being impressed by the solemnity of this ritual. Beware: Saundersfoot station is miles to the north of the village itself, with not a waft of ozone in the air.

You need imagination and old photographs to appreciate the nature of the harbour at Saundersfoot. On both quays there were coal loading hoists for the railway coal drams on the side past the present yacht club and beneath the cliff. Under sail and by steam, in the early days of the industrial revolution this was a small but significant port, potentially more prosperous than Tenby following the dredging of the harbour and the construction of the east pier. In 1849 the Customs Officer based in Tenby had moved offices to Saundersfoot, though he was still required to check vessels from Tenby plying their trade across the Bristol Channel to the west country and to patrol that stretch of coast each side of Saundersfoot to prevent "petty smuggling between the villages and crews of some trading vessels trading with coal and culm to the adjacent bights and inlets."[13] No doubt in common with much of the coastline of Britain, south Pembrokeshire experienced regular incidents of smuggling, especially as the coal transportation was, in law, subject to duties even between British ports. Loading by night on a beach would greatly enhance the profit margins of the boatman.

In common with the train station, the village church, St Issell's, is some distance from the seaside Saundersfoot we know: it occupies a wooded, secluded hollow to the side of the B4316, a fine, impressive setting. You may visit this seaside resort and be unaware of either. The tower, font and other sections of the church are Norman, but as in so many churches much was 'improved' by the Victorians. The church in its dedicated windows and plaques reflects the power and influence of the Vickermans and the Child

family. St Issell's is remarkable for the extent of its graveyard and the fact that it has a stream running through the middle of it, the only such I have ever seen. Close to the edge of that stream are two military graves commemorating RAF officers who died in a crash in 1943.

The best place to stay or eat in Saundersfoot is, arguably, the St Bride's Hotel above the harbour. This large white building with its spa and infinity pool was originally the Carrington and built in the 1920s. The present hotel is equipped for business conferences, and rugby and soccer teams use it for R&R. On their website two long-haired beauties lean, as it were, over nothing except the reaches of Carmarthen Bay. There's a never-ending stream of warm water playing into the pool. Enjoy; don't worry about Green issues. You get the point. Lunch is affordable and this was our regular taking-Mum-for-a-treat stop. It's worth driving or walking up for the view, anyway.

From there you can imagine the small village with its railway line running around to below the hotel for coal loading. There would have been a row of houses along by the Cambrian Hotel, but none of the bungalows, caravans and shops would have been present until the 1950s. In truth, we rarely go into Saundersfoot and, apart from the prospect of lunch at St Bride's, we would rather avoid the car congestion and the one-way system. Having said that, the beach is fine, long and sandy and you can walk/clamber right round to Wiseman's Bridge eastwards, and to Monkstone Point to the west when the tide is fully out. On very rare occasions it is possible to walk from Tenby to Saundersfoot almost entirely on sand, though you have to allow plenty of time and be sure of the tides. I worked for one school holiday at the Booths amusement arcade opposite the car park entrance, so may have negative feelings about the place. I wore (like a self-appointed mayor) a long important-looking chain of keys for the machines and sorted out change and the frequent jamming of the works.

Near the wall where miners and boatmen would congregate for work there is the Tourist Information Office which, like the one on the Parade in Tenby, is stocked with maps and those free guides which are sufficient for most day or week-long visitors. Just back up the steep one-way hill from the Hean Castle Hotel is a traditional iron-mongers shop, Frosts. It's the sort of place where they will probably stock that nut, or screw or flange-thing you can't name and can barely describe. The nice young man who served me when last I called provided the nut I need for the lawn mower, but also recounted the bass he'd caught the previous weekend off Lydstep Headland. All in Pembrokeshire time, which has a variable relationship with GMT: I could smell and taste those two bass. In 1895, it is claimed, Bill Frost of Saundersfoot was the first human to fly, eight years before the Wright brothers and several more since Icarus. He powered his contraption with some sort of combustion engine and rose off the ground only to catch the top of the hedge and ruin the machine.[14] Apparently, he tried to persuade the Secretary of State for War to invest in further research who assured him that "the nation does not intend to adopt aerial navigation as a means of warfare."[15]

Less than fifty years later the skies over Saundersfoot and the coast from Tenby to Pendine were thick with flying machines. In 1943 Operation Jantzen was staged in the area. This was one of the major practices for the D-Day landings that were planned to liberate Nazi Europe. The flat sands were similar to those beaches at Normandy which would the following year be forever re-named as

Utah, Omaha, Gold, Juno and Sword and the Pembrokeshire coast was by 1943 out of sight of the crippled Luftwaffe that had so devastated the oil reserves at Pembroke Dock and which had landed one bomb on Tenby.

The pub at Wiseman's Bridge proudly claims that Winston Churchill stayed there to witness the vast rehearsals. No doubt he found a sandwich easier to obtain at the Wiseman's Bridge Inn than I did on my last visit on a hot day in May. I felt like invading France myself to obtain decent service. There was no lack of discipline in in June 1943 when most of the roads and communications from the surrounding area were under direct military control. Some one hundred thousand troops were deployed but the only visible record of this huge and strategically vital event are the consequences of the bulldozers and heavy machinery used in the exercise which further destabilised the sea defences of the village.

AMROTH

Amroth has always fought an unequal tussle with the sea. Where now you look out from the road right across to the Gower there was a line of houses in the nineteenth century; these and their gardens are long washed away. Somewhere too on Amroth beach there is buried the rusting remains of a landing craft. Of necessity, there is now a vast rock and boulder sea defence which protects the road and village, but which cuts one off from a natural access to that beach.

Like Wiseman's Bridge and other Pembrokeshire fishing villages Amroth has a rash of bungalows from the dreadful 1950s and 60s, but either the walk from Saundersfoot or the tortuous drive down from the A477 is worthwhile. The sea is clean and the beach is broad with rock pools and the promise of fossils or remnants of a sunken forest to delight the imagination of children and shore foragers of all ages. Near to the coast road you can see the cave of what had been a lime kiln. Tell the kids it's full of trolls.

Amroth Castle, built on coal money,[16] is an eighteenth century building on a Norman site (it was once an asylum for the disturbed); now it and its grounds have been developed into a self-catering and caravans site; quite tastefully done, as those things go, though it's no Manorbier or Carew. But there is history here, as much of the lands in the triangle between Tenby, Amroth and

Narberth were wooded: the forest of Coedrath is referred to on many occasions in older manuscripts and George Owen of Henllys reminds us that in 1151 in that forest Cadell ap Gruffydd was attacked and badly wounded by soldiers from Tenby; that led to the virtual destruction of Tenby and the massacre of inhabitants by Cadell's brothers Maredudd and Rhys in 1153. The castles of Pembrokeshire, unlike the promontory forts, were about coercion as much as defence: the wild Welsh had to be subdued, made safe.

The most famous inhabitant of Amroth is Roscoe Howells the historian and novelist. He has done more to keep this small village in the public eye than anyone. In his nineties as I write this book, he is as passionate and forthright about the county and its "development" in the last century as anyone.[17] His trilogy of novels, *Crickdam, Heronsmill* and *Roseanna*, is set in this area and covers family stories from 1800 to the 1980s. *Woodreef* is also set largely in Amroth and has a plot line from 1700 to the 1990s. Perhaps most remarkably Roscoe Howells has traced a surprising connection between Amroth and Stepaside and the Mormons in Utah.[18] In that state, where that strange clan have records on everyone and anyone, there is the journal of Daniel Williams who converted to the Mormon cause very early, in 1847, and who preached (as they do) to all who would listen and even more who wouldn't. He must have worn more than a few down because it is reported that in 1851 there were congregations of 'saints' numbering over one hundred and fifty in south Pembrokeshire, from Angle to Amroth. Williams had become disillusioned with the sectarianism of the Baptists and other non-conformist communities and seems to have trained and committed himself to the Mormon cause in Merthyr Tydfil, returning to his native Pembrokeshire (he was born in Penally) to enthuse the populace. He worked at the Grove ironworks and, with four other Mormon men, set about spending all his spare time walking far and wide to spread the word.

In July 1851, his journal recalls that, having walked twelve miles the previous day, he set off another twelve miles to Stepaside. He was, unsurprisingly, somewhat late, but, "Elder Sykes had addressed the council at some length before I came – then I had to speak for a short time showing the impossibility of man becoming perfect without the Milchisidec priesthood, and urged on all the exert themselves in the offices that they held, that they might be found worthy to be exalted in due time etc."[19]

What is clear is that the Amroth, Wiseman's Bridge, Stepaside,

Kilgetty area was well populated and worth the Mormons' efforts. A people working exhausting hours and living close to the poverty line, and often just beneath it was in need of hope and inspiration, possibly escapism and dreams.[20] Several families followed that particular and peculiar dream of that mid-west Moses, Joseph Smith and his Mormons, risking much and losing some in the Atlantic passage and the trek across half a continent. How could they have imagined what they would find in the blistering heat of Utah as they gazed out over the sea at Amroth?

Those pious pioneers were leaving behind their chapels and the established church. Half a mile up a narrow road to the north of the village is the parish church of St Elidyr. It is a fine little church in a good situation with a Norman font and memorials to local families of rank, including Fawleys and Biddulphs. Most striking, for me, is the commemoration of Richard Fawley from 1743, given by his widow Rebecka:

All born on Earth must die. Destruction reigns
Round the whole globe and changes all its scenes.
Time brushes off our lives with sweeping wing
And to the graves our earthly tents doth bring
Where they shall lie till Christ's reviving day
When glorious souls shall wear refined clay.[21]

The artist Arthur Giardelli (1911-2009) visited Amroth as a boy and returned first to live in Pendine over Marros Mountain to the east and then Warren, as a mature artist.[22] He talks about Graham Sutherland's painting of the county as an inland and inlet reflection of the landscape, but says that for him "the glory of Pembrokeshire is that the next stop is Mexico. This infinite stretch of ocean, the power of it is overwhelming...". Giardelli's boyhood visits recall the essence of the village and its vulnerability: "Quite quickly we became integrated into Amroth and were at that time its only 'foreigners'; the village was entirely inhabited by people who had lived there or thereabouts for generations. Every year an important occasion took place called 'Big Day' when people from nearby came by cart or car to Amroth for a day's outing, and in the evening there was a concert at which I would sing or play the viola. All this happened before the great storm and the disappearance of the cottages on the seaward side of the beach road." He describes the poverty and hardships of the Depression years and how growing vegetables, rabbiting and scraping coal cut "out of the side of the cliff" was essential to their survival.[23]

These boyhood idylls were not to last, of course. First came the soldiers of the Second World war and then the post-war development: "Amroth became so delectable a place to live in that the little cottages began to be bought or leased by 'foreigners'... The old village community that we knew is finished and we witnessed the end of it." That encapsulates the continuing dilemma for the county: new money and life-blood needs to come in to Pembrokeshire, but the landscape must be respected and the indigenous population and its memories negotiated.

LUDCHURCH

This village is en route to Narberth on the road from Carmarthen that branches right and northwards from St Clears. The church at Ludchurch is dedicated to St Elidyr, situated prominently above the village. This has a fifteenth century tower and a notable 1920s memorial to William Bauch Allen of the Cilrhiw estate which incorporates work from a fireplace in the gentleman's house, originally inset with peacock feather pattern tiles designed by the notable Arts and Crafts potter William de Morgan. Historian Richard Fenton passes through on his way to Tavernspite and notes that the village is "most curiously situated on a limestone rock, which has been worked all around as far as the sacred precinct would admit of, leaving it almost insulated. The quarry lies in horizontal strata, is black, beautifully veined and enlivened with the likenesses of various shells in white, and furnishes slabs for chimney pieces that take the finest polish." Lewis in 1833 confirms that such industry is still active, noting that, "The substratum is limestone of very superior quality, which is worked upon an extensive scale: this stone is susceptible of a beautiful polish, and many slabs raised from these quarries have been manufactured into elegant mantelpieces, and used for other ornamental purposes: it is also burnt for manure, there being no fewer than six kilns for this purpose in constant operation, for the supply of the more northern parts of the county."[24] In truth, you will, like Fenton, pass through, rather than linger here, though to do that you would have to branch off the A477.

LAMPETER VELFREY

Lampeter Velfrey also has a strong traditional of lime quarrying and lime kiln burning for it is set in a richly wooden valley. St Peter's church, though not as dramatically positioned as that of Ludchurch, has several seventeenth and eighteenth century tombs of interest and a fine mid-nineteenth century window of the Tansfiguration. Lewis remarked that this village had "a parochial school, for the gratuitous instruction of poor children... supported by subscription." Coarse fishing enthusiasts may be drawn here by the White House Trout Fishery; most visitors will simply drive through. They'll miss the church, but enjoy the trees.

COLBY LODGE

This property and its grounds are well sign-posted from the A40 and it is best reached from this direction rather than from the winding coast road from Amroth. A sense of poignant beauty is underlying the Colby Lodge gardens, eight acres of them, administered by the National Trust since 1979, and certainly worth visiting for the rhododendrons, camellias, magnolias, Japonica, hydrangeas and azaleas in their seasons, and the stream-side walks. The stable and other blocks to the east of the main house are now the shops, tea rooms and offices of the National Trust. The path from here to Amroth takes you about a mile and three-quarters down to the coast. Our intrepid traveller Lewis in 1833 reported that he found here, "An excellent mansion, seat of Captain Protheroe, [is] beautifully situated in a romantic dell opening at one extremity towards the sea, of which it commands a fine and interesting view."

This is indeed a delightful location and there is evidence of Roman and other early settlements in this place, though whether Lewis could actually see the sea from this far inland is doubtful. As with Amroth itself, the coal and iron works of the area brought wealth and built this house and estate, specifically from the fine anthracite mined from the Redlangoige Colliery in the early nineteenth century. The Scourfield Lewises who now live in Colby Lodge itself are known to me through the Contemporary Art Society for Wales. They kindly showed me around the remarkable summer house in their walled garden, which is not open to the public.[25] It was designed by Wyn Jones and built in 1975. The garden is open to visitors, but the summer house isn't normally and they use it for occasional dinner parties. This white wooden structure at the top of the garden is indeed striking with its clean lines and trompe l'oeil decorated interior walls. It is built over a spring which sends water trickling down the centre of an ornamental path to a small circular pond.

The estate is named after John Colby, who, with Lord Milford, mined the area in the early 1880s. He built Colby Lodge in 1803 to a John Nash design, as a holiday home for his family. The next owners, the Kay family, in particular Gladys Kay and her husband, developed the western woods and the impressive gardens. There has been a property here for centuries and the earliest recorded name for the place was Rhydlangoed. Where the gardens are now developed there would have been a drive and entrance from the south, linking the estate to the coast. Two monuments placed on either side of the valley commemorate the Chances, the couple who completed the gift of the estate to the National Trust in the 1960s.

The National Trust indicates that around 25,000 visitors enjoy this place each year. The Lesser Horseshoe Bat now roosts in the outbuildings at Colby Lodge, so you might be lucky and be able to add a rare creature to what I have always found to be an inspiring visit. Colby Lodge is one of those Pembrokeshire locations which refreshes both mind and spirit.

Notes

1. Fenton mentions, "Sir Thomas Canon, a man of great wealth, power and learning, in the reign of James the First."

2. The Kilgetty mine and the Grove mine were connected by an 870 yard pathway underground. The proliferation of shafts and workings must have left a honeycomb of history below this area.

3. See my visit to the Master of the Hunt in Cresselly. And, of course, sadly the reference to Jim's funeral in endnote 21. Jim was greatly helped in his final weeks by the Paul Sartori Hospice at Home Foundation, a Pembrokeshire-based organisation of great worth.

4. George Owen of Henllys does not mention the place by that name.

5. At the end of the eighteenth century Lord Milford planned to build a canal from Stepaside to Wiseman's Bridge to greater facilitate this trade, but it was never fully functional. For more details of this and many other aspects of this area, see books by Roscoe Howells, the pre-

eminent local historian of this coast; *Old Saundersfoot: from Monkstone to Marros* first published in 1977 and reprinted with additions by Gomer in 2003.
6. As always M.R. Connop-Price is excellent on the production and shipping of coal from the Saundersfoot area. *Pembrokeshire: the Forgotten Coalfield* (Landmark, 2004).
7. The road called 'The Incline' which goes down to the main car park follows the route of the Bonville's Court pit railway worked by an ingenious weighted coal-dram system.
8. The tv and film actor Kenneth Griffith (see Penally and Tenby) has his family roots in Stepaside. "I can distantly recall talk of Loveston colliery, Swallow Tree Bay, Coppet Hall and 'Big Day' (fair) at Amroth. The place names re-echo the vivid ghost memories of long ago. I can remember the colliers walking between Kilgetty and Saundersfoot with black faces. I can remember the little railway. I can remember so much of the beauty and character that has now gone." Foreword to the first edition of Roscoe Howell's *Old Saundersfoot.*
9. Possibly named after a fourteenth century landowner Nicholas de Bonville.
10. In fact, that wealth had been dissipated by the end of the century and Hean Castle became the property of William Thomas Lewis, first Baron Merthyr of Senghenydd.
11. See francisfrith.com. Incidentally, not to be confused with the pub of that name in the centre of Saundersfoot; that is neither splendid nor wealthy and the last time I went in was for my twenty-first birthday party in 1967.
12. The Romany community which had existed on the Common for a hundred years and more is now invisible and fare from the main road. Romany Gypsies are still the largest ethnic minority in the county. They have contributed to the agricultural and trading life of Pembrokeshire and their traditional way of life is celebrated in an educational caravan which tours schools in the county. This is in contrast to many other parts where, especially on continental Europe and the former communist countries they have been persecuted.
13. From the Pembrokeshire Record Office, quoted by Connop-Price.
14. Roscoe Howells is convinced by this story. See *Old Saundersfoot* p 53.
15. This was not the only example of pioneering aviation in the county. In 1913 Howard and Herbert James of Clunderwen were possibly the first locals to fly any distance in Pembrokeshire; they had been taught at Hendon. A year later they managed to fly out of the county all the way to Carmarthen. A photograph of their plane (a light wood and string struts biplane) may be seen in Narberth Museum. The previous year the Englishman Denys Corbett Wilson took off from Goodwick near Fishguard to make one of the first successful crossings of the Irish Sea. He took 100 minutes, which is less than a modern airplane if you count the check-in time and other inevitable delays at modern airports. Wilson went on to be a pilot in the RFC and died in the Great War. Herbert James went to be a notable test pilot in the 1920s and flew in the RAF in the Second World War.
16. "This parish, which is situated on the western shore of Carmarthen bay, abounds with coal of a peculiarly fine quality, which, burning without smoke or any offensive smell, is much in request for the drying of malt and hops; for this purpose, considerable quantities are shipped from a place called Wiseman's Bridge, in vessels of fifty or sixty tons' burthen, and sent to Bristol, and other places on the banks of the Severn." *A Topographical Dictionary of Wales*, S. Lewis, 1844.
17. See the note in the South section about his dispute in the *Tenby Observer* about Haile Selassie. A vice-president and former chairman of the Pembrokeshire Historical Society, he was also a founder member and chairman of the old Pembrokeshire Records Society.
18. See *From Amroth to Utah* (Gomer, 2001).
19. I do not advise any reader looking up Milchisidec unless they have hours to spare – man or angel?
20. Howells quotes the amusing outrage of an Irishman at a Mormon meeting at Monkton when he tore up a handbill and "pressed forward through the crowd fugling as if he was going to strike us." In nineteenth century Pembrokeshire when you threatened someone with your

fists you were 'fugling'.

21. St Elidyr's is where my friend James Mervyn 'Jim' John was buried on December 29th, 2010 when this book was already in the hands of the publisher. He was described in the Kilgetty section. I gave the oration at that funeral and a few days later worked on the following poem:

St Elidyr's, Amroth

Six men straining to carry you to rest, Jim,
on a day when the trees are heavy with December mist
and the vicar's words are beaten down
by the weather and the sea.

All born on Earth must die. Destruction reigns
Round the whole globe and changes all its scenes

Then the sprinkling of fine soil on your lid
and the glint of sliced earth ready under its faux-grass cloth.
So cold. With the solstice tide
beating like a heart – shush, shush, from the grey beyond.

Time brushes off our lives with sweeping wing
And to the graves our earthly tents doth bring

Saint Elidyr invited underground by the little folk
played their games and lived on saffron milk
until his greed for their gold brought him back
to the everyday world. Then to Christ. Then repentance.

Where they shall lie till Christ's reviving day
When glorious souls shall wear refined clay

Lives such as ours journey down to this: no further.
Coastal our people, farmers and miners, being
rooted to the land, hearing the sea. Saint Elidyr
breaking open the earth to find nothing.

22. See the West section.

23. *Arthur Giardelli: Conversations with Derek Shiel* (Seren, 2002). The most notable art now in Amroth are some of Geoffrey Yeomans's prints on display in the otherwise unremarkable Amroth Arms.

24. *A Topographical Dictionary of Wales*, S. Lewis, 1833.

25. It's worth checking, as recently, and at certain times this has been open to visitors.

NORTH

HAVERFORDWEST

I'm climbing up a ladder into the upstairs of a lock-up garage just down from Castle Street. At the top there is a windowless room guano-ed with paint and high with the smell of oil. David Tress has invited me into his studio and I am amazed to discover the place where his stunning paintings are made. David now the outstanding painter of expressionist landscapes of Pembrokeshire. He has memorably painted churches (including Gumfreston and Stackpole), seascapes and towns in the county and in London, Dublin and France. In his large *Chasing Sublime Light* exhibition he retraced the journeys of Turner, Sandby, Girtin, Cox and others through the Scottish, northern England and Wales landscapes in which they sought out the Sublime experience of nature in its terrors and glories. His torn and multilayered works on paper, both drawings and paintings, have a hard-won energy and engagement with the ruggedness and later despoilation of the land.[1]

You'll be hard pressed to see his work in Haverfordwest: there is no art gallery in the town. Haverfordwest is where you go to sign forms and to be healed or to die, for Withybush Hospital to the north of the town is the main medical centre for the county.[2] The little airport is also on that road out to Fishguard, as is Poyston, the birthplace of Sir Thomas Picton (1758-1815) who served in the West Indies, then in the Peninsular War and who died at Waterloo.[3]

Haverfordwest was founded by the building of a castle by Tancred the Fleming[4] in 1110, much celebrated in 2010, of course. It grew to become the principle town in the county from the Act of Union when Tudor patronage was added to its strength of location – centrality, the fort on a hill and trade by tidal access on the Cleddau. In 1748 William Pitt the Elder visited the town and observed that he "liked the place because it had the appearance of trade… but it was a devil of a town to walk in." That may still be the case; there are hills and something of a confusion of focuses. When Lord Nelson visited Milford in 1802 he was presented with the freedom of "the opulent town of Haverfordwest" which was also described as that 'little Bath'.[5] But high society had to step carefully around the squalor of the lower orders. Much slum clearance was necessary and, much later, development of a predictable nature has blighted the town – the recent New Market development on the river, for example, is undistinguished and the whole town seems to be moated by roads and concrete. The major access point was a bridge to the north, donated in 1726 by the Philipps of Picton Castle where the new supermarkets are and at a crossing of the river which Henry Tudor would have used on his way to Bosworth and the Crown. But you are likely to enter the town now over a bridge opened in 1837 and initially guarded by toll gates returning revenue to William Owen, the county surveyor whose scheme it had been and who had been instrumental in persuading the GWR to extend their railway line to Haverfordwest.[6] You now pass between the County Hotel and the Masonic Hall. There is no toll.

One of the most significant artists of the twentieth century, Gwen John (1876-1939)[7], was born here (in 7, Victoria Place; her blue plaque is on the Lloyds bank building) and her brother Augustus John described the vibrancy of the town during their childhood years: "On market day... the streets and squares were full of life and movement. Noise too, with the continual lowing of cattle, the screaming of pigs, and the loud vociferation of the drover."[8] Now the winding and steep High Street has a confused identity and the town has lurched down to the shopping development on the Cleddau and to the supermarkets in the west.

The fine church of St Mary's, St Mary the Virgin, set above High Street and given great prominence in the town is worth a visit. The Pesvner Guide compares it favourably with both Llandaff and Wells cathedrals in terms of its thirteenth century preservation, its

Tudor carved oak roofs and its sixteenth century clerestory. There is too the sun dial over the south porch from 1656 and a later inscription beneath it – 'My house is the house of prayer, 1771'. There are thirteenth century features, many of them vigorous and surprisingly secular and rude – a fiddler pig, an ape playing a crwth,[9] grotesque faces and heads. The wooden ceiling is well restored and there are many memorials to the notable families of the area, including two stained-glass windows in the porch poignantly dedicated to young men killed in the First World War. There is a particularly impressive marble memorial to Sir John Philipps, with bust and cherubs, ('large playful reclining putti', as Pesvner has it) who died in 1736. The Philipps of Picton have been significant patrons of this church and Sir John, the fourth baronet was also an important figure in the SPCK and a commissioner for the building of new churches in London. His contacts with the organ makers Harris and Byfield in due course led to the installation of the 1737 organ which is essentially that which you see in St Mary's today.

The bells of St Mary's are a particularly impressive peal of eight, originally by Thomas Bayly in 1765, and over the years they have attracted visiting teams of campanologists. In 1648 when Oliver Cromwell came to the town a 'joy peal' was rung in celebration. The bell ringers were paid by the council: better safe than sorry.

The churches of St Martins, St Martin of Tours, and St Thomas, St Thomas a Becket, are also substantial and it is worth seeing the late Victorian stained glass and the 1960s Virgin and Child in the former. St Martin's church is the oldest in the town and is situated close to the castle. It has also a fine stained glass window designed by Burne-Jones. In August 1771 John Wesley preached at St Martin's and "strongly applied the story of Dives and Lazarus, and many were almost persuaded to be Christians." Also, from the heights of the graveyard you can look down to the north at the prospect of Tabernacle Congregational Church and its schoolrooms. Its crown announces 'Built A.D. 1774: Restored A.D.1874'. George Whitefield preached at the Tabernacle in 1768.

The castle is now the County Record Offices; it had been the

county gaol. In the last two hundred years the building which had dominated the town and its skyline has been eroded and diminished in importance. By the early 1960s the constabulary had departed, and the council completed the demolition of the gaol buildings within the walls.

In Bridge Street which linked the castle area to the river quays there was a thriving Dominican Friary, St Saviour's, established in the thirteenth century and supported by Henry III. Under another Henry, in 1538 it was taken over by the Crown as part of the Dissolution process. The Priory and the important merchants' houses on the Cleddau quay are clearly shown in the Bucks' engraving of the town and they completed a version of the Priory itself (1740). This priory was first established at the beginning of the thirteenth century by Robert FitzTancred and was an important centre of religious learning and practice until the Dissolution of 1536. In recent years CADW, the body which preserves and administers ancient buildings in Wales, has done considerable work on the Priory; this is best viewed from across the Cleddau as you approach or leave Haverfordwest to the east.

Haverfordwest was also a centre for the Quakers from the early nineteenth century: the Nantucket whaler *Starbuck* came across from Milford to the Friends in the town where, much earlier, John and Janet Bateman had been prominent, and persecuted, Quakers in the years following the American Revolutionary War. John Wesley preached in the town on fourteen separate visits to great effect, but the Wesleyan Chapel in Perrots Street is now a warehouse, though the Calvinistic chapel further down that road is still active. Between the site of the ruins of that Wesleyan chapel and the surprisingly ornate 1830s terraced houses of Barn Street is the Mariners Hotel. This has imposing shields in its stucco from the AA and RAC and the claim that an inn had stood on the site since 1625. The manager stops short of claiming that date, but is pleased to show me some impressively old beams in the bar. The Mariners has twenty six bedrooms and is centrally-placed if one wishes to stay in Haverfordwest.

The imposing former Shire Hall across from the Castle Hotel in the main square at the bottom of High Street has been converted into two restaurants, and converted rather well. You now have the choice of either the Italiano Mambo or the Black Sheep: both do very reasonable lunches and are probably the best places to eat in the town centre.

Turning right out of the old Shire Hall and bearing down Quay Street takes me to the main commercial area of medieval Haverfordwest, for the town was, of course, connected to the Haven and the world by the western Cleddau. I remember that Jeannette John at Wooden had told me that when she worked in the council offices here they would see otters, salmon and even seals in the Cleddau at this point. What remains of Quay Street's shipping past is a 1930s post office, some former warehouses and the eighteenth century inn The Bristol Trader. Returning along the river bank one day I spotted what looked like a run-down gallery with an easel in its window, a Ray Howard-Jones painting. The side door was ajar so I ventured in. John Mitchell came down the stairs and explained that he ran a frame shop there, Robel on the Quay, established for nearly thirty years, and that the building had been the site of his father's business since 1946. The Ray Howard-Jones was in his own collection and not for sale. He was, however, generously prepared to loan that and others of her works to an exhibition I planned for 2013 at Tenby Museum and at the University of Glamorgan. Over the years he and his father had framed work for David Tress and other artists in Pembrokeshire and beyond and he remembered Ray Howard-Jones coming to the shop and at other galleries. She was inclined to divest herself of clothes, or at least anything that covered her up respectably, at every opportunity. John remembers his mother remonstrating with her once when she appeared naked in front of him and his siblings. As her subject-matter was Ramsey, Skokholm, Skomer and the coastline around St David's, this remarkable artist, one of the few women to become an accredited war artist in the Second World War, will not feature greatly in this book as her subject matter was in the north of the county. But, as I have mentioned, she is well represented in the collection at Tenby Museum and claims to have become a painter after a stay in that town when she was a young girl. Certainly, her summers on Skomer in the years when it was privately owned produced some of the most notable work on birds and seashores produced in the county in the second half of the twentieth century.

I am in the front room of a 1950s semi to the north of Haverfordwest standing in front of an enormous horn that stretches way above my head and takes up almost a third of the room, rather like an installation by the artist Anish Kapoor. But this is a functional object and from it comes an orchestra-backed crooner:

A perfect sea, a sunny sky
There was she and so was I
What could we do?

Martin Langer lifts the chrome needle arm from the record and responds to my request for some jazz by putting on a Satchmo record from the 1920s. Louis Armstrong's trumpet against a background percussive drum slapping never sounded so authentic, so archival. Then it's Adelina Patti the soprano of her age in a 1904 recording done in her bedroom at her Swansea Valley mansion Craig yr Nos.[10] Between these carefully handled period discs, each time Martin removes the tiny bamboo needle with triangulated point the end of which he snaps and sharpens with a device rather like a pair of silver scissors. This large cabinet and its thirty-inch diameter horn is a 1930s EMG Mark 10b, he says. And because the sound is amazing, unique, taking one into a time-warp, I don't argue or doubt it.

I've come to visit Martin's partner, the painter Maurice Sheppard, so this horned concert is a bonus. In 1947 this notable painter of water-colours was born in the Cleddau fishing village of Llangwm. He went to the Royal College and was a contemporary of my friend and former colleague Alan Salisbury. We take tea in the conservatory beneath a very large oil by Carel Weight, Maurice's professor at the college.[11] While Alan's work has gone into adventures with the portrait, involving influences as diverse as soccer players and the Old Masters, Maurice has established himself more conventionally as a landscape painter. For decades he has been based in Pembrokeshire and like the older John Knapp-Fisher at Croesgoch he has made his living exclusively by painting. He has offered to gift to the National Museum of Wales a large and impressive oil painting by his former teacher at Haverfordwest Grammar School, Ronald Lowe.[12] Like many in the circles of Welsh art I had forgotten, or had never really considered, this painter, but Maurice is very enthusiastic and keen that Lowe's achievements be recognised and his reputation secured. Indeed Lowe made a significant contribution to Haverfordwest, helping to secure notable exhibitions in the town in the early 1960s by some of the leading British artists of the twentieth Century – Jacob Epstein, John Piper and Stanley Spencer. Maurice and other pupils helped to carry the works in to St Mary's Hall on Tower Hill. It was Ronald Lowe who helped to found the town's Civic Society and to work to preserve older buildings. He even enlisted the support of the President of the Royal Society, Sir Hugh Casson, to try to ensure that the buildings of High Street were painted appropriately and presented sympathetically. Alas, there is little evidence of those principles now.

Maurice has painted scenes throughout the county especially, of course, around his native Llangwm and tells me that his cousin, Michael Roberts, a retired head teacher, still holds one of the licensed boats, K8, for compass net fishing out of that village. The poled nets are hauled up spilling silver water and weighed with salmon. Maurice's words paint a picture of this and I resolve to meet Michael.

PICTON CASTLE[13]

This castle is one of the oldest and finest houses in west Wales with forty acres of woodland and gardens featuring an exceptional collection of rhododendrons and azaleas. It can be traced back to the original lord, Sir John Wogan in the fourteenth century. It is now administered by The Picton Castle Trust and the walled garden and grounds can be visited in the summer season. Those who can enter the castle will find, amongst other fine features, a wonderful eighteenth century Great Hall and Library. As Richard Fenton observed, there was: "an air of great baronial magnificence, and his lordship's superb establishment is commensurate with this appearance, and justifies his pretensions as to family rank, property, and influence in the county."

Picton Castle[14] remained in the Wogan family until the middle of the fifteenth century when it was acquired by Sir Thomas Philipps whose line would include Sir Richard Philipps who became Lord Milford in 1776.[15] He and others extended and modified the castle in neo-Norman and other styles which survived until its occupation in the Second World War, after which considerable repair and remedial work was undertaken. Much power and influence has been rooted in Picton Castle over the centuries. It was a Royalist stronghold in the English Civil war and was besieged by the Parliamentarians, though an amicable truce was arranged and the property, unlike Pembroke Castle, came to no great harm.[16]

The Philipps family later served as Lord Lieutenants and in other high offices in the county and they had considerable mining interests – at Begelly, St Issells, Amroth and Freystrop – and, in addition, the Pembrokeshire Iron and Coal Company and the ill-fated Saundersfoot Railway Company. There were even coal workings in the vicinity of the castle itself. The Philipps grew wealthy and travelled widely; for example, Erasmus Philipps brought back from his Grand Tour in 1740, among other souvenirs, a 'St Sebastian' by Guido Reni. Viscount St Davids whose connections with Lydstep I have mentioned, was a Philipps, and their properties and interests extended throughout the county

My particular interest in Picton Castle stems less from its present use as a venue for conferences, family visits and as a location for short courses from Pembrokeshire College, but rather from its art heritage. In the 1740s it was the subject of a Nathaniel and Samuel Buck print, and again in 1779 by Paul Sandby, but the twentieth century it was to be an inspiration to Graham Sutherland (1903-80), one of the most important painters in Europe. Sutherland's work was transformed by visits to Pembrokeshire, beginning in the 1930s and continuing after the war until his death.[17] He wrote: "From the first moment I set foot in Wales, I was obsessed. I have worked there, especially in Pembrokeshire, every year since 1934...I have contin[ued] my visits in order to make my studies and to soak myself in the curiously charged atmosphere, at once both calm and exciting, to meet the people, so kind and optimistic, and to benefit on good days from the extraordinarily clear and transparent light." He explored and drew and painted around St David's Head and in the Marloes and St Bride's district.[18] One day, missing the direct road to Dale, he discovered one of those narrow inlets or 'pills' of the Cleddau: "we missed the road and found ourselves descending a green lane buried in trees, which, quite unexpectedly, led us to a little cove and beach by the banks of a narrow estuary... The whole setting is one of exuberance – of darkness and light – of decay and life. Rarely have I been so conscious of the contrasting of these elements in so small a compass."[19] Sutherland was introduced to the Philipps family in 1944 by fellow artist John Craxton and from that time the castle became an important place in his career, though he lived for much time after the war in Menton in the south of France.[20] Sutherland's descriptions of the county reflect the poetry of his visual responses as he expressed his wonder and delight at the workings of light and natural forms, trees, rocks and the narrow winding roads: "Yesterday we were spell-bound at sunset by the effects of the sun coming through holes in the clouds and making orange red patches in the blue black mountains."[21] Visitors to the county will have had such moments of epiphany: this is a landscape which may well move you further and deeper into your life.

Sutherland converted to Catholicism in 1926 after meeting his wife Katherine and he found on the banks of the Cleddau at the south of the Picton Castle estate root, rock and tree forms which twist into the agonies of Christ, and speak of the human condition. From specific places in Pembrokeshire Sutherland developed a vision that would resonate around the world. His war work and the contribution to the re-built Coventry Cathedral are stunning. His late paintings, completed specifically to be shown at Picton are majesterial. It is to be greatly regretted that for some years they have not been shown as a group. The National Museum of Wales and the Philipps family had come to an agreement whereby a Sutherland gallery was established in the courtyard and stables of the castle; that opened in 1976, but that arrangement, for some reason, ended and for over a decade most of the works have been locked in store. Efforts to re-establish a Sutherland Gallery in the county continue. Watch this space: this empty, annoying blank wall.[22]

SLEBECH

> The entertainment consisted of a cold collation, sewen excepted,[23] which were taken from the water, broiled on the spot, and so served up. The board was most liberally spread with every luxury of the season, and the guests involved all the beauty and fashion of the country. Pines, grapes, and the choicest fruit enriched the dessert, and the wines were no less distinguished for variety and excellence. To enliven the festivity, a military band was most judiciously stationed, whose music came mellowed to the ear from behind an intervening screen of foliage. All the company parted in great good humour, some in carriages, and some on horseback, whilst the barge, freighted with beauty, gently glided down the tide with the setting sun, through a landscape of unrivalled variety, the charms of which all nature at that moment contributed to heighten by the richest tints and the happiest distribution of light and shade.

So wrote Richard Fenton of his visit to Slebech Hall.[24] A little further east from Picton Castle along the A40, south of the road, after Canaston Bridge and what for Fenton in the eighteenth century was nothing more than a brisk walk from Picton, is Slebech. The estate is close to the hamlet of Rhos,[25] and its hunting tower may be seen from the main road. Slebech Park has fifteen finely appointed rooms and suites around its courtyard, many of them with specially-commissioned wall-hangings by Riita Sinkkonen Davies. The restaurant offers an excellent Sunday lunch followed by the possibility of several good walks along the banks of the Cleddau.

Slebech was a principal centre for the Knights Templar in this area in the Middle Ages, and many of its eighteenth century characteristics survive.[26] The hall, available for weddings and conferences now ('the perfect backdrop for a dream wedding') retains its fine position overlooking the eastern Cleddau.[27] The Barlow family acquired the land and established the original house and park after the Tudor Dissolution. Roger Barlow was a notable traveller and writer, accompanying Cabot on his second voyage of discovery in 1526, and translating Enisco's *A Brief Summe of Geographie* while in Slebech in the early 1540s.[28]

The house's late seventeenth century terraced gardens on the river bank are particularly impressive. The property was acquired late in the eighteenth century by Nathaniel Phillips whose wealth had been made, as was often the case at that time, by sugar and slavery in the West Indies. In fact, in 1793, he bought Slebech from a bankrupt slave-owner, William Knox, and continued to draw revenue from his estates in Jamaica, though he never returned to them, and spent his days between London and Pembrokeshire.[29] In 1833 Lewis in the *Topographical Dictionary of Wales* describes the place thus: "The church, formerly the conventual church of the commandery, and the only remaining portion of that ancient establishment, is a venerable and ancient structure, in the Norman style of architecture, pleasantly situated near the bank of the river, and embosomed in the luxuriant groves which surrounded it." Baron de Rutzen who acquired the house through marriage in 1822 was, evidently, more interested in the 'luxuriant groves' than in preserving this ancient church.[30] Only the ruins of the original place of worship remain today. There are headstones for recently deceased members of the Philipps family, and in a branch of the Cleddau oppsite the restaurant is Dog Island, where the family pets are buried.

Slebech, in common with Picton Castle, might have been a significant location for twentieth century art. It almost figured largely in the life of Augustus John, for in his autobiography *Finishing Touches*[31] he tells of staying in Picton Castle and enquiring about the ruined hall nearby which offered a "foothold in the heart of my own country... a place in which I could work, and a kind of ivory tower in an enchanting ambience...". His host, Sir John, declared that it was the property of his sister and that the famous artist might have it if he undertook a portrait of her. It was not to happen: "tragedy rudely intervened: poor Johnny died in his bath. The drawing was never done and Slebech was sold."

CANASTON BRIDGE

The Slebech estate has had considerable trouble with Canaston Bridge and the Cleddau on its land. The river has traditionally been a source of salmon and sewin and Canaston Bridge, at the junction of the A40 and the A4075, continues as the most successful location for coarse fishing in the county. Weirs and wattle gates facilitated this for many years. Of course, the Cleddau was for centuries navigable up to this crossing and bridge, which encouraged the transport of flour and iron at various points in its history. Fenton says that he reached Canaston by river but at that place, "for many years noted as a great iron forge and fishery", and "deeply embosomed in oak and beech of most luxuriant growth and character", he took to his horse as the tidal river was not reliably passable.

This crossing point of the river has been vital to passage between the south and north of Pembrokeshire, lying as it does at the northern edge of the forest of Narberth where hogs, honey and timber sustained the locals. Since the time of the Knights of the Templar the river crossing and its environs has been valued. When Slebech had passed down to the eccentric Baron Rutzen he attempted to put a check on poaching and it is recorded that in 1830 there was some violence between his retainers and the Llewellyns, notorious local takers of fish. Their coracles were seized and subsequently they were charged in court in Haverfordwest.

Two centuries earlier Blackpool (well sign-posted on the Tenby road) was developed as an iron forge, the combination of wood, anthracite and ore making it a potential success; but this had declined before the time of Baron Rutzen. The iron forge was replaced in 1813 by the existing mill which was built by Nathaniel Phillips and which is worth a visit. The mill as a tourist attraction was developed by Lady Dashwood. It has a craft shop, cafe and exhibitions of the mill's history. It's also worth stopping for the stunning views of the river and the wonderful bridge, though the whole area has been radically altered by the 2010 road improvement and its new roundabout, both much needed. The Forestry Commission has marked out a circular walk taking in Minwear Wood which has amongst other attractions, American red oaks and good spots for observing the bird life of the Cleddau.

LLANGWM

War has shaped Wales more than any other force through the last century and each of us will at some point in our lives acknowledge that. Wales had enlisted men in the Crimean and the Boer Wars, but in 1914 Wales, in common with the rest of Britain, was caught up in a wave of patriotic fervour: as many men served in that conflict as worked in the essential mining industry which fuelled the fleet and the factories. From the Somme, at Mametz Wood and through Passchendaele, up to the armistice in November, 1918, Welsh regiments and divisions served widely and suffered greatly on the

Western Front. It is surely part of most of our families' histories. My Pembrokeshire grandmother's cousin, James Charles Thomas had been a member of the Pembrokeshire Yeomanry[32] and served in the Middle East before being transferred to the Machine Gun Corps on the Western Front; he was killed in the German counter-offensive at Cambrai in December 1917. His body was not recovered until the following January. Some corner of the village of Caudry is forever Tallyho Farm, Llangwm.

Augustus John remembers the oyster women of Llangwm coming to market in Haverfordwest, "in their distinctive and admirable costume, carrying creels of the famous oysters on their backs."[33] There are no such sights now, though there are traditional fishermen's cottages and the church of St Jerome is worth a visit – a Norman font and an interesting knight effigy – and at Great Nash there is a fine dovecote.[34]

However, in the summer months there is some chance of catching sight of one of the six remaining compass fishers of Llangwm and there is a link to those picturesque sellers which Augustus John saw. The skill of compass net fishing was brought in the nineteenth century to the coal fields of Pembrokeshire by two miners from Gloucestershire where the practice is called 'stop net' fishing.[35] Ormond and Edwards are commemorated by two of the fishing 'stakes' on the eastern branch of the Cleddau, for each position on the river is thus designated – Home Stake, The Stones, The Bite, The Grim Bank and so on. The compass fisherman secures his boat by a line threaded through the bow and along its length to stakes on each bank of the river. A frame of crossed poles, up to twenty feet long, and often cured by burying in the bank side mud for many years, is used to hold the net which is then lowered into the Cleddau to catch the salmon returning downstream to the sea. A counterweight, stone, concrete block or lead, is used to lever the net and fish up and back into the boat which has been held broadside to the often swift-flowing Cleddau.

I visited one of those remaining licensees, Michael Roberts, introduced to me by the painter Maurice Sheppard. Michael is a retired school headmaster whose family has a tradition of compass fishing. He said that the fishing is now restricted to the months of June, July and August and from mid-day Monday to Friday; also, that the salmon are increasingly scarce. This is honoured as a tradition, rather than a profitable seasonal occupation. The men still use the Little Milford Quay for their boats and the tradition is passed on from fisherman to his 'endorsee', often a family member. Michael's boat is fibreglass, replacing his traditional tarred wooden boat which was damaged some years back.

On a frosty December day Michael walks Margaret and I around the village and the shoreline from the pill or 'lake' to the slipway. He has "three or four boats" and points out K8, his compass fishing boat and its predecessor, broken planked and skeletal on the grass bank. He explains that he has made his compass poles from larch trees he himself felled in Benton's Wood along the western bank of the river. The edge of the field we pass, Cunnigar's Field, (a Norman word for rabbit warrens, he says) is marked by trees the roots of which are eroded and exposed like those which inspired Sutherland at Picton just a mile or so up river, as the Cleddau branches towards the east.

The day is cold and clear and remarkably quiet: this is a Pembrokeshire entirely distinct from the county we inhabit. Here one's life is defined by the river, not the sea; though of course the tides dictate the sea's bidding translated far inland. Across from us are the oaks of Sam's Wood, the old limestone quarries and, beyond and just around the eastern Cleddau's curve is Landshipping where, Michael tells us, a friend of his is developing a house from one of the old mine buildings; he also points out the top of Picton Castle in the woods to the north. There is a rich, sour reek of estuary mud; and so many birds – mallard, shelduck, teal, waxwings, dunlin, redshank – then a glorious curlew that rises from the river's edge and calls its name across the water until it's out of sight and sound.

We round Black Tarr rock and return to the village, past the competition longboats – 'Cunnigar Stinger', 'Will O' the Wasp' – up a pony lane and across the fields past the rugby ground where Llangwm Wasps play. Michael and I are contemporaries and must have played schools rugby against each other. Michael then played for Llangwm and, as with the sailing club, had a hand in running things there for years. He says that a local derby against Haverfordwest might draw a crowd of around five hundred. This hamlet must shake with that much noise and excitement.

We thank him and his wife, Elena and walk back to our car. "I wonder whether my people, the Barrahs and the Thomases may have had boats?" I say.

"Farming folk and river folk don't mix," Michael says.

LANDSHIPPING

Directly across the Cleddau is Landshipping, a village now remembered for a most unfortunate reason: this was the site of a serious mining accident on St Valentine's Day in 1844 in which forty-four miners died. The Garden Pit disaster victims included women and children, for they were commonly used at that time. At the end of 2002 the local community erected a memorial listing those victims whose names were known. This is a simple but effective concrete block with a Celtic cross incised that stands at the edge of the river which flooded the mine. It is particularly poignant to read 'Joseph Picton – 11' and 'Miner John – Child': this despite an act of Parliament a couple a years before which sought to ban such child labour. *The Times* later that week reported that:

> The colliery has for very many years been in full work, giving employment to a large number of men, women and boys. It appears that on Monday last a lot of men and boys were set to work in a level which was about a quarter of a mile long, and extended a considerable distance under the bed of the river Daugleddau, and which had not for about three years previously been worked, for the reason, it is said, that it was not considered safe to carry on operations there, the colliers having reported that in one place there was a leak of saltwater over their heads... The greater portion of the men who have thus met a violent and untimely death have left wives and large families to deplore their loss. In addition to the incalculable amount of distress and destitution which the surviving relatives must inevitably sustain, the injury to the proprietor, and the other colliers in his employ, is tremendous, as it is thought that all the works on the estate communicate internally with each other, so that it is probable that water has extended through the whole, which may possibly occasion a total cessation of them...

Obviously, the disaster marked the end of this small Pembrokeshire village as an industrial centre, cutting a swathe through the population and rendering the Owens' mining business a serious blow.

The quay still evident here was built for Hugh Owen of Orielton to facilitate the transport of that coal. The Owens also built an impressive house at New Landshipping from those coal profits and this faced across the Cleddau towards the fine house at Slebech. Another impressive house lies about a mile away but can only now be discerned by the bricked and terraced ornamental gardens and water features.[36] Fenton remarked that Sir William Owen lived there "in a style of hospitality but little known and practiced these days." Landshipping is now a quiet village little visited and the coal, which had been mined since the eighteenth century, is long lost.

FREYSTROP

We are in a 1960s house on Moorland Road in Freystrop which although relatively undistinguished from the front is at the rear where we are having coffee, a remarkable place. This is where the weaver Riitta Sinkkonen Davies lives and has her studio and her looms. Ritta is Finnish and was captivated by weaving as a very young girl in her grandmother's house; in rural Finland they were practising self-sufficiency long before the colour supplements caught on to it and it became a moral imperative.[37]

Freystrop, in common with Hook, the nearest village, is situated on a hooked promontory around which the western Cleddau and its mud flats curl on its way from Haverfordwest. Each village is generally remembered, if at all, for coal: firstly bell-pits and inclines, then some deeper shafts. These villages were linked by their own railway/tramroad which in turn connected to the GWR line passing north and south close to Rosemarket.[38] Colin Davies says that there can be ground instability in the area, which means that new houses will often have a metal mesh laid beneath them to prevent subsidence from the old mine workings. There is still some evidence of an industrial landscape around Hook, if you seek it; but Freystrop's coal history is now all but invisible.

Riitta's place is a veritable cottage industry, though. She is one of the outstanding weavers in Wales, with an international reputation from San Francisco to Tokyo. She sells her smaller rugs, scarves, table runners and framed woven landscapes from her house and in a number of galleries, including Cardiff's Craft in the Bay. But she also works to commissions, some of them large and prestigious: she designed and wove the rochet worn by Rowan Williams at his enthronement as Archbishop of Canterbury. She has work at St Michael's Church in Oxford, Shakespeare's birthplace in Stratford and the Sutton Hoo Visitor Centre and can re-create the relevant historical techniques for such places. As we have noted, at Slebech Park just to the north and on the eastern branch of the Cleddau,

Ritta was commissioned to create large wall hangings for the public areas and for each bedroom. She tells us that she has just completed a range of weavings for an architect's house close to Haverfordwest, including one large rug which he has fitted into a sunken aperture in the living room.

She was formally trained in textile arts at Turku College of Art and Design in Finland and moved to Pembrokeshire with her Welsh husband, Colin Davies, almost thirty years ago. The landscape of the county and west Wales has obviously fed into her art. She dyes the wool herself and each piece therefore has a unique quality. She also combines linen, silk, angora and other materials in her scarves, framed pictures and hangings. In 1996 she created an installation work 'Through the Snow' for the European Textile Network Conference which was a large linen piece with a motif of woven flowers through which, over several months, grasses grew and, as it were, reclaimed. For the National Trust's Dinefwr Castle near Llandeilo her series of wall hangings are inspired by the trees on that estate: her art is reflecting nature back at itself.

The Freystrop workshop is packed with three large looms, one of which is linked to a computer's design programme, as well as other small looms on which she tutors others. There is work in progress on each of these. Riitta's studio is open to the public in the middle of the week in season, but she holds classes throughout the year. What she learned from her grandmother and her ancestors, she passes on.[39] She tells us that her grandmother grew flax in the fields for her own linen: "All we bought in those days was salt and yeast," she says, "Everything else was produced." That old lady's spinning wheel for turning flax into linen stands in the corner. As we leave, Margaret swings her new wool and angora scarf around her neck.

ROSEMARKET

In this apparently unremarkable village are at least two remarkable associations. The first concerns an ancient mansion, long ruined, formerly the seat of the family of Walters, in which was born Lucy, daughter of Sir Richard Walters, the favourite mistress of Charles II, and mother of the ill-fortuned Duke of Monmouth: Rosemarket could have produced a king. Fenton in 1811 describes the place as "a village now of very mean appearance, lying on the edge of a cheerful little vale well wooded and watered by a small stream." But he goes to describe a visit he made in London to the house of Dr Johnson in which lived a companion, Miss Anna Williams, born in Ros Market, "who served to alleviate his recent grief for the loss of his wife."[40] Her father had been a doctor who had chased the dream of calculating longitude by means of magnetism and moved up to London to make his name and secure his fortune. His daughter, who was blind, was befriended by Mrs Johnson and became a close companion to her and later to her widowed husband. Boswell and Johnson took tea with Anna most evenings. Dr Johnson said, "she acted with prudence and bore with fortitude...". Fenton, who was a barrister in chambers there, reports that "she displayed fine taste, a retentive memory, and strong judgement... finding I was a Welshman, she increased her attentions; but when she had traced me to Pembrokeshire, she drew her chair closer, took me familiarly by the hand, as if kindred blood tingled at her finger ends, talked of past times, and dwelt with rapture on Ros Market." Miss Williams received financial support not only from Lady Philipps of Picton Castle, and wrote 'On the Death of Sir Erasmus Philipps, Unfortunately Drowned in the River Avon', but also from Garrick who staged a benefit night at the Drury Lane theatre for her and helped to publish her poems. Anna Williams's modesty mirrors that of the village in which she grew up:

> For me, contented with a humble state
> 'Twas ne'er my care, or fortune, to be great.

During the research for this book, for me there has emerged a third remarkable aspect to Rosemarket: my family, the Barrahs, were rooted there, rather than at Jeffreyston, as I had thought. My distant cousin David Barrah, in 2010, kindly guided Margaret and I around the village and to Sardis where a number of my ancestors are buried in chapel grounds and churchyards. The Barrahs, Thomases and others owned or at least farmed at Tally Ho, Llangwm and Lower Bastleford. David and his wife have built a house in what was the orchard of the latter farm and he has done much work to trace our family's connections. Many things he showed us, but two especially: a photograph of our men in Pembrokeshire Yeomanry uniform posed with their horses. All but the sergeant are short and stocky. Then we visit the medieval dovecote in a Rosemarket garden, originally part of the Walters estate and now on a ridge overlooking a set of beehives. This is in a

remarkably good state and is worth the detour to this village.[41]

And one thing he gives to me: a cup and saucer inscribed to "Stephan Thomas Barrah from his sister Matty August 25th 1876". It is lettered in gold and has a well painted flower pattern. It was probably a twenty-first present for my grandfather, Stephen, who is buried in Jeffreyston churchyard and whose pony and trap accident led to the loss of the farm there. The name is misspelt and there is no record of anyone named Matty in our family records. I shall pursue that mystery in more research.

MILFORD HAVEN

Milford Haven, the largest town in the county, takes its name from one of the finest natural harbours in Europe, is crucial to the energy economy of the whole of the UK; and has the only live theatre in the county. It could have been central to the development of the British Navy and the expansion of the Empire, but despite the attention of Lord Nelson himself, and the Hamiltons,[42] what military attached to the county was destined to be sited across the water at Pembroke Dock. Milford was a significant fishing port, but that role declined in the second half of the last century. This despite the fact that in Tudor Britain it was described as "the most famous

port of Christendom".[43] Not only that, but in Shakespeare's *Cymbeline* Imogen says:

> How far is it to this blessed Milford? And by the way
> Tell me how Wales was made so happy as
> To inherit such a haven.

Milford's name probably originates from the Vikings and certainly those raiders (ravishers and traders both) left their mark. It had strategic importance, at first for the military and then for commerce. French forces landed in support of Owain Glyndwr here in 1405. It was further along to the west that the future Henry IV landed, at Dale. And in the last years of the seventeenth century the Nantucket whalers, mostly Quakers, established a base here with a whale oil store.[44] This, incidentally, marks Milford as the first place to have Starbucks: for so were named some of those whalers.

The Starbucks and other Quakers "a most industrious well-disposed people... whose character and abilities make their small capital useful in different branches of business" were well established by the end of the eighteenth century. In Priory Street there is still a Friends meeting house built in 1811 for those whaling families encouraged to set up at Milford by Charles Greville. Inside, some of the original benches are still in position, while in its graveyard there are some headstones commemorating members of that community who died in the town. They are remembered simply by their initials.

The port was ambitiously and greatly developed by Sir William Hamilton and his nephew Charles Greville and by the beginning of the eighteenth century was a thriving port and ship-building centre:[45] the *Milford*, a naval ship of seventy-four guns was launched in 1809. Richard Fenton visited the dockyard, managed by Mr Louis Barallier, 'a foreigner', and witnessed the construction of another ship of war, "this gigantic monument of the improvement of science". Then was pointed out to him a "curious circumstance, that a thrush had built her nest in the rope-yarn hanging loose between some of the timbers of the ship" and that "the noise or sight of the workmen had no effect so as to frighten her from a discharge of maternal offices to her young." It's a moment of accidental theatre and poetry which we can only read now with a knowing irony.

At the height of its ambitious establishment Greville and Lord Cawdor had even instituted an annual Milford boat race, on the first of August, the winner to receive a cup to the value of £30, a considerable sum in those days. There was too the important link with Ireland: "The packets here stationed are five in number, of about seventy tons each, fitted up with every convenience for passengers, by which daily intercourse is kept up with Waterford."

The fishing industry in Milford goes much further back, with George Owen describing the oyster trade: "Milford haven yields most delicate and of several sorts and in great abundance, and is a commodity much uttered in many shires." There were stocks at Lawrenny and Llangwm, but in the Haven oysters and another fish were "taken by dredge" from the bottom and, as with the Tenby stocks, the enterprise was destined to be unsustainable. Deep sea fishing in the Irish Sea and beyond was thriving in Milford Haven in the twentieth century up to the 1950s, but it declined and continues to be overshadowed by the oil and gas industries. The coal workings in north western Pembrokeshire were planned to access the Haven's shipping at Newton Noyes, over Castle Pill to the east of the town, but the scheme was delayed and missed the economic moment.[46]

Now the main attraction all year round in the town is the Torch Theatre in St Peter's Road. It has live productions, touring professionals and local groups, Christmas and Summer Season specials, a cinema and cafe. Here you may catch some of the better films which don't appear in the other Pembrokeshire cinemas, tribute bands, celebrity talks, occasionally dance and opera. The artistic director Peter Doran has driven forward some notable original productions and the Torch has been an important contributor to the Schools Shakespeare Project in which pupils perform in half-hour versions of the plays.[57] My anthology *The Poetry of Pembrokeshire* was launched here in 1989, when old Greenhill contemporary Clive Merrison[58] took part in readings.

In common with many smaller theatres the Torch constantly struggles to maintain its original productions and the quality of its offerings when squeezed by the local council's grant system and the assumed priority of Olympic Games spending and other national cuts.[59] However, when we last visited a production of *An Inspector Calls* had been doing good business, the Joanna Field Gallery[50] was hanging a new show by Alan Rees-Baynes based on the words of Torch theatre-goers and the coffee bar was nearly full; this is probably the safest bet for a lunch in the town.

We talked to Bernard Prettyman, one of the front-of-house staff who, it turned out, had known my parents and had worked in a Tenby shoe-shop with my mother in the late Sixties. He showed us the studio theatre and the main auditorium and explained that the Torch had a couple of years before undergone a modernisation costing some five million pounds. The building's outside appearance may resemble that of a discount warehouse, but inside it is impressive. In their forthcoming programme I note not only *Jack and the Beanstalk* as the Christmas panto, but original plays – *The Man who Walked through Walls, Augustus John, You Turn me On!* and live music – Preseli Pete and the Bluestone Boys – dance companies and 'Live transmission from the Metropolitan Opera, New York in HD' – *Boris Godunov, Don Pasquale* etc. In truth, the Torch may be a visitor's main motive for visiting Milford; for the town has a confused air about it. There are fine houses along Hamilton Terrace, including the Lord Nelson Hotel, and below along The Rath, but the octopus Tesco has squeezed too much of the life out of the town's single shopping street.

Disappointingly, the museum down on the harbour/marina opens sporadically, but a new art gallery has been established on the waterfront in Vanguard House. Pure Art/Gelf Pur is run by Leslie Crascall who, he tells me, aims to show a range of serious artists. Certainly, the Graham Sutherland exhibition of drawings and prints at the end of 2010 signalled that intention. A serious gallery in Milford is a challenge: I wish him well.

The harbour still has a working fleet of fishing vessels and on The Rath there is a rather fine monument to the town's fishing heritage. I am reminded that the Hakin district to the west of the town was celebrated obliquely by Sir Lewis Morris [51] in 'The Fishing Lass of Hakin':

You must have heard of Milford Haven
All harbours it surpasses,
I know no port this side of Heaven
So famed for handsome lasses.

...If ere you saw a cuttle fish,
Her breasts are more inviting,

Like shaking blubbers in a dish,
And tender as whiting.

Well you get the point; even allowing for this page three bit of fantasising, what is clear is that Milford is being written up as a most desirable place. Hakin itself proved unexpectedly desirable in the year before Lord Nelson's visit, for King George IV's ship from Ireland was storm-forced to take shelter at Hakin in September 1801. Robert Greville saw the opportunity to enhance the port's reputation and a celebratory crowd and band was organised, with a royal salute from the guns at Hakin Point as the King proceeded by coach to London. A fawning plaque – 'violent and succeeding tempests... refuge and security in the capacious and safe anchorage of Hubberston Roads' – was made to commemorate the royal landing and placed on the spot. It can be seen now attached to the Victoria Bridge.[52]

At least George IV's visit was not as unfortunate as that of Richard II in 1399. That year he left for Waterford in Ireland from Milford to try again to enforce the power of the Crown in that unruly country. When he returned to the port two months later he was told of Henry's return from exile with a support sufficient to overthrow him and take the throne: it's all in Shakespeare. With a

fair bit of dramatic licence.

In March 1915 four liners were torpedoed in the Irish Sea and those who survived (one hundred and five men. women and children died) were landed in Milford where a plaque commemorates their loss and the Germans' outrage. The fact that Americans were lost in these actions increased the pressure on their nation to commit to the war.[53]

In the big freeze of January 2010 fleets of tankers berthed at Milford, each one carrying enough super-chilled gas, Liquid Natural Gas (LNG), to run the whole of the UK for eight days. The journey can take two weeks from Qatar on the Gulfl[54] and then the terminals on the Haven at Herbrandston[55] and South Hook store, heat and transform the liquid gas into gas for the pipeline that runs nearly two hundred miles to Gloucestershire (at a construction and laying cost of one billion pounds)[56]. This system, it is claimed, can supply one fifth of the gas needs of the UK. That did not prevent a series of demonstrations and active interventions by protesters in south Wales and in Herefordshire and Gloucestershire during the construction. Some local councils were put under pressure to facilitate planning permissions and action group protest camps were set up along the route and in Milford Haven itself. The *Sea Empress* disaster still informs people's responses to further developments in the area.[57]

Richard Fenton described the surroundings thus: "The situation of the town of Milford is most singularly beautiful, as occupying a point of land with a gentle slope on all sides." However, the sad truth is that the town, its 'situation' and its survival, now depends on the ugliness of oil and gas importation.[58] I first realised this in the early 1960s when I played for Tenby Golf Club 'Conies' against Milford. The town's course gives wonderful views down over the Haven, but nudges up against the unyielding metal of the refinery. It's an incongruous juxtaposition. Milford will now attract the visitor – for its theatre and for its complex history – rather than the tourist.

NEYLAND

Neyland's fate was always connected to that of Milford, but poor Neyland was always going to be the bridesmaid. The town can be quite specifically dated from April 1856 when Isambard Kingdom

Brunel fixed on that position for the terminus of his railway.[59] He is commemorated by the impressive statue situated on the quay bearing his name.[60] As well as the railway, Neyland was an embarkation point for a generation of iron-clad steamers. I remember crossing the Cleddau from Hobbs Point in Pembroke Dock to visit a distant cousin of my father's who managed the Co-op in the town; my father making my mother and I get out before driving the little Austin on to the bobbing ferry. The landing stage after that few minutes' crossing was the very same that Brunel's great ships used. There was no Irish ferry looming over us, no hint of an oil tanker. Now you are aware of the marina on Westfield Pill as you cross the Cleddau Bridge.[61] There's money on the water at Neyland, but perhaps not enough of it washes over the town where older terrace houses sit uncomfortably next to developments of flats overlooking the Haven. It's not sure how much to forget and what lies ahead.

From Brunel Quay

I look over to Hobb's slipway
where my father would drive us on to the chugging ferry
for its short drift here across the Cleddau;
years before that concrete bridge framed the sky
and river to link the county.
One of the anglers has pulled out a green-grey wrasse
glinting from the brown waters of the Haven.

This stretch of estuary mud and water
is where my Uncle Ivor took us on his new boat
up the disappearing curves of the Cleddau
– Mill Bay, Beggars Reach, Llangwm Pool –
all the way to Haverfordwest quay
one calm and sunny day in fifty-eight;
that was after the refinery had paid him a fortune
for the Old Rectory and his fields of earlies
and just before his heart gave out.

On Brunel Quay where the Great Western
would connect us to the world
the engineer's plinth has been stripped of its statue,
– that tough little man with stove-pipe hat and a fistful of plans –
sawn off in the early hours and scrapped for bronze cash;

but now the evening comes alive with the wriggling fish
this angler weighs and measures
then lifts to his lips like a lover.

He bites through the line an inch from its open mouth
and drops the old lady, y wrach, the wrasse
back into the gentle slap of the tide.
These new hooks dissolve, he says.
It all dissolves.

DALE

I can see the attraction of Dale for those with families and a need to have a water holiday, though I have never shared their enthusiasm for the place. It is a flurry of sailing and other activities on the water, for this landing spot for the future Henry IV is remarkably sheltered, turning its back on the west and the weather and curling round its protective arms. You can be taught surfing, wind surfing and power boating here; the West Wales Wind, Surf and Sailing Centre can be reached through their website. They also have courses in Cornwall, while the surf shop is run by Pete Broads, formerly a Welsh champion surfer and world surf traveller.

John Wesley was not impressed by his visit to this village in 1771. "It seemed to me that our preachers had bestowed here much pains to little purpose. The people, one and all, seemed as dead as stones – perfectly quiet and perfectly unconcerned. I told them just what I thought. It went as a sword to their hearts."[62] That may not be true of Dale today; however, the twentieth century alterations to Dale's castle have rendered it as 'dead as stones' with its red sandstone walls and rather forbidding appearance. This was never a castle in the military sense, though Dale was perceived as having strategic importance as Milford Haven's potential as a major naval base grew. The peninsula has the Western Blockhouse which originates in the Tudor politician Thomas Cromwell's schemes. This was rendered obsolete in the later nineteenth century when rifled cannon were developed, but in the Second World War the position was armed again. Dale Fort is much later, being another of those mid-nineteenth century coastal fortifications which never fired its considerable artillery in anger.

On Dale Point there were Bronze Age and Iron Age promontory forts and one can still see the raised defensive mounds which protected those small communities. Now there is a community of study at the Dale Fort Field Centre which runs courses, clinging to the sides of the eastern cliffs. Castlebach Bay, Watwick Bay and Mill Bay are viewed though not accessed from the Coastal Path, though on this walk and further round on the Coastal Path at St Anne's Head the views are fine. A chapel was said to have been built on the Head to mark the coming of Henry Tudor in 1485, a landing of forces that would culminate in his victory at Bosworth. Nothing remains of Henry's chapel but the lighthouse, still working and run by Trinity House, is striking. The Dale peninsula is still dominated in its interior by the extensive ruins of Second World War camp buildings. The ghosts of the RAF and Naval staff still linger and it is difficult for one not to start humming Marlene or Vera, or to click fingers in time to the memory of Glenn Miller's 'In the Mood'. The air base, Coastal Command Station 19 Group, an extension to the base at Talbenny, which occupied most of the peninsula was active between 1942 and 1943 and was used by a Polish squadron, a notably brave and decorated unit. Though it was a Manchester class bomber on a training flight from Talbenny which almost crashed into Marloes Junior School; only the skill and bravery of the pilot Flight Sergeant Dickenson, saved the day when he managed to belly land the plane in a nearby field.[63] In 1943 the base became a Fleet Air Arm station called HMS Goldcrest.

MARLOES AND ST BRIDE'S

The splendid Marloes Sands appears on the OS map as a long walk up and northwards from St Anne's Bay, but I have only reached it by road from Martin's Haven after trips to Skomer. This is a fine beach with excellent rock pools, made more notable by Gateholm Island which extends, in effect, the north eastern arm of the coast. The island is only really an island when the tide is in. Obviously, it was a promontory fort and still has an appealing challenge for invading children and their parents. It is possible to discern outlines of the huts which covered the island and these may date back to the Iron Age.

From the southern edge of the beach there's a fine view of the end of Skokholm Island, which often looks as if it is an extension of Gateholm and that the promontory extends for miles further; but that stretch would be a deadly swim and, often enough, a bumpy boat ride. Towards the south east end of the beach there are the prominent tall rock towers known as 'The Three Chimneys'. Stand at the foot of these and imagine riding a sky rocket.

Marloes village was a Flemish farming settlement when they were encouraged to come to the county to develop the local agriculture. Fishing sustained the people, though they would have supplemented this by the taking of both rabbits and gulls' eggs on trips to Skomer and the other islands. Between Marloes and Martin's Haven is the National Trust land Marloes Meer. This is now a protected wet lands, though until 1811 it was common property and a useful source of leech-gathering; it is said that these were exported as far as Harley Street, when such blood-sucking practices were the cutting edge of medical treatments. I mean the leeches, not the fees.

When one goes on to Martin's Haven to catch the boats to the islands, there are the walls of the former deer park to the left side of the road. This haven was the site of an Iron Age settlement and fort.

The lands became the property of St Bride's, a castellated mid-nineteenth century manor house to the north, past Musselwick Sands, near the Nab Head, itself the site of a Stone Age flint factory. The manor house had extensive and sophisticated gardens and grounds; it is now a property bond development business. There's progress.

Also of note is the church of St Bridget in the hamlet of St Bride's which has memorials to the ubiquitous Philipps family as well as to the Lords Kensington of St Bride's Castle. St Bride's Haven has the remains of a lime kiln and evidence of the coastal trade that flourished until the late nineteenth century. St Bride was Brigid of Kildare, a late fifteenth century abbess from Kildare who had churches named in her memory in Cornwall and on the continent. The cliff walks around the smuggler's bays such as Dutch Gin and Brandy Bay are beautiful, especially in the setting sun on clear evenings. Intoxicating, one might say.

BROAD HAVEN, DRUIDSTONE, LITTLE HAVEN

It is a fine end of August afternoon at Broad Haven, its mile and more of flat golden sand stretching wide with the tide far out and stunning views to Skomer and to the north to St David's. Broad Haven has been much developed in the final decades of the last century with apartments and shops. As we drive in from St David's a police man and woman are booking cars which have parked on the single yellow line on the front. Quite right too, because the road has been kept deliberately narrow to slow down traffic. And why on earth would anyone want to drive quickly past such a view? Whether you've come from north or south the roads and lanes will have slowed you down to a philosophical crawl anyway. Broad Haven, Druidstone and Little Haven are the three beaches of Haverfordwest, some six miles inland, but the two Havens are also much favoured by visitors. They stay at the usual variety of camp sites, caravans, rented houses and B&Bs along this coast and on the roads from Haverfordwest.

We have been visiting the painter Brendan Stuart Burns in the final week of his residency as artist in residence at Oriel y Parc in St David's. This, the newest gallery in Wales, is a collaboration between

the National Park and the National Museum of Wales. It's on the edge of St David's as you drive up from the south – a functional and well-designed building which houses a permanent exhibition of art from the national collection, and it is especially good to see again those works by Graham Sutherland. The situation of the Graham Sutherland works is a problematic one, as I have said. The crumbling banks and undermined trees fallen or perched precariously over the Cleddau fed his imagination and were at the core of many of the paintings which would establish Sutherland as a leading figure in European art. His twisted root and branch forms, the gnarled wood and bright foliage against a theatrically backdropped sky pierced by the sharp flight of birds established an imagery which Oriel y Parc exhibits again. After his time in the south of France it was to Pembrokeshire, where in a sense it had all started, that he finally returned. It was only in the last days that he revoked his desire to be buried in the county.[65] Sutherland's reputation is no longer as central and one wonders to what extent the disappearance of those major works from the public's perception has to do with that?

Graham Sutherland's legacy is carried on by artists in the county with a cutting edge that goes beyond those endless representations of the surface reality of the landscape. I have mentioned David

Tress in Haverfordwest and Brendan Burns is another significant artist working in the county. He has had a productive year on the beaches of Pembrokeshire north of Little Haven. But that has been the case for over a decade now. His wife Ruth, the textiles artist, was born in Haverfordwest where her mother still lives and they travel down from Cardiff to stay whenever possible. It is at Broad Haven and Druidstone that he has walked, photographed and drawn for years; these researches becoming fine works in themselves and the journals he has kept providing a unique record of a painter and his commitment to capturing the essence of an experience, the essential, spiritual quality of a place. These are no coastal views, no landscape or seascape representations of the Pembrokeshire coast; they appear as abstract expressionist works on linen, canvas or board, but, in fact, are accurate responses to the minutiae of weather and light as they change the appearance of rocks and pools on the sea shore. His paintings are as much to do with the 'inscape' of the coast as the 'landscape' of the coast. His best works are both dramatic and meditative; they pull one into the core of the tides, pools and rocks.[65]

Brendan shows us his studio which is filled with drawings, rock rubbings and paintings of great vigour and a new redness which he says he has taken from the cliffs and stones of Caerfai Bay. His residency is at an end, but his commitment to the county will continue, of course: it's his locus genii and, like Sutherland, will no doubt inspire his work throughout his career.

At Broad Haven a tall, bronzed Lifeguard is taking in the flags of safety and beginning to pull up the kayak they use for rescues. He says that it's been the usual busy summer season, with six incidents that day – cuts, sand in the eyes, strains. A Fishguard lad, he's just graduated in manufacturing engineering at Loughborough: no job has been kept for him by his sponsors, a firm in Bristol, so he's off to Australia to guard more lives. Melbourne; we wish him well.

There's a decent coffee at the Ocean Café on the front before driving on south. It's only later, having read *Pembrokeshire: the Forgotten Coalfield* that I realise that even this area has the remains of the coal industry. The seam which surfaces from under Carmarthen Bay around Amroth and Saundersfoot makes its way diagonally north westwards across the county and stretches as far north as Newgale. At the back of these coastal villages inland there are the ghostly depressions and rusting residue of small mines. The trench of water back from the beach at Broad Haven is a man-made

coal washing point. The winding valley back inland from Little Haven held several coal workings too. Almost no-one remembers or notes these things and they play no part in the life and image of contemporary Pembrokeshire.

At Broad Haven and Druidstone, now for me Brendan Burns's beach, the cliffs have tumbled into rock formations and pools the colours of which shift in the wind and weather magically. The limestone and sandstone twists of strata give the coastline a sculptural beauty. As Peter Finch wrote in his poem 'Out at the Edge': "I get the feeling that if there is/An edge to this world then it is here."[66]

The rock pools have anemones, seaweeds, mussels and lichen and, as everywhere in the world flotsam and jetsam of the passing world of telegrams and anger. These things continue to inspire artists and beach visitors with their children.

At Little Haven the car park serves also as a boat park and there we meet two men who are preparing to go out in a Celtic longboat, one from Haverfordwest and one from Abingdon in Oxfordshire. They are middle-aged professionals and say that they are preparing for a Charity row down 22 miles of the Thames at the end of the summer. Their longboat is called *Kingfisher* and has among its sponsors Dale Sailing, the people who run boats to the islands of Skokholm and Skomer.

There are several pubs and places to eat in this tiny village. The Nest Bistro looks classy, with a suggestion that if you want their seafood platter then you'd be best to book the previous day. We choose to shelter from a sudden squall in the Swan Inn which is perched on the left hand side of the little bay. Two halfs of Rev. James beer and, on impulse, a shared starter of moules. This is delicious, served in a white wine and garlic sauce sponged up with hunks of rosemary bread. This small, two hundred year old pub has a cosy feel. If you walk on past up the path to the end of the rocky bay then the views are wonderful: back down to the bay and the village, along the strata of the cliffs to the north and south and out into the Cardigan Bay with its islands and tankers nudging into the setting sun.

SKOKHOLM ISLAND

Skokholm is an island of approximately half a square mile, essentially red sandstone, lying two miles south of Skomer and less developed in terms of visiting. From the mainland and from Skomer it is a low shape like a basking whale. Its name is rooted in the Norsemen's 'Wooded Island', though there is little evidence of that now. There is however evidence of human habitation dating back to the Bronze Age. The island was bought from the Earl of Pembroke for £300 in 1646 by a lawyer, William Philipps, and it was kept in his family for over three hundred years. It has been farmed and was a profitable source of rabbits, both for the Normans and much later in the nineteenth century. It is an SSSI and, of course, part of the Pembrokeshire National Park. Ray Howard-Jones, the painter I'm researching, painted both Skomer and Skokholm over several decades. Well into her seventies her skinny dipping exploits provided visitors with an extra dimension to their appreciation of Pembrokeshire's wild life.[67]

The island is home to the third largest colony of Manx Shearwaters in the UK and is one of the most important breeding sites in the world for Storm Petrels and Puffins. Consequently, it is not generally accessible, though regular trips around the island are possible from Martin's Haven and there are also day trips in season which go round The Neck and land at Hog Bay (details from the Wildlife Trust, which took over the administration of Skokholm in 2006).Development of an improved landing jetty should facilitate visits and this has been worked on by teams of volunteers and by public and private financial support. Skokholm is one of those special places which focusses ideals and actions. Both from the cliffs and from boats there is a good opportunity for seeing seals and dolphins and there are boat trips organised out of Neyland marina for this. A trip around the island gives great views of the variations in the colours of the rocks and cliffs – purple, green, red and grey, and at Hog Bay and elsewhere you are certain to see seals.

Like Skomer Island and Orielton, Skokholm drew the attention of the naturalist Ronald Lockley; he first leased the place and its ruined farmhouse in 1927.[68] He had the idea of raising rabbits and large profits from Skokholm; and there were clear precedents for the island had been an important source of food for the mainland since the early fourteenth century. A ministerial record from 1387 records that "3120 carcases from the islands of Scokholm, Scalmey and Myddeleholm," were sold. Lockley planned to breed Chinchilla rabbits whose pelt was worth up to a pound in 1928. I wonder what he planned to do with all that meat? In any case, the 1929 financial crash put an end to the fur markets and he became more involved with the birds he saw on Skokholm.[69] He developed the farm cottage and set up an ornithological base, arguably the first such in Britain.

He gradually became a naturalist rather than a farmer. He was especially fascinated by the Manx Shearwater, a bird which nested in burrows and commuted nocturnally to the island. In July 1937 he persuaded a British consul from Italy to take two of the Skokholm birds to Venice and release them: in the fifteenth day one bird had returned and Lockley calculated that it had either crossed the continent, some 930 straight miles or, as most probable, had navigated by sea some 3,700 miles. The other appeared on Skokholm the following March. His brother John assisted Lockley by releasing shearwaters in the high Alps in 1939, before his entry into the war and capture by the Germans.[70] His captivity was, no doubt, made more bearable by the fulsome letters of bird life on Skokholm which Ronald regularly sent him via the Red Cross mail. Lockley leased the island and wanted to use it for profit; he came to see the place as having its own integrity and to realise that he was merely a man passing time and passing through. "When I see our ravens, I have a feeling, almost, that this island is not mine but theirs. They have been her since time immemorial."

There are many bird hides now, though most twitchers will be seeing them from the boats which circle around Skokholm, and ravens, choughs, fulmar and guillimots are among those regularly to be seen. Lockley wrote *Dream Island* (1930) about his early years on Skokholm and it may well be that his observations on the lives of the rabbits there influenced Richard Adams's *Watership Down*. Lockley left when the military occupied the island in the Second World War; although he was to play a crucial role in establishing the National Park status of Pembrokeshire, he never again lived on Skokholm.

There has of necessity been a lighthouse on Skokholm since the eighteenth century when the strategic importance of the sea approaches to Milford Haven as potentially a major naval base was paramount. The striking white lighthouse at the south west point of the island, looking out over Wildgoose Race, dates from the mid nineteenth century when it was manned and serviced from the mainland, but it has been automated since 1983. It is an isolated cliff edged enclosure (with a helicopter pad) and the only evidence of current human intervention, as the cluster of farmhouse dwellings are now no more than ruins.

GRASSHOLM

Grassholm is another island named by the Vikings and at various times used for sheep grazing by successive mainland communities. The only way to see this small island now is to take one of the inflatable commercial boat trips; Grassholm is a bird sanctuary, owned since 1947 by the RSPB, and one cannot land. In truth, you would not really want to for the whole place is dominated by raucous gannets (around forty thousand of them from February to November) and decorated by their guano. It's that which paints the place into a white capped view in your binoculars. Not matter how powerful they may be or how tightly focussed you can apply them you will never come close to experiencing the noise and smell of the birds. This is one for the serious twitchers probably; or for those in search of myths, for Grassholm may well be Gwales, the island from the *Mabinogion* on which the severed head of Bran was kept alive for eighty years while his men feasted and slept oblivious until they opened a magical door and gazed out across to Cornwall. The moral may be that Sir Benfro, Pembrokeshire, should be all one needs and that there was never any point in looking out to Cornwall, Ireland or anywhere else.

SKOMER ISLAND

Elvis has left the building. Well, 'All the Puffins have gone' says the chalked notice at Martin's Haven as we queue to take the boat over to Skomer: "the pirate island with the cruel Norse name/where seals and smugglers have felt at home."[71] It's early August and although, we are assured, one puffin was spotted a few days ago, the birds for which this island is famous, over 10,000 of them, have now bred, grown and migrated. Even the Warden of Skomer can't tell us where they've gone. There has been recent fitting of geo-locators on some birds, and the general consensus is that they go back north in the direction of Greenland or Iceland, but no-one is sure. The Puffin described by R.M. Lockley as "that extraordinary clown-like bird with the aldermanic air…" is truly extraordinary and we know it to be so because of his work.[72]

Still, this is one of finest days of the summer, pleasantly warm with the odd decorative cloud carrying no rain. Martin's Haven is not the easiest place to reach, not too bad from Haverfordwest down the B4327 signposted to Dale, but from south of the Cleddau you have to cross over the bridge and strike west from the A477: in short, you need a map to reach Marloes and then the OS map or its equivalent to locate Martin's Haven.[73] There is a National Trust car park and a short but steep walk down to the small inlet from which the Skomer boat leaves. It's the *Dale Princess* run by Dale Sailing and runs from the first of April through to the end of October. You have a fifteen minute trip and, though the tides can be high and strong, is not subject to the extremities of, say the journey to Bardsey Island off the Lleyn. We have to line up on the high path to the jetty on the left side of the haven and it is strictly first come first served. There are some 14,000 visitors each year. The boat service is independent of the island which is run by Ymddiriedolaeth Natur/Wildlife Trust, a charity which has some Assembly capital support, but which relies on charity and many volunteers.

While waiting for the *Princess* I talk to Nathan Walton who is supervising the loading of wooden planks on to an inflatable; they are laying extra boardwalks for the paths near the Wick on the south side of Skomer. He has been employed by the Wildlife Trust Wales on a four day week during the recession, but thanks to some Heritage Lottery funding things are looking better. *The Dale Princess* returns with a dozen or passengers, including a family with suitcases and other luggage who confirm that they have been staying on Skomer for a few days; "Wonderful," a young man says, "And I caught some mackerel." Mackerel don't really count, I thought, they're too easy; but enjoy.

As we head out into the widening mouth of Milford Haven we pass six tankers waiting to unload at the refineries' terminals; could not those huge and hugely profitable companies spill a tiny bit of largess to keep things going? Through my binoculars I try to read the names: *Bio Anna*, or is that *Bro Anna*? But one of them has quite clearly along its flank *Golden Energy*. Of course it's in everyone's interests hereabouts to put a responsible spin on the oil refineries and the new liquid gas terminal and pipeline. Although the big surge in employment which is associated with such large developments is bound to be short or medium term, there must be some permanent or long-term benefits to the Haven's economy. Certainly, this sort of ferrying and the other coastal employment must needs be seasonal.

The *Princess*'s skipper is Keith, who is happy to let me sit in the cabin and chat. He's been at this for a number of years, after straining his back and leaving the gas fitting business. Karl, the ticket collector and rope man is a local man too. Both of them are employed by the owner John Reynolds at Neyland over the winter on the maintenance tasks of overhauling and painting the *Dale Princess* and other work at what seems to be a pretty substantial ship yard. The firm also builds what Karl calls 'Gentlemen's boats', the sort of classy cruisers you see on the Med; Neyland to Nice and Antibes. Once clear of the tiny inlet that is Martin's Haven, Keith flicks a switch and takes his hands off the wheel. This unassuming craft has a sat nav steering system which he says is a lazy man's job most of the time, but essential in these currents which swirl treacherously as the Irish Sea with the force of the Atlantic is diverted around Grassholm, Skokholm and Skomer before it hits St Anne's Head and the south Pembrokeshire coast. "A mist can come in and before you know it you could be turned around one hundred and eighty degrees," he adds.

"And those tankers could stray a bit close," I wonder.

"No, they're out at that distance because they are queuing and they want to avoid unnecessary port charges," he explains.

On the island each boatload is met by one of the wardens and their helpers. Jo Milbarrow and her husband are the current wardens and the quayside helper is Jennifer, a volunteer who also

admits to being an ecological consultant. I linger after Jo's brief introduction to the routes and the rules of Skomer and ask her about the running of the place. They have six volunteers at any one time in the season and anyone may apply; all are seriously considered and, she insists, they have no oddballs or time wasters; you don't have to be a consultant ecologist, but I guess that would help. The wardens now live in a modern, wood-clad building overlooking North Bay where we have landed. This building also houses study facilities and a library. Skomer has a serious research role which the residential flats and day visitors help to support. Each visitor pays a fee to land.[74] That is the only aspect of commerce on Skomer for there is no shop, no drinks or snack machine; you bring on to the island the food and other consumables you need and you leave with the packaging; there are no waste bins. We saw no litter at all in the four hour walk around the island. Toilets? There are two which you reach by ascending the stairs at the side of the Old Farmhouse block which has the general volunteer and rented accommodation. You climb stairs to the loos because (of course) they are non-flush degradable loos; perfectly respectable toilets which cover building-tall pipes which lead to dark oblivion and to which you add a scoop of sawdust each time you use the facility. What our American cousins would call 'the comfort station' is also a learning experience on Skomer.

There are several ways to see Skomer and the *Skomer – Maps, Trails and Information* booklet you buy at the landing is excellent, clear and concise. Margaret and I take the island circuit – 'Approx. 4 miles. Approx. 2.5 to 3 hours.' And, after our packed sarnie lunch in the Old Farmhouse's picnic space, we head off to the north to cover Skomer's coast in an anti-clockwise direction. This covers everything, for at most points you can look across into the middle – gorse, bracken, a couple of ponds with water birds and several clusters of rocks and stones which, we are assured, are evidence of habitation stretching back to prehistory. At the end of the nineteenth century Edward Laws says, "The number of these hut circles is so great, that had they been inhabited at one and the same time, it would certainly have been necessary to import food from the mainland." But there would have been fish in abundance and surely some livestock.

On the first section of the walk, between North Pond and Green Pond over to Garland Stone off the north coast we look out for the Short-eared Owls that can be seen feeding in daylight hours. Nothing today; nor do we hear the curlews that are also possible. Apart from the ubiquitous gulls, the birds we encounter most frequently are the corpses of the Manx Shearwaters which litter the whole island and all the walks. Nature is red in tooth and claw and if you come into a natural reserve such as Skomer you simply have to deal with that. Especially on an island which hosts the largest colony in the world – some 120,000 pairs nesting. The adults spend all daylight hours out at sea fishing and return under cover of darkness to feed their chick. These big fluffy chicks are monitored in the burrows, some stolen or inherited from rabbits, and you can see live and recorded activity on the video displays in the exhibition room back at the Old Farmhouse. As John Stuart Williams wrote of the birds on neighbouring Skokholm:

In the iridescent morning air
Below the singing bird-shot sky,
Their sharp wings spread like arms,
The lost shearwaters lie
Eviscerated by the gulls.
Those without deep shelters die.[75]

Eviscerated is the word: the gulls consume the whole body and the head, leaving each pair of feathered wings and the headless vertebrae. It is nature's way and it must make sense to sacrifice hundreds so that the thousands who survive and thrive in their rabbit-designed underground nests may leave each autumn to cross the Atlantic and winter over in Brazil and Patagonia. Where the Shearwaters went, so went the Welsh. After four years the grown young return to Skomer, often, it is said to exactly the same spot.

On the way north you have the option of taking an historical loop to see evidence of the stone age settlements; in truth, it is difficult to make out precisely where they are in relation to the rocky outcrops, particularly when the bracken is summer high. They are there and can be clearly seen from the air. Toby Driver's book has them visible from several hundred feet. So too are the outlines of field systems around the edges of the island and on the Neck itself. Driver describes Skomer thus: "[it] ranks among the finest archaeological landscapes in Britain", because most of the island was not subject to ploughing in recent centuries. He says that the prehistoric founding communities would have benefitted from a light covering of oak woodland and a plentiful supply of fresh water from several streams. Fishing, together with the collecting of eggs and seaweed would have supported their keeping of livestock.

At Garland Stone you have a stunning view of the south end of Ramsey Island to the north and to Ramsey's left is the cluster of rock-islands, the Bishops and Clerks with the lighthouse island of South Bishop. There's Stack Rocks to your right and beyond, further up the coast a hint of Broad Haven sands. Garland Stone itself is a large outcrop some 110 metres from the cliff: here and at Mew Stone past the Wick, you just want Monet or Sisley to get the brushes out. Another one of the Volunteers, Gill, a council worker from Liverpool and now Gloucester has set up a scope. I spot a couple of cormorants on the Stone, or are they shags, smaller, slightly greener? Gill says there are no seals yet but with her Nikon Fieldscape we can look south towards Grassholm. It's an island almost perfectly dissected diagonally black and white. The black is the rock at this distance and the white are the tonnes and generations of deposits of guano. Beyond, and at a distance of some 25 kilometres is the Smalls lighthouse: this is a really clear day.

But it's clear too of some of the attractions of Skomer and until we reach Pigstone Bay we see little of real interest, apart from the brown and plump rabbits which abound. After eating our remaining

sandwiches and a whole fruit bar (crisps and cans are really not the thing on Skomer) we look out to a deceptively calm sea where the currents run fiercely and where gannets and porpoise may appear. Nothing. The sun, the freshest air and occasionally the high glint and growl of airliners heading for America, which Peter Finch on the Coastal Path thought "maybe…just isn't there".[76] But then below us in the bay itself the torpedo body of a grey seal which saunters in and basks in the turning waters of Pigstone. What mammal is more at ease in its element than a seal? This one has a greasy-smooth insouciance; it's a lounge-lizard at this edge of the Atlantic and we watch from above for as long as it's there.

We cross the trickle of Wick steam and at the Wick itself we take in the sheer height of the massive cliff. This has a multitude of birds – kittiwake, fulmar and guillemot. A man alongside us has seen a peregrine falcon, but my eyes or my binoculars are not up to following the directions he gives. To the right of the cliffs and opposite is a huge slab of rock angled low into the water. Puffins, in their season, congregate here after fishing, their mouths full of sand eels.

On from Wick we take the option of looping around the South Plateau. At the southern point rears up Mew Stone which has the dramatic presence of Cezanne's 'Mont St Victoire'. Only closer. Again, it cries out for Sisley, or Monet or Cezanne; a rock cathedral with a choir of birds and the stained glass of the ocean and sky. A man and his son have been scoping the view and say that there are choughs. And then I have them – a pair and then one more; quite clearly choughs with their red beaks and feet swooping past, cruising the cliff's edge in front of us with Mew Stone as a backdrop.

We descend through by the narrow paths through bracken and heather along Driftwood Bay in the South Haven where four motor yachts have moored for lunch and an afternoon read. Then up and on to the landing place for our departure. On the way back on the *Dale Princess* we see that none of the tankers has moved; we see to the south, off St Anne's Head, the white form of the departing ferry for Rosslare. These fierce waters are now full of commerce; how brave or desperate must those pre-historic, pre-ferry, pre-*Princess* people clinging to a living on Skomer, Skokholm and Grassholm? And what isolated bliss must days like this have been even for them haunted by the constant need to find food and warmth.

Notes

1. You can find David's work in the Boundary Gallery in London, Beaux Arts in Bath, the Tegfryn Gallery in Ynys Mon, the Albany Gallery, Cardiff and Myles Pepper's West Wales Arts Gallery in Fishguard. See also, *David Tress* by Clare Rendell (Gomer, 2002) and *David Tress; Chasing Sublime Light* (West Wales Arts Centre, 2008), a bi-lingual text and commentary by David.
2. On a sunny afternoon in March 2009 I held my mother's hand as she died there in her ninety-first year. In the bitter winter of 1963 I almost died there – an infection after an appendix operation. The ex-army huts in which I split my stitches during an episode of Steptoe and Son are recorded by a photograph in the entrance hallway of Withybush.
3. There is a huge needle monument to Picton on the old Carmarthen road at Job's Well. Also, the local comprehensive in Haverfordwest is named after him.
4. Gerald of Wales described the Flemings thus: "a people, I say, well versed in commerce and woollen manufactures; a people anxious to seek gain by sea and land in defiance of fatigue and hunger; a hardy race equally fitted for the plough or the sword...".
5. *The Story of Lord Nelson and Sir William and Lady Hamilton's Tour in Wales*, E.C. Freeman & Edward Gill, 1962
6. The Owens, especially Williams' wife, were also benefactors of schools and the workhouse in the town.
7. See Tenby Museum for more about this artist. Augustus was born in Tenby.
8. *Chiaroscuro*. Augustus also remembers a camping trip from Tenby during his Slade days: "falling in with a party of Irish tinkers, we profited by their company and conversation, which was rich in the wisdom of the road... Encamped within the picturesque walls of a Priory at Haverfordwest" from which they were forced by a man "flourishing a pitchfork and foaming

at the mouth."

9. A traditional Welsh stringed instrument played with bow.

10. Adelina Patti (1843-1919) was the outstanding soprano of her time, greatly admired by Verdi. The Patti Pavilion in Swansea commemorates her. Martin's record would have had her singing at the age of over sixty.

11. Carel Weight (1908-1997) visited Haverfordwest several times, staying with Maurice and his mother. He was a Professor at the Royal College and had served as a war artist in the Second World War. Maurice Sheppard in 1984 became the youngest President of the Royal Watercolour Society. He has regularly exhibited in the Royal Academy's Summer Exhibitions for decades.

12. Lowe was art master at Haverfordwest from 1959-71 when he became HMI for art in Wales. He exhibited widely, and the critical attention which Maurice Sheppard seeks for his work is long overdue.

13. Signposted left off to A40 four miles short of Haverfordwest.

14. Also the name of a training ship based in Nova Scotia. 'Picton Castle' has graced other ships, including a British naval vessel in the Second World War.

15. The buying of peerages is not new. In 1611 Sir John Philipps bought his, the money being used to pay for James I's campaigns in Ireland. There is an irony in that the original owner Sir John Wogan had been Justiciar of Ireland from 1295-1313.

16. Fenton retells the story of a trooper, under the guise of a white flag, snatching a child from an open window and forcing the castle's occupants to sue for an accommodation; page 155.

17. He had planned to be buried in the county, but changed his mind a matter of weeks before his death.

18. Sutherland's work, including many of the Pembrokeshire works, in is all the major collections, including the Tate and the National Museum of Wales.

19. From 'Welsh Sketch Book' in *Horizon*, April 1942.

20. One of the Philipps, Nicola Jane, has had a successful career as a portrait artist, notably a double portrait of the Princes William and Harry in 2009.

21. A letter of December 1939 to Kenneth Clark, later of *Civilization* tv fame, who commissioned Sutherland as an official war artist and who championed his work. Tate Gallery Archive collection.

22. Following Brendan Stuart Burns's residency at Oriel y Parc in St David's (2009-2010) a number of important drawing and paintings were shown in that gallery, curated by Burns.

23. The sewin, a sea trout, is caught by line and coracle in the Towy and Tefi rivers. It is rarer and more delicious than salmon. Never baulk at the price; just savour it. See my poem 'Mapping the World' in *Crossing Over*.

24. Fenton pays great attention to Slebech, eight pages of commentary and an engraving.

25. There are fine aerial photographs of the estate in Toby Driver's book. The castellated stable block is of the same vintage as that of my golf club at Wenvoe Castle, just outside Cardiff.

26. See also Templeton in the Central section.

27. The Knights had constructed a tunnel from the house to the banks of the Cleddau: this passage was re-discovered during the Second World War by nurses based in the military hospital at Picton Castle who were out walking. See Maxwell Fraser's *Introducing West Wales*, (Methuen, 1956). For this source and some others I am grateful to Dillwyn Miles's book *A Pembrokeshire Anthology* (Gomer, 1983).

28. *Marine Plans and Charts of Wales*, Olwen Caradoc Evans (The Map Collectors' Circle, 1969).

29. There are extensive papers relating to the Jamaican estates of Phillips at the National Library of Wales and in the county record office.

30. The county record office has a copy of Lady de Rutzen's recipes and household hints – how to take spots out of marble, cures for corns and sea sickness, hare soup, calves' feet jelly, that sort of thing.

31. Jonathan Cape, 1966.
32. The Yeomanry was established in 1794 on the national orders of Pitt and organised by Lord Milford and the future Lord Cawdor of Stackpole. Cawdor formed the Castlemartin Troop and in 1796 they were used to subdue disturbances in Pembroke town resulting from bread shortages. They were more patriotically deployed against the drunken French invaders at Fishguard the following year. 'The Pembrokeshire Yeomanry' by R.L. Howell in *The Pembrokeshire Historian*, No 2, 1966.
33. Michael Roberts confirms that there is clear perception still that Llangwm's society is matriarchal.
34. Each June there is a scarecrow competition in the village, too.
35. See *Nets and Coracles* by J. Geraint Jenkins (David & Charles, 1974). And an article in *The Countryman* by F.F. Nicholls in Summer, 1961.
36. See a fascinating aerial photograph of these raised gardens in the Toby Driver book p. 188.
37. www.rasdavies.co.uk Their house has a substantial garden with fruit and vegetables in abundance.
38. M.R. Connop-Price, again, has maps and photographs and numerous details about this are of the coalfield.
39. Riitta and Colin's oldest daughter is a fashion designer.
40. Her *Miscellanies in Prose and Verse*, was published in 1766 as a quarto edition by Thomas Davies with Johnson adding a preface and several prose and verse pieces; she also wrote a play.
41. Rosemarket also has a nine-hole golf course, though it's of little interest; except that between two of the fairways they have a grass landing strip for aircraft. I am grateful for this information to Colin Butters, an old school mate of mine and retired airline pilot. Colin tells me that he has landed a light aircraft at Rosemarket. You have to phone them up an hour or so to give your ETA so that they can warn the golfers and clear the space.
42. Sir William Hamilton who had inherited land in the area got a bill passed by parliament in 1790 to allow for the development of the port. Nelson visited in 1802 and a local hotel, The New Inn, was re-named after him to commemorate the visit. The hotel has undergone considerable alterations over the years, but still retains the original staircase.
43. George Owen in *The Description of Pembrokeshire*. In the Shakespeare play, set in Roman Britain, scenes are set in the 'Country near Milford Haven'.
44. The Quakers were active here for about twenty years only and had been encouraged to come over as a result of the American War of Independence and trading levy problems. The most famous whaling association with the county was the filming of *Moby Dick*, starring Gregory Peck, though episodes of the successful tv series *The Onedin Line* were filmed at Milford in the 1970s. The world has moved on (apart from the Japanese, perhaps) and rather than processing the whale, Milford now has a seal hospital.
45. See the Skomer section for contemporary boat building.
46. See M.R. Connop Price pp 138-40: the Milford Haven and St Bride's Bay Light Railway was an ambitious proposal linking the pits from above Nolton Haven to Milford Haven. It eventually petered out in the First World War.
47. In 2010 the Youth Drama Festival celebrated its tenth anniversary back in Milford and was featured on tv.
48. See the Tenby section. Clive has had a great noughties decade with continuing work as the radio *Sherlock Holmes* and in *The History Boys*.
49. The Amoco oil company was generous in its initial sponsorship of the Torch.
50. Named after one of the company's earlier actors and supporters.
51. See his poem on Lydstep Caverns in the South section. The Hakin and Lydstep poems are in my anthology *The Poetry of Pembrokeshire*.
52. K.D. McKay, *A Vision of Greatness* (Chevron, 1989).
53. *Pembrokeshire Shipwrecks*, T. Goddard (Christopher Davies, 1982).

54. Qatar has the largest natural gas reservoir in the world.
55. This is one the 'Thankful Villages' (there are fewer than forty of them) which did not lose any of the men sent to the Great War.
56. The pipeline was completed in 2007. There was also a considerable degree of concern and opposition from locals. Nicholas Young, a farmer from Rosemarket, quoted by the BBC, was not untypical: "I'm concerned about my children's' future and putting a bomb in the backyard does not make me feel very good."
57. See the section on Angle.
58. It is unfortunate that a fine house, Castle Hall, built in the last decade of the eighteenth century for John Zephaniah Holwell, a former governor of Bengal and survivor of the Black Hole of Calcutta, was left to decline and demolished by the Admiralty in 1937.
59. Brunel was appointed the chief engineer of the G.W.R. at the age of twenty-seven in 1833. His *Great Eastern* was for a time docked at Neyland for refurbishment.
60. Unveiled by Prince Charles in 1999.
61. Opened in 1975 after being delayed by construction problems and a fatal accident.
62. *John Wesley in Wales*, A.H. Williams (University of Wales Press, 1971).
63. Dickenson and his crew went missing in a Lancaster raid over Wismar in Germany within weeks of the Marloes incident. *The Pembrokeshire Life* magazine (always worth buying) in its September and November issues in 2010 has interesting articles about the war in this area.
64. He is, in fact, buried elsewhere.
65. Brendan is a colleague at the University of Glamorgan where he teaches on the Foundation course. He has twice won the Gold Medal at the National Eisteddfod of Wales and been Artist of the Year in Wales. Together with the Haverfordwest-based painter David Tress, he has come closer to the core of beauty and significance in the Pembrokeshire landscape than anyone since Graham Sutherland and John Piper.
66. Included in *The Poetry of Pembrokeshire*.
67. Ray Howard-Jones (1903-96) was a remarkable, individualistic artist who, though born in Berkshire and brought up in Penarth, made the Pembrokeshire coast around St Martin's Bay her home for each summer over decades. Many of her paintings reflect her commitment to this coastline as a place of physical and spiritual inspiration. Maurice Sheppard knew her over many years and was a member of the same Anglican congregation at St Martin's in Haverfordwest.
68. See the section on Orielton. His *Letters from Skokholm*, with illustrations by Tunnicliffe, was re-published by the Dovecoat Press in 2010. Many of the letters were those sent to his brother-in-law John Buxton who was a prisoner of war in Germany. See also Roscoe Howells's *The Sounds Between* (1968). Lockley's writing is more than a record of his bird observations and has the force of literary writing: see his description of ravens killing and eating a pregnant ewe – p 46-7.
69. This after many attempts to cull the indigenous population of wild rabbits, including cyanide gas and the introduction of the recently invented myxomatosis.
70. Pages 196-200 in *Letters from Skokholm*.
71. From Raymond Garlick's 'Expedition Skomer' in *The Poetry of Pembrokeshire*.
72. *Letters from Skokholm*, p121.
73. Ray Howard-Jones lived at Martin's Haven and alone or with her long-time partner Ray Moore (they never married) spent many summers on Skomer drawing and painting the birds and the cliffs.
74. In 2009 this was £7 for adults with concessions for senior citizens and children. The *Dale Princess* is also very reasonable – £10 return for adults. Accommodation is short stay, self-catering and around £35p.p.p.night.
75. From *The Poetry of Pembrokeshire*.
76. *Ibid*.

WEST

JAMESTON, HODGESTON AND LAMPHEY

Beyond Lydstep on the Pembroke road you pass, probably quickly and without regard, the villages of Jameston and Hodgeston: the first is rather charmless, though it has the Swanlake Inn, which serves to remind you to trek down to the coast to Swanlake Bay. But Hodgeston is worth stopping at because of the remains of its moated hall and its church.[1] You may find the porch doorway blocked by a wire and wood frame, but this is simply to keep out the birds and you can undo it and enter. The place is now one of five Pembrokeshire churches supported by the Friends of Friendless Churches and, though no longer used for worship, is reasonably well preserved.[2] It has Minton floor tiles and mid-fourteenth century stone seats, sedilia, for the priests, by the same hands as those at St David's and Lamphey. The choir stalls were brought there by the Friends and are by a notable Edwardian designer, W.D. Caroe.

More obviously significant is the church of St Tyfei and St Faith at Lamphey.[3] with its imposing fifteenth century tower and Norman font. This is well-kept and, it would seem, well-used with a neatly trimmed churchyard which has at least one mysterious grave to 'Our unknown shipmate' lost when the USS Coastguard Clipper *Tampa* was torpedoed in September,1918 in what they call the Bristol Channel, but probably meant the Irish Sea. The gravestone is just about legible but what draws you to it is the rusting American Legion star on its spike stuck in the ground before the stone. 'Thy way is the sea, thy path in the great waters' is the inscription in Arlington Cemetery, Washington D.C. for the one hundred and thirty one sailors lost: one of whom is here in Lamphey.[4]

The house next to the church was a staging inn called The Venison, but across from the church in the former vicarage is a decent hotel and restaurant, Lamphey Hall, which serves good food and which has some of its original features. In fact, Lamphey also has a decent pub, The Dial, and a Best Western hotel, the Lamphey Court Hotel, in the splendid setting of the former Lamphey Court, reached by a long drive and several bridged streams. It is a Greek revival house of the 1820s which retains many good features, some by Charles Fowler, the architect of Covent Garden market.

To the left of the entrance to Lamphey Court is the car-parking for Lamphey Palace, the grand ruins of a grander bishops' palace for the see of St David's; their pleasure dome in the south, as it were. Built first from the early thirteenth century to the middle of the following century, there were two large courtyards and two large halls. The Western Hall has some its original paintings still discernable. It fell into the hands of Henry VIII in 1546 and thence to the powerful Devereaux family[5], the earls of Essex, who held it until the Civil War. "The Devereux of Lamphey assumed the first place in South Pembrokeshire society," remarked Edward Laws.

The Owens of Orielton then owned the land and the ruins, but it was better maintained by Charles Mathias of Llangwarren in north Pembrokeshire and more recently and to the present day by CADW, of course. There is much to see (allow a couple of hours) but on a fine day try to imagine the combination of spiritual contemplation and quietude, combined with the good life, for to the south west there was a walled deer park and to the north east an elaborate system of breeding and feeding ponds for fish; there were orchards and pastures, dovecotes and mills. There was an abundance of limestone for building and for local kilns. The priests ate well and could sustain themselves through the cold dark winters. As we can with the more than adequate provisions in this small village. Originally reached by water, Lamphey has a station on the Tenby-Pembroke line and a devilishly twisting road.

One Sunday driving to lunch at Lamphey I stopped the car between Lydstep and Jameston at the vision of an athletic woman dragging a sledge–on-wheels towards us. Rosie Swale-Pope MBE is one of the most recognisable people in Pembrokeshire.[6] She is amazingly fit, hugely idealistic and, quite possibly, a bit bonkers. I mean, she's my age! She is unique. Built like a lady whippet. We stopped and talked that day as traffic slowed and negotiated our obstruction. I reminded her that she had been a guest in my series of theatre evenings of 'Desert Island Books' in the Dylan Thomas Centre in Swansea some fifteen years before. She'd already been walking for years and is walking still. She has walked around the world, raising over a quarter of a million pounds, and has been walking for much of her adult life, and all of it for good causes, charities; and for her own sense of a purpose, of course. She has lost two husbands to prostate cancer and has survived many broken bones and running related injuries. That day she was practising for her latest self-appointed challenge – twenty-six marathons of

twenty-six miles in twenty-six days, for the Ty Hafan children's hospice. We put some money in the jar she keeps in the sledge-tent which is home for her on her epics, and wish her well. In the middle of lunch I feel guilty and know that I should have gone into my wallet for notes. I shall send her some via her website. We all should. www. rosiearound the world. co.uk

PEMBROKE

You might be forgiven for imagining that Pembroke was the county town, though it is, in fact, Haverfordwest. It is also the case that this Norman-castled town had fallen into a decline and has only significantly revived its fortunes in the wake of the naval expansion which created its now poor relation Pembroke Dock in the first quarter of the nineteenth century. The map maker John Speed said of Pembroke in 1610 that he "found more houses without habitants than I ever saw in any one city throughout my survey", though Daniel Defoe a century later noted a bustling market. What is certainly bustling now is the main street – one way and almost impossible to cross Main Street safely during working hours because of the relentless stream of traffic.

Like so many towns and cities Pembroke exists because of water: the castle offered security, branched by the dividing tidal waters and easily defended in the manner of a promontory fort since prehistoric times.[7] Trench and earthwork fortifications were the original protective line of the eleventh century conquerors and Gerald of Wales says that they threw a slender fortress of stakes and turf across the neck of the land. In the twelfth century Pembroke was the eponymous Earl's administrative centre for south Pembrokeshire and a long straight road of houses developed to and from the castle gates, with gardens dropping down the slopes from them on either side of what now is Main Street. There are two churches on Main Street – St Mary's and St Michael's – though their Norman and later features have been given the Victorian treatment, to no great effect. The religious building of most obvious note is the Wesleyan Chapel which was placed proudly at the point of St Michael's Square in the last quarter of the nineteenth century, but which now and for some years has been used as an antique centre. Wesley, so enthused by his welcome a few miles east in Jeffreyston in the 1780s, would surely have been perplexed by this turn of events. The spot from which Wesley preached in the town is at the rear of the York tavern, one of the more interesting of the town's pubs.

On our family visits to my uncle in Pwllcrochan in the 1950s my father would swing the car (any of that bewildering succession of cars) down below the castle and out on the B4320 to Hundleton and then swing up to the south side of the Haven again. We rarely stopped in Pembroke or ventured in again from those deep country weekends. Though I remember a trip to the cinema with my cousins. The late Fifties – John Wayne?[8] Probably John Wayne. The cinema was Haggar's, one of the oldest in Wales with the Haggar family now rightly remembered by film and social historians, as William Haggar was one of the pioneers of film making at the cusp of the twentieth century.[9] We certainly never visited the castle.[10] William Haggar shot what was probably the first British film drama *The Life and Death of Charles Peace* in nearby Pembroke Dock. William Haggar Jnr and his beautiful wife Jenny Linden set up the cinema in Pembroke and had performed plays, notably *The Maid of Cefn Ydfa,* in South Pembrokeshire with their travelling troupe. The cinema proved so successful that the Haggar family developed the business into the Assembly Rooms ballroom and a restaurant, now, sadly, all gone.[11]

Despite frequent earlier Viking raids, after development by the

Normans Pembroke and its castle was impregnable until the Civil War when, in common with Tenby and other Pembrokeshire towns the allegiance of the garrison swung and wobbled from one side to the other. The destruction wreaked by Cromwell's forces in July 1648 after a bitter seven week siege saw the castle partly destroyed and its dependent town slump into decline. John Poyer of the Royalist sympathisers drew the worst of three lots and was executed. What you can see now when you visit the castle is largely due to restoration by first J.R. Cobb in the 1870s and then Sir Ivor Philipps of Cosheston in the first half of the twentieth century, though the Great Tower and the Barbican wall on the town side are medieval.

In 1456 in Pembroke Castle the son of Jasper Tudor, the boy who would be Henry VII, was born.[12] He would found the Tudor dynasty, and, in a sense, be the first Welshman to wear the crown of England. He defeated Richard III at the Battle of Bosworth Field in 1485. Henry VIII, his son, appointed Anne Boleyn (his second wife) Marchioness of Pembroke.

Visitors to the castle today find a large lawn and benches which can be a pleasant spot to meditate on the history of the place, particularly out of the high season. You can also walk along sections of the walls and climb to the top of the Great Keep, built by William Marshall around 1200, almost fifty feet wide at the base and rising to seventy five feet. From here you can survey much of the surrounding countryside, and feel impregnable. Note below the castle to the north the Mill Pond which harnessed the tidal rise to power a corn mill at Pembroke Quay. And to the south, above the Orange Gardens area, the lower level where you will probably park the car has been tidally flooded in earlier times; there are two defensive towers to your right, just as you swing left for the Bosherston and Freshwater West road.

From this tower you can also see across the road and river to Monkton. It was here that Cromwell set his cannons and bombarded the castle. Monkton is now a rather non-descript village, a suburb of Pembroke really, though there are some remains of the Priory incorporated into the parish church of St Nicholas, one of the most impressive parish churches in the county, and a well restored medieval dovecote. The church grounds afford an excellent view of Pembroke town and it was from this spot that Richard Wilson painted the castle. There are impressive tombs of the Owen and Meyrick families, both substantial land-owners in the area (for example, Orielton, and what became Pembroke Dock). Also, the Priory Farmhouse has a good Flemish chimney. Arnulph de Montgomery had founded the Benedictine Priory at Monkton in 1098 though it was almost certainly a much earlier Christian site. The new Priory was the daughter house of the Abbey of Seez in Normandy and was served by a quay on the river. There were Bronze Age finds at the Priory Farm Cave during an excavation in 1908, evidence that the Pembroke promontory and the high ground of Monkton have been inhabited for many centuries. Monkton Old Hall was restored by the Landmark Trust in the 1980s and may be rented; as it probably served as a guest house for the Priory, this seems especially appropriate. Though whether those guests would have afforded nearly £3000 for week in the high season, is less likely. It does sleep seven.

In truth, Pembroke is a one street town needing another stage of development which the local council have still not managed to secure. The cinema is long gone and there are too many shops vacant. There is a decent deli and on alternate Saturdays a farmer's market held in the town hall. On our last spring visit we met Pat Bean from the Manorbier Springfields nursery selling asparagus and daffodils. She's there to support the idea and principle of the market, though all her asparagus had gone by lunchtime. The town hall is notable now largely because of the extensive painted murals on the ground floor and going on up to the dusty council chamber. There over a dozen large panels by George and Jeanne Lewis which were completed in 2006. They are as skilled as the Bradforth piece in Tenby market hall and less mannered.

Apart from the castle, you may linger only for a bookshop, the two churches and the two antique/bric-a-brac places which now occupy the large, and now ungodly Baptist and Wesleyan chapels.[13] The castle itself is best viewed from across the inlet to the north west, the views used by Turner and the Bucks and just about every other artist who passed this way.

PEMBROKE DOCK

This town will not be high on the visitor's itinerary of Pembrokeshire unless they are catching the ferry to Rosslare. But what may seem to be unprepossessing is, in fact, an interesting example of modern town development. Pembroke Dock was, in a sense, born when the Admiralty determined to expand its operations in Milford Haven across the water to the south side where, close to the village of Pater, a dockyard complex was built. This attracted workers from all around the Haven and eventually their houses were built close to the dockyards. 'PD' was always predicated on war, rather than fishing, though nearby Pennar was a centre for oysters until the late nineteenth century.

Edward Laws describes this as a purchase of "a poor sheep-walk developed into building land" and commends the "wisdom of Mr Meyrick's action."[14] He goes on to underline the vast expenditure on the defence of the Haven at this time. Lord Nelson and the Hamiltons had visited to survey the prospects for a major British Navy base in Pembrokeshire. Remember that blue plaque in St Julian's Street, Tenby? Laws cannot resist digressing from military matters to that of Mrs Hamilton. And, of course, neither could Horatio Nelson. "All this [expenditure] may be indirectly ascribed to the fair face of Lady Hamilton, but if the grumbler thereat (whether he be a shareholder in Milford Docks, or a taxpayer criticising the modern ruins of Dale Fort) will go to Stackpole Court and there view one of the twenty-four portraits of Emma painted by Romney, I verily believe he will forgive all the naughtinesses of her life, and the wasteful folly which has pursued the property purchase by a transfer of her charms."

Pater Dockyards was soon in action though and saw the launch of two British navy ships, the *HMS Valorious* and the *HMS Ariadne* in 1816. And in the nineteenth century, until 1922, two hundred and sixty-three Navy vessels were built there. There were also notable constructions for other navies; of particular interest was the *Hiei* built for Japan in 1877 which occasioned an official visit by Hechahiro Togo, who later became a national hero in naval battles against the Chinese and the Russians. So important was the military and commercial potential of the Haven that no less a figure than Thomas Telford was commissioned to build the new road from St Clears on the border of Carmarthenshire to Hobbs Point. Telford died before he could undertake the scheme but his plans were followed and the Tavernspite Turnpike Trust[15] oversaw the construction. The greatest challenge proved to be the spanning of the stream and gorge at Stepaside. You will go over this if you take the road from Kilgetty village across the new (and dangerous) junction with the A477 to Stepaside village.

The 31st Regiment left for the Crimea from these docks and the scene was described by a Mrs Peters: "The ground on that (February) morning was covered with a sprinkling of snow, and the

air was bitterly cold and cheerless. The soldiers marched from the Hill to the Dockyard steps amidst much excitement and many tokens of grief from wives, families and friends who accompanied them in order to bid them farewell". A local poet called Samuel Cozens wrote:

> It is thus with the soldiers as they march to the shore
> To embark in the beautiful ship, Imperadore;
> Safe she rides at her moorings in beauty and pride,
> And her steam curls aloft as she swings with the tide ...

During this conflict reports of the war's progress were read to the townspeople at meetings at the Clarence Hotel.

Pembroke Dock was, clearly, a major centre of military importance, defended with the rest of the Haven by blockhouses and forts, including two Martello towers ('Palmerston's Follies' – see image page 171) at the entrance of the dockyards.[16] These survive and one houses a small museum with original guns and models of the aircraft stationed here. It is best seen from Hobbs Point towards the south west before the ferry terminal. Visiting the tower is easy as it is well sign-posted and is reached by a raised walkway over the edge of the sea. Children will enjoy clambering up the winding metal stairs and seeing the gun which points across at the oil refinery. There is a short and interesting video and uniforms and clear explanations of the tower's purpose.

The most notable of these defences was the Defensible Barracks, built in the 1840s to house the Royal Marines and their artillery, and still a landmark in the town.[17] It was bought for a song some years back, but is currently undeveloped and not accessible to the public. Two listed-building hangars remain in the dockyard, but the site has also been developed for housing. In fact, there is a scheme to greatly develop the old barracks area for a marina and housing – called Martello Quay, it may be delayed by the recession at the end of the noughties. Certainly, 'PD' needs investment and a lick of paint.

Little could be done to defend the huge oil tanks at Llanraeth, just below the Defensible Barracks. In the afternoon of August 19th, 1940 three Junkers bombers appeared without warning and destroyed much of the oil reserves, causing a fire which burned for eighteen days and was, at that time, the worst bombing incident of the war. I imagine my father on coastal searchlights near Angle would have heard those massive explosions and seen the smoke

clouds which covered the area for weeks. Pembroke Dock and the Haven became more strategically important in the Second World War than it had in the first. In 1931 a squadron of RAF flying boats (the now forgotten Southamptons) set up base at the Dock. But during the war this was the base for the beautiful and effective Sunderlands, one of the most elegant of aquatic planes, and the means by which for over two decades the British Empire was reached by the rich and important. Pembroke Dock was, in fact, the largest such base in the world in the 1940s. Some 120 foot long, the Sunderland was the largest aeroplane in the world at that time powered by four engines which produced 4,000 horse power.

On one of my parents' trips down to see my Uncle Ivor I remember being taken into the Dock and allowed to clamber aboard the Sunderland that was on show. Even to a boy it felt cramped. I had laboured long and hard to assemble the Sunderland from an Airfix kit, so could remember the smooth lines and boat hull of the craft. The inside of the actual plane was much more Meccano than Airfix: awkward metal struts and a dank smell of old leather and so

little light apart from the cockpit. Something that day undercut the fascination with war and planes: these things were real and heavy and no place to die.

There is now a Sunderland information centre, which opened at the end of 2009, where you can see a selection of photos and come closer to experiencing the aircraft's unique characteristics. This is run by the Flying Boat Trust which aims to raise and renovate one of the earliest Sunderlands, T9044, which sank at its moorings in a gale in November 1940.[18] This trust, like the information centre, is run by a group of volunteer enthusiasts, including former Sergeant Signaller Ron Boreham who flew Sunderlands after the war. The group has access to public funding and are seeking both public and private supporters to raise the aircraft. A million quid would come in useful. When I last visited, one of engines had been recovered and was being renovated. The town and Pembrokeshire needs to further explore, articulate and celebrate its important links with the war and this aircraft.

This was also the home base for the USAF's Catalina squadron, the first in Europe, and almost one hundred flying boats were stationed here for much of the war. The RAF left Pembroke Dock in 1957 and the Short Sunderland was soon decommissioned; it was the last such aircraft to be flown by the RAF.

Before modern warfare the town had been developed on a military grid system out from the dockyards themselves. The remains of the medieval Paterchurch tower remain in the present dockyards, but that original hamlet was subsumed into the expanding town of the nineteenth century.

There is a military cemetery in the Llanion area of the town, on the east side, just off the A477, established in the nineteenth century for the burial of those drowned or killed in the dockyards. This has forty World War One graves and thirty three from the Second World War, including four Australian airmen who died when their Wellington crashed at Milford Haven. Llanion was the site of an eighteenth century mansion owned by the Meyrick family, who, in fact, owned much of the land on which the town was built. The 'grave-spit at Llanion' has others; for example, "Sian, her WVS uniform in full/Fold, pairs her ankle-bones to the town" in Roland Mathias's poem 'A letter From Gwyther Street'.

Pembroke Dock struggled to survive and prosper after the Depression years of the 1920s. Ironically, the war brought activity and money and the re-building of houses following Luftwaffe attacks brought some older streets into modernity. But the promised riches that the oil industry would bring have proved short-lived. A large call centre was closed in 2000 and the town has an out-of-work atmosphere; many shops in Dimond Street having closed in 2009.

ANGLE

You reach Angle on the B4320 from Pembroke: you may have come through Monkton (see above) or Hundleton. In any case you have to pass 'the Spec'. The Speculation Inn is so named after the original investors. The landlord is Gerry Wilson, a Plymouth man who came down in 1969 for oil refinery work. He is knowledgeable about the area and the development of the refinery which dominates the coastline along the south side of the Haven. In the small front bar hangs a letter dated 1916 from Mr William Gwynne on behalf of the Orielton Estate warning the landlord against "allow[ing] the house to be used directly or whilst in connection with rabbit catching or poaching" or young men leaving their horses outside and "frequenting the house in the evening." The Spec dates back to the beginnings of the nineteenth century, at least. Its position gives good aspects of all the approaching roads (and customs men).

On the rise before you swing down right into Angle you will pass The Rocket Cart House on your right; this a strangely castellated place which you may have taken for a church as you approach from the east. It was once used as a store for coastguard rocket life-saving pieces and as a watch tower over the Haven, and dates from the end of the nineteenth century. The village of Angle itself dates back to mediaeval times, but most of the surviving houses were built in the nineteenth century by the Mirehouse family who owned the Hall. Lt. Col. Richard Mirehouse (1849-1914) returned from service in the Boer War and developed the rows of flat-roofed houses which are such a distinguishing mark in the village. They are not particularly attractive, having a building block squatness. He became High Sheriff of the county and his descendants still have involvement in the politics of Pembrokeshire. The car park at West Angle is free in perpetuity, thanks to the generosity of the Allen Mirehouse family.

The church of St Mary dates from the thirteenth century, and has Mirehouse memorials, but as with so many others, was worked on by the Victorians. There is a fifteenth century seamen's chapel in its grounds in which were left the remains of drowned sailors. Such tragedies were not uncommon; more remarkably the remains of a crew of Japanese sailors are buried in a corner of the graveyard. On a more comic note the sailing ship *Loch Shiel* ran on to the rocks of Thorne Island in 1894. The crew was rescued by the local lifeboat but seven thousand cases of Scotch were also salvaged as jetsam. Two locals were drowned in efforts to secure the bounty and another was said to have died from drinking too much of the stuff. For decades afterwards bottles were still being discovered, secreted or at the bottom of the sea. The Angle lifeboat station was reequipped with a state-of-the-art Tamar class boat in 2009, so swimmers and those who mess around in boats can do so more safely. Don't mention the possibility of another oil tanker disaster. Both Angle Bay and West Angle Bay are part of the Coastal Path; the former is an SSSI and is particularly rewarding for sea bird watchers, while the latter is more accessible and family friendly with an adjacent caravan park and boating activities.

There are a number of forts along this section of the coast, from the Iron Age promontory fort at Castles Bay to those of the Second World War: in fact, a battery of anti-aircraft guns was positioned right next to the ancient works. The fort at Popton which is now a Field Studies Centre, dates from the middle of the nineteenth century and was part of the defensive system protecting the British navy in the Haven from the threat of attack by France.[19] This fort, in common with the East Blockhouse, built three hundred years later by Henry VIII, and that at Chapel Fort from the late nineteenth century, saw no action, of course. Though it had a considerable fire-power when operational, with over two dozen guns covering the sea approaches. The only threat to Pembrokeshire between the Civil War and the Second World War was the farcical landing by French forces at Fishguard in 1797 when a disorderly and probably drunken force of some fourteen hundred, commanded by the Anglo-American Colonel Tate, was repelled and then captured by Lord Cawdor's militia, aided by many Welsh women in traditional costume mistaken for Grenadiers. The Tudor fort, about a mile to the west along the coast from the village, has only three walls remaining now, the fourth having collapsed into the Haven.

The remains of a hut at North Hill may well be the position at which my father served in the first two years of the Second World War. From here a search-light crew scoured the skies for mining and bombing raids by the Luftwaffe. Above the village to the west there was also an airfield from which Hurricanes and Spitfires were operational.

The fort at Thorne Island, just off the coast to the west, was run as a hotel in the 1990s but is now being extensively developed as an even grander and bigger hotel. This is the fort which you look out on from West Angle beach and which appears to be situated on the headland to your right. The von Essen Group has promised "An international hotel... (which) will encompass a fabulous sea-water spa, preview cinema with editing suite, and a contemporary seafood restaurant.... a romantic retreat linked by cable car."[20]

Though now a beautiful spot in the lee of industrial development, Angle Bay took a mighty blow from that industry on the fifteenth of February 1996. A tanker called *The Sea Empress*[21] entering the Haven on her way to deposit its cargo of North sea Crude oil at the Texaco refinery hit rocks in the middle of the channel, punctured her hull and started to lose oil,. Some seventy three thousand tonnes of the stuff spewed out and washed up along the

Pembrokeshire Coast National Park. It was international news and the tv reports quite rightly predicted extensive damage to the wildlife and natural environment, not to mention that other major business in the county, tourism. The RSPB set up an emergency bird treatment centre, but thousands of birds were lost, the Common Scooter being especially vulnerable. It took the local authority and many conservationist organisations and volunteers five years to clean up the coast of south Pembrokeshire. Miraculously the seal population escaped and so did the tourist business. Try *Sea Empress* out on visitors at a local pub quiz. They can phone a friend.

BOSHERSTON, BARAFUNDLE, FRESHWATER EAST AND ST GOVAN'S

St Govan's Chapel is one of the most unusual places of worship in the whole of these islands. Only accessed by the descent of (apparently) innumerable steps, it perches in a shadowy cleft of limestone cliffs, the western edge of which is the boundary of the MOD's Castlemartin artillery range. The steps, so the legend goes, will never be counted identically between your descent and your ascent. Quite honestly, who cares when you have spent time in one of the strangest spots on the coast of Wales, the sense of an ancient truth or superstition, the green ocean's tide and the sun's track as the only reminders of time passing? Those steps, "worn smooth by the feet of the curious, the superstitious and the invalid"[22] have to be taken with care and the chapel, sadly, is not accessible for anyone with any physical problems.

Invariably the inside of the chapel will be dim and dank; the sun tries to work its way in, but you will be left with the feeling that this is a place of austerity and solitude. You don't want others there, in fact. Try to time your visit when there are few about. Imagine that the cliffs have opened to offer you refuge. Listen to the sea and drink in its green purity. There is fresh water from the spring between the chapel and low tide, but surely those seeking enlightenment and contemplation in this place would have had to climb back into the world to obtain provisions? Fish would be difficult to land and you can't live on fresh air and green and limestone solitude, can you?

St Govan's story and the origin of the chapel is somewhat apocryphal, but it is likely that he was an Irish priest called Gobhan who followed the teacher St Ailbe at Solva in the north of the county. By the sixth century the trade between Pembrokeshire and Ireland, in goods and religious ideas, was certainly well established, despite the hazardous prospect of crossing the Irish Sea. Gobhan, now an Abbot, visited Rome and returned through Wales to spend time at Solva. It is said that he was attacked by pirates, probably those based on Lundy Island, and evaded them by taking to the cleft in the cliffs at this point. The chapel has a man's ribcage formation of stones in which it is said he hid. There is also a Bell Rock alongside the chapel which is said to contain a silver communion bell stolen by the pirates, but returned by divine intervention and secreted within. St Govan was able to tap the rock and hear the bell.

The chapel is probably no older than the eleventh century so, as with many legends of faith, the narrative of special significance has been elaborated and stitched onto the place and the historical facts.[23] There is a slab altar and faint inscriptions, but, alas several instances of contemporary graffiti. The usual properties of healing were ascribed to water dripping in the chapel and the external well. In 1902 King Edward and Queen Alexandra visited the spot. I

wonder if they agreed on the number of steps down and up? Or whether servants did the counting?

Freshwater East is a fine long beach, but the development of chalet-type blocks has done nothing to enhance it. Margaret and I spent an hour watching the gulls fishing along parallel lines to the beach, the glint of a catch as thrilling as if we'd had lines in the water. In David Wilson's book of black and white photographs Pembrokeshire there's a fine landscape of the dunes and beach looking east towards Manorbier. That's the best way to regard and remember the place.[24]

Bosherston is reached on the B4319 south from Pembroke; it's nearly six miles from the town. Its unusual name may be explained by its being a village given by the Norman lord De Stackpole to one of his retinue called Bosher. There are three outstanding reasons for visiting Bosherston: the church of St Michael and All Angels, the lily ponds and Broad Haven (South) beach. They should be visited in that order as the lily ponds and beach can be quite tiring, especially if you come with children, and you may be tempted to skip the church.

St Michael's is late thirteenth century, with relatively modern windows depicting among others St Govan and St Teilo. Lord Cawdor of Stackpole, the first earl John Frederick Campbell, paid for the extensive renovation of the church in the middle of the nineteenth century and the Cawdor arms are represented in the floor tiling.[25] There is a crusader tomb and that of a dowager duchess. In the church grounds is a preaching cross. The church is colourful and light-filled and prepares you for the long walk around and through the lily ponds.

The ponds have filled three limestone valleys which were dammed by the Stackpole Estate in work carried on in the late eighteenth and nineteenth centuries. Coarse fishing permits in season may be bought from the Olde World Cafe in the village.[26] There are several routes through and around the ponds and all provide a walk of tranquillity and beauty.[27] These ponds consist of three stretches of water – the 'Western Arm' which is the closest to Bosherston village, the 'Central Arm' which is the shortest stretch and which is bridged by the main path and the 'Eastern Arm', the longest and largest, which spans almost due north and which is bridged close to the Warden's Office and Study Centre on the path and which gives the shortest route to Stackpole Quay. At the top of this arm on the western side is the site of the former Stackpole

Court.[28] This was a Palladian house of great style and substance completed in the 1730s after a precarious existence as a fortified position, perhaps since the Normans and certainly through the Civil War. By the end of the eighteenth century the lakes and their distinctive eight arched bridge had been completed by James Cockshutt for the Cawdors. From that bridge try to imagine a Palladian villa with two bays, walled garden, ice house, summer house and flower gardens.[29] The estate had extensive wooded lands for hunting and rolling pastures. All that within a walk of some of the finest coastline in Britain. James Fenton described it as "a large and magnificent pile and well adapted to its site." Tragically, it did not survive the rough use it received by billeted troops in the Second World War and was subsequently demolished.

Still, what's left is ours and all routes around the ponds, 'a charming piece of water admirably planned', offer beautiful views of flora as well as the possibilities of otters, large dragonflies and kingfishers.[30] Of course, the lilies have their season, late spring and early summer, but at any time of the year there is bird life and a sense of complete escape. Even at the height of the season it should be possible to find a spot where you can enjoy the scene in comparative peace. And contemplate what had been: "the hills skirting the lake on the house, and forming its boundary, are richly wooded in every

direction, as are the pleasure grounds and shrubbery in front, beyond which, but completely hidden, are the gardens, including the hot-houses on an immense scale."

Man-made magnificence may have been lost but we still have the shock of pleasure and awe as you burst onto the bright yellow sands of Broad Haven, a funnel of beach that focuses on the Church Rock rising from the sea. From the correct angle this is indeed a convincing church shape, as if one were in Cornwall looking out at St Michael's mount in the distance or Mont Sant Michel in Normandy. You could plan to carry a picnic and settle on this unspoiled beach. However, if you have the energy and time it might be wise to carry on eastwards on the Coastal Path and climb over Saddle Point and the headland that is Stackpole Warren on over Stackpole Head to reach the most stunning beach in Wales.

Barafundle Bay can, of course, also be accessed by parking in Stackpole and walking westwards over the cliffs.[31] The coast here is owned and managed by the National Trust, so there are no ice cream sellers, souvenirs or deck chairs. Anyone playing loud music or dropping litter is struck down by the presiding spirits and will be haunted by guilt for the rest of their days.[32] Barafundle is often referred to as the most beautiful beach in the country and even appeared in the top ten beaches in the world in a website a few years ago. It has a smooth curve of fine, bright sand backed by dunes and some pines to the western edge. Of the bay's appeal in winter the poet John Tripp wrote:

> It is a proud and stubborn line of rock,
> Impatient under moon channels,
> Waiting for the late Atlantic lash,
> Turning a storm-eye on frivollers
> But welcoming the rough-weather guest.[33]

And there may be a truth in those lines for much of south Pembrokeshire. If you can visit away from the summer and the school holidays the place becomes more your personal space. I have walked across to Barafundle from the Stackpole car park in a late summer, late evening and found the place almost empty. The sight of someone's heel or stick written names in the perfect sand did no more that heighten the sense of the place having a special force for us. Those sand-written names are framed by that stone arch through which you descend the steep path to the sand. Such things invariably remind me of John Tripp and our visits to Pembrokeshire:

Dexter
&
Daisy
SEREN FREUD
written in the sand, letters five feet high…

…The last fishing boat turns away
from its implausibly orange lobster buoy.
One by one I throw
my pebbles at the sea.
Barafundle – *the Atlantic lash,* as you said,
will turn *its storm eye on all frivollers* such as we –
Dexter and Daisy and Seren, the sand-scratched names,
John, the living the dead.[34]

WARREN AND CASTLEMARTIN

It's a blustery but dry November morning in 2009 in the small church in Warren, a tiny hamlet some five miles from Pembroke off the B4320. Locals, family and artists from afar have come to say goodbye to Arthur Giardelli M.B.E., painter and art collector and educator who has died, aged ninety-eight.[35] As a painter, but particularly as a maker of three-dimensional pictures and constructions, Arthur was one of the most original of artists working in Pembrokeshire. His constructions used salt-washed cork and wood, string, slate, watch parts and sea shells to explore the movement of the sea and its moulding of the coast. Some works are specifically based on the landscape and places of west Wales – 'Carmarthen Bay', 'Laugharne Panel', 'Pendine Panel' (he and his first wife had lived in Pendine from the late 1940s – while others demand more philosophical responses – 'Eternity the Other Night', 'A Shoal of Time' and 'Black Fugue'. He told me: "If one can make a woman's body out of marble, why not the sea out of torn paper, shell and watch parts. I like giving discarded things a new life."

From 1969, he and his second wife, 'Bim' Butler, both worked and lived in The Golden Plover, the former village school in Warren. Arthur was one of the twelve painters I interviewed for my 1996 book *Welsh Painters Talking,* and Margaret and I visited them on many occasions. The Golden Plover was a treasure trove of sculptures, drawings and paintings by many hands. Was that a Picasso print in the toilet? A Zoran Music print behind you at the dining table? There was certainly a Walter Sickert drawing on the stairs and a magnificent Ceri Richards 'The Rape of the Sabines' doing its own Picasso thing in the living room. Arthur had known many artists and had brought work directly from them. He owned 'Manawydan's Glass Door', one of the most important larger works by David Jones, the greatest poet-painter since William Blake, and had travelled in Europe after the war to represent Eric Estorick's gallery.[36]

Arthur was from an Italian family and was born in London. He was educated at Alleyn's School in Dulwich and read French and Italian at Oxford, where he also attended classes at the Ruskin School of Art.[37] The family had holidays at Amroth, but Arthur first came to live in Wales near Merthyr in the Valleys as an evacuated schoolteacher in the war. He soon declared himself a Conscientious Objector (he had heard Gandhi at Oxford) and consequently lost his job. He worked on in Dowlais for the WEA and met Cedric Morris and Heinz Koppel.[38] When he moved to Pembrokeshire it was at Amroth that he first settled; Arthur contributed greatly to art in Wales and specifically in Pembrokeshire by his example as an artist and by his extra-mural lectures for the University of Wales.

I never heard Arthur play, but he was a pianist and viola player – a broadly cultured man and wonderfully welcoming. He and Bim had a full size table tennis table in the large room at the end of The Golden Plover which had been the school hall. I never saw them play, because that table was always piled with their works on paper, which visitors were encouraged to buy (we did). Arthur's description of moving to The Golden Plover may resonate with readers who are contemplating a life-change (or have already moved) to Pembrokeshire: "We took this place which stands alone out in the country after it had been empty for a year. For some years before it had been neglected, so that it was nearly derelict. We have been fighting to stop rain and wind from beating in, round and under and through. We have had floors up to stop dry rot; we have painted and papered walls and ceilings. We haven't nearly enough furniture or anything else... [it] was once a school and then a pub; one schoolroom was converted into a bar and the other into a ballroom. We shall use the ballroom for hanging pictures so that people can come there and buy them if they want to. And the bar we are converting into studios."

At the back of that house was the strangest of conjunctions: The Golden Plover is on the north boundary of one of the largest tank and artillery ranges in the UK. It was not unusual to have one's cup and saucer, and sense of well-being, shaken by very loud explosive noises just outside the kitchen window. Tanks, both British Army and other NATO forces, fire down towards targets between Warren and the coast. Arthur and Bim would not flinch or hesitate mid-sentence. Bim had been a navy wife in her first marriage, stationed in the Med and part of a bright, partying young officer set that included the Prince of Denmark: no, not Hamlet, but Philippos of Greece and Denmark, later the Duke of Edinburgh. She was evidently bred to be calm under fire, and I suppose the war-time C.O. had simply got used to it and carried on painting. The hedge between them and the Panzers[39] was mainly hawthorn and some of Arthur's most memorable watercolours were of these wind-bent trees, often in a crucifixion of three. When I pressed him about the religious significance of these trees he said, "You're quite right. Of course, I thought about the crown of thorns... I don't think that nature is a machine which will be one day understood. In that sense it's a miracle, it is beyond human comprehension."[40] In the post funeral reception at his son Lawrence's Bosherston pub the St Govan's Inn, a projection of the Contemporary Art Society for Wales film of Arthur played on one wall and there were fond memories and warm, genuine respect for this most enthusiastic and inspired of Pembrokeshire's artists. As I write, The Golden Plover is empty and rather forlorn.

A Topographical Dictionary of Wales, 1833, described the Castlemartin area thus: "The whole of the district abounds with numerous military works and fortifications, thrown up during the frequent contests which took place between the Danish pirates who infested this part of the coast, which, from its exposed and defenceless situation, was much subject to their attacks, and the native Welsh, who resolutely repelled their aggressions." That heritage is re-enacted on the 6,400 acres of limestone plateau which, since 1938 has been the Royal Armoured Corps firing range at Castlemartin and through the ghostly abandoned farms, trench systems (German style defences were recreated for D-Day training) inland from the dramatic limestone rocks in curving folds that constitute the most spectacular cliffs. All these are, for the most part, forbidden to the public, from Castlemartin itself down to the Linney Head, though the National Park organises certain nature and archaeological tours throughout the tourist season.[41]

At the main gate of the Merrion camp on the B4319 you can see the two specimen tanks – a Centurion Mk 12 main battle tank and a heavy-gun Conqueror tank, both dating from the post war/Cold War period. Inside the camp gates, though not open to the public, are two others – a Churchill Crocodile flame-throwing tank used by the 79th Armoured Division and a German Leopard Mk 2 tank from the 1980s. More peacefully, in the village of Castlemartin stands St Michael and All Angels church, which dates from the thirteenth century. It underwent extensive renovation in the 1850s by Lord Cawdor. It has a granite plaque commemorating the Canadian servicemen who trained in the village in the Second World War. The churchyard has a late nineteenth century lych gate with iron handles shaped as fists, and a medieval preaching cross. Note at the west end of the village an animal pound whose circular stones probably represent the first roundabout in the county.[42] On the Castlemartin range there are the ruins of several interesting period houses: Brownslade, Flimston and Pricaston. Brownslade is the model farm developed by Mirehouse, but you can only access these sites when the National Park organise safe, no-firing days. Check to see whether they run guided tours too.

On weekends when the army are not firing it is possible to drive or take the coastal bus down the track across the range, passed the ghostly church and hamlet of Flimston to the car park near the cliffs. From here it is a short walk westwards towards the Green Bridge of Wales, an astonishing natural arch created by the sea's workings, and a breathtaking view back along the cliffs to the east. There is a viewing platform for the inevitable and irresistible photographs and sufficient guide rails to encourage you not to stray too near the edges. I have a nervous aversion to cliff edges, but on this section of coast one would be just as silly not to peer over. Back a few hundred yards towards the car park and we come to the view of the Stack Rocks, two inconceivable free-standing towers of limestone left by the sea's erosion. I am determined to view and walk over to the promontory fort at Flimston. Here you can clearly see and have to negotiate the raised earthworks which protected the families which huddled for safety before the sheer drops of the cliffs. Flimston Fort curves back on itself, leaving a witch's cauldron of vertical sides which fall hundreds of feet to the sand and sea: I see a chough which turns into a raven, and there's rock samphire clinging to the clefts of rocks.

There is an easy way back along the MOD roadway, but I prefer to take the cliff path and look back west to the Stack Rocks and Green Bridge. To my left I see a group of figures on the cliff face, climbing and playing ropes. By the time I've walked round they are at the top and moving on. They are, they explain from London and Warwick climbing clubs. This coast is one of the best climbing sets in the west and the climb which I've viewed from across the bay was 'Flimston Slab'. They have one more challenge and are anxious to press on, rather than entertain a tourist.

From the next promontory fort I see that their leader, a man almost my age, is already setting up to absail another cliff and organise the climb back. We shall take another ten minutes on the coast path to approach Bullslaughter Bay (photo p.179), painted by Piper, and one of the most secluded and inspiring beaches anywhere. Harder to access than Barafundle (you have to clamber down a narrow almost-track) it also has the challenge of negotiating a tip of sea-strewn flotsam and jetsam before crossing the rocks and walking on the beach. I wonder why the National Parks Authority don't clear this stuff – wooden pallets, trainers, ropes, nets, plastic boxes and containers, part of a vacuum, a diver's canister – or could not the MOD arrange for a squad of soldiers to clear it and/or burn the stuff away?

Still, the beach is a wonder. The sea a patchwork of azure, greens and blues on this changeable afternoon. The cliffs and their half a dozen caves are blacks and reds and ochres and greens. It is breathtaking; I take a long, slow hour.[43]

On the MOD track back to the car park I see a gaggle of yellow hammers above a tapestry of yellow, and blue and red heathers and gorse, greater knapweed, bird's foot trefoil, carline thistle and other plants. Back at the car the MOD warning signs and the distant view of the refineries stacks bring me down to earth and the present.

STACKPOLE

The Stackpole Inn has Good Food Guide, Michelin Guide and AA recommendations for its food. It has accommodation and is one of the more pleasant pubs in the county, though the village itself is not particularly distinguished. You may need a pub break if you take on the whole circular walk from Bosherston to Stackpole. The little harbour is one of the smallest you'll see, a "buffeted, butting slab" which gave shelter to "Good grizzled captains. Salt-whacked, trawler-buried, all carried down to the sea mist."[44] From above it looks like a curled fore-finger afterthought in one of those sea captain's dreams of safe mooring. Too small to be true.

It's the last week of September and the sun is shining with a few clouds coming from the north west. Sunday lunch at the Stackpole Inn is decent lamb roast, but an over-generous and over-sweet pudding. A walk is required after these pub lunches.

Stackpole Elidyr church is situated a mile from the village in a wooded dell. It was first established by Elidyr de Stakepole and referred to by Gerald of Wales. It's a lovely spot, well kept and still in service as a place of worship. There are a number of notable memorials, including in the Lort chapel the seventeenth century tomb of Roger Lort and his wife. Though not as ornate or well preserved as that of the Mercers in St Mary's Church in Tenby, this is a fine monument with the conventionally kneeling children – twelve in this case – at its base below their praying parents. There are two large wooden coats of arms of the Cawdors and Campbells, lords of the manor at Stackpole, the family who built Stackpole Court.[45] And a slab commemorating the Hon. Ronald George Elidor Campbell, Captain the 1st Battalion Coldstream Guards who served as a staff officer and 'fell on the Zlobani Mountains' on March 28th, 1879 'in the performance of a most gallant deed'. He was buried where he fell by colleagues 'under the fire of the enemy'.

On the west wall behind the Lort chapel is a plaque in memory of George Ellis who died in 1659 aged thirty five.

Let us not boast of youth or strength
Of years or houres or of their length
Loe here lies one that scare out ran
King David's one halfe age of man
Yet whilst hee fed a humane sence
He feared God and loved his prince
Lets study all whilste we have breath
To live this life and die his death

Following that advice is easy on such a day. The walk from Stackpole Quay across to Stackpole Point is both easy and inspiring: there's a handful of people on Barafundle beach, a small tanker swaying out in the bay waiting its turn to enter Milford Haven, Lundy Island clear and close to the south and Manorbier's castle and church across to the left and east.

There are horses grazing on the headland and a couple of angling boats around the coast. At several of the red climbing markers there are heaps of haversacks and clothes with ropes secured leading over the sheer edges of the cliffs. Heads appear: the first is a man of about thirty. He's from north Wales, Llanberis, and is down for the weekend. He is secured by three strands of rope fixed, I think precariously, by jamming metal wedges between rocks at the edge of the cliff. He tells me that the climb is called 'Adamant'. We look across at the Church Rock off Broad Haven beach and beyond to St Govan's Head, looking back along the coast which we had seen on that walk from Castlemartin.

Further round the point and overlooking the spectacular Gun Cliff Bay with its spire rock and inviting caves. There is no access to this remarkable inlet, except to descend by rope as the guy in his forties from Manchester tells me. He has just come up the climb called 'Seal Hunt'. He explains that he has a five hour drive each way and has been waiting to climb here. There is no activity allowed from March to late August because of the birds breeding. "This is a premier place for the sea cliff climbing community," he says. I am impressed. But reason that the only real motivation for risking oneself in this way would be to then spend the day on Gun Cliff, alone, on that unspoiled sand and the promise of a couple of seals.

On the way back I see twenty or so children playing beach baseball on their sand diamond at Barafundle, organised by three or four adults. The birthday boy's granny explains that it's what they'd planned, with wet suit rock hopping to follow before tea.

"Such deprivation, how mean," I say. "Why didn't you arrange for them to enjoy a burger party at McDonald's?" We laugh: the sea is emerald and calm, the sky still blue with the promise of a harvest moon to rise.

ORIELTON

On the way to Freshwater West and Angle, just three miles south of Pembroke, and not far off the Coastal Path, is Orielton, one of the fine old gentry houses of Pembrokeshire, "a mansion that has maintained high rank for centuries", said Richard Fenton at the end of the eighteenth century. Turning towards the intriguingly named village Maiden Wells[46] off the B4319 you go on to pass the gate and lodge houses, North and West (each has a Gothic charm) with a sign which proclaims that Orielton is now a Field Study Centre.

That fact would have made proud the previous owner, Ronald Lockley (1903-2000), whose 1977 book *Orielton* was a popular account of how he acquired the property in 1954 and developed it as both a family home and a place of the natural sciences. This followed his Skokholm island adventures, which I described in the North section.

The fact that he could buy Orielton in 1954 for the sum of £5,000 gives some indication of the decline of the property, but also of the regard with which he was held by the aged owner, the widow Alice Gaddum.[47] Lockley had lived in Gumfreston after his time on Skokholm and sold the rectory at Gumfreston to buy Orielton. Alice Gaddum knew that Lockley and his family would bring the place back to life and respect the natural heritage. In fact, Lockley undertook serious research into the breeding of rabbits for the British Nature Conservancy. He also played a prominent part in the opposition to the oil refinery developments around Milford Haven in the 1960s.[48]

Orielton was established as a seat of one of the Norman conquerors, the Wiriets, who built a fortified dwelling on this prime spot, elevated and close to a spring.[49] It was acquired through marriage (Elizabeth Wyrriot) by Sir Hugh Owen in the reign of Elizabeth and remained in that family for the next three hundred years. The Owens were regularly returned as the parliamentary members for the county, but in the 1840s the cost of buying such a privilege, together with the excesses of John Lord a relative who had been left the estate by Sir Hugh Owen, had left the estate bankrupt and the house passed out of the line which had stretched through the Owens back to the Wiriets. The Georgian frontage is much reduced and the most impressive reminder of its former splendour is the central staircase and hall with its early nineteenth century ironwork. The stable block and walled garden survive, together with the American Garden, to the south of the main house, so called because it was planted with large American pines in the nineteenth century.

Lockley is particularly intrigued by Sir Arthur Owen, Whig MP and barrister at Gray's Inn, who in 1736 entertained his neighbour John Campbell, a Cawdor of Stackpole Court and the prime minister William Pitt and showed them all 'the rarities of his house'. Campbell wrote: "One thing I thought odd, and that was Sir Arthur called for his horse. I thought it was to send us part of the way home, but that was to ride about his gardens to show his plantations.

He was extremely pleased with Mr Pitt for approving his designs." Those designs, in the manner of the eighteenth century had established woods, gardens, walled gardens and ponds, paid for in part from the profits of the Owens' considerable coal mining interests in the county. They had interests in mines at Jeffreyston, Reynalton and Hook and owned the considerable pit at Landshipping. The monies they earned in the county did not stay in the county and the Owens, like other Pembrokeshire gentry engaged with the London season and could be at the centre of 'society;'. In 1811 "the beautiful and accomplished Mrs (Charlotte) Owen of Orielton is among the present leaders of fashion in the gay metropolis, and (we understand) that Owen bonnets, Owen scarfs and Owen caps Are all the rage."[51]

Shortly after the property was lost to the Owen family there was established at Orielton's lake a most remarkable feature. The duck decoy was a system of tunnels down which migrating ducks would be lured: it was first built in 1868 but had fallen into decline during the First World War. Originally they would have been killed for food, but from the 1930s the system was used as a means of ringing and tracking the birds – wigeon, mallard, teal and others.[51] This was organised by the Wildfowl Inquiry Committee and later the West Wales Field Society. In this and other aspects of the development of Orielton Lockley was supported by his friend Sir Peter Scott, the eminent naturalist and artist. In fact, Lockley, Scott, Julian Huxley and the architect of Portmeirion Clough Williams-Ellis were among those who campaigned for the designation of the National Park and Coastal Path in the county. The lake and decoys had been put out of bounds to the RAF personnel billeted at Orielton during the Second World War and was resumed in 1945, but the practice ceased at the end of the 1950s.

Lockley's book tells of his children growing up with the rabbits and a variety of co-inhabitants including – four Spanish workers, two married couples, white owls, badgers, sparrow hawks, a raven called Odin, greater horseshoe bats,[53] a variety of spiders and the lesser mason bee. Lockley's greater horseshoe bats have gone, but pipistrelles have thrived (over 1,000 were recorded at Orielton in a1990) survey. The underlying respect for natural life and the commitment to understanding more about these animals and birds is what the more formal and institutional Field Study Centre now promotes with its courses and residencies.[54] They cater for groups of students and families.

FRESHWATER WEST, RHOSCROWTHER AND PWLLCROCHAN

Freshwater West is far superior to Freshwater East. There is not the constant feeling that the development of flats and houses are looking over your shoulder. It is best approached by the B4320 from Pembroke. Freshwater West is highly rated by surfers and my son and his friends count it as one of the best rides in Wales.[55] The expanse of beach is unspoiled, so unspoiled that is has become a favourite with film companies. Gareth, my son, and the surfing fraternity are jealous of their prime locations, though there are guides available for the cognoscenti.[55] We have had wonderful days on this beach with Gareth and Madeleine and Huw Arthur; Huw eating mouthfuls of sand while his parents take it in turns to paddle their surf canoe out and around the western point to the next bay. One day on the way back to the cars I notice for the first time a small war memorial with poppies grouped around its base. War and the practice of war are never far from this coast.

Gareth has fallen in love with this area, but would not remember his first encounter which was when Margaret and I re-visited the site of the Old Rectory in Pwllcrochan, which I can date to the late 1970s, because I wrote a poem.[57] After staring at 'an ache of absence' where the old house had been, we walked down the lane and left the road at the little bridge to go on through the rushes to the crushed shell and pebbly beach.

> As we walk back to the car, stepping from
> bank to tussock, the marks of our weight in the mud stay,
> draw an ooze of mud to rainbow our way.

And again, twenty years later, I returned because "This is one of places it begins,/the diaspora of feelings." And I remembered the excitement of shooting (my oldest cousin David was old enough to carry a shotgun) and fishing (nothing but tiddlers and some dogfish they'd throw back) and egg collecting with my cousins; the cooking smells from the huge kitchen range, the smell of potatoes you'd pulled yourself an hour before from Uncle Ivor's fields. For a council house boy from Carmarthen this was a Fern Hill dream years later I'd recognise when I read 'Fern Hill'.[568] And only I am witness to that which was lost for profit and progress. The fields to the east, all the way down to the Pennar Mouth of the Pembroke River, were also taken for a power station that was quickly out-dated and lasted a fraction of the time that the Old Rectory served this tiny parish. Though the church has long gone; and the school (being converted into a house) and the barn (derelict) where we tried to pitch-fork rats, and the orchard and the orchard wall against which my father wintered his caravan for hire which, uninsured, was split in two when lightning struck one of the oaks. All gone, unless we write the poems and tell the stories.[59]

And telling and re-telling the stories was what Emma Dixon did; she is buried, strangely, in Pwllcrochan churchyard under a large stone with a metal commemorative plaque. "A sincere friend of the Poor and a doer of much good... She rests in peace – her work lives on". As Emma Leslie she was a popular novelist whose children's books are still in print. With titles such as *Fanny the Flower Girl, From Bondage to Freedom: A Tale of the Times of Mohammed, The Orphan and the Family* and numerous publications in the 'Church History Series', it is clear that Emma Leslie had a Christian readership and Victorian values. She was a writer of her own time and inclinations. She lost her sight and then moved to live with her son, Ernest, a geologist employed by the Geological Survey of England

and Wales who was based at Pwllcrochan for his surveying work. She died there on December 1909 aged seventy-five.

The church is now shut, though around its edges and the former grounds of my uncle's place, the Prince's Trust and Chevron have established an attractive boardwalk through the rushes with two bird watching hides. Ignore, if you can, the backdrop of the Chevron refinery and you can enjoy the birds; they seem to be able to get by, despite the roars and crackles of the plant.

The last time I walked down the lane to the bridge I photographed the bay of Pwllcrochan Flats; the water draining off the rushes was cold and clear, the fields where I helped to pick and plant early potatoes were ploughed. But the cleft of the Haven beyond the narrow driftwood and shell beach was entirely filled by the broadside of a tanker berthed across the narrow Haven.

The next village, Rhoscrowther was swallowed up, first by BP and then by Texaco. They left the fourteenth century church of St Edmund and in its grounds a little jewel of a building, the 1851 National Schoolhouse, which is still used by what's left of the community, and the ruins of Eastington, a fourteenth century tower house. And little else, particularly after two near disasters, in 1992 and 1994, when two explosions rocked the refinery and the whole

surrounding area. In 1992 those residents who had stubbornly held out against the dollars on offer took the money and left. Two families who remained were also frightened from the place of their birth and families' lives when two years later, after an enormous electrical storm, the refinery proved too vulnerable to the lightning and widespread damage was done. Two years after that *The Sea Empress* spewed oil over the peninsula and beyond. My Uncle Ivor who had sold the Old Rectory to the oil people in 1960 for a large sum (and who could blame him?), died within a year of leaving Pwllcrochan. "How far is it to this blessed Milford? And by the way/Tell me how Wales was made so happy as/To inherit such a haven." It's bloody Shakespearan.

Notes

1. The remains of the hall are past the church and off the main road to the left. Not easy to find.
2. See later note for Rhoscrowther.
3. Originally Llandyfai, or the church of St Tyfai.
4. In March 1984 another USCGC *Tampa* was commissioned: she bears the same inscription.
5. Sir George Devereux was implicated in the proceeds from piracy when a tun of Gascon wine was discovered at the palace, courtesy of the Elizabethan pirate John Callice. In Sybil Edwards p.133.
6. See her book *A Little Walk Around the World* (HarperTrue, 2009).
7. The Wogan cave discovered beneath the castle contained finds from the Mesolithic period.
8. Haggars had the cinema until the early 1980s. Walter Haggar (1880-1953) ran the place until his death; he had acted in his father's films, including *The Poachers, The Life and Death of Charles Peace* and *The Bather's Revenge*. Copies are held by the BFI and Wales National Screen and Sound Archive in Aberystwyth. His grandson taught drama at Greenhill School Tenby. He recalls, "The War brought a new audience: service men and women from all over Britain and the Empire – Poles, Czechs, Dutch and then – the Yanks. The cinema was a godsend to them, a place of some warmth, comfort and entertainment in a bleak world. The Sunderland crews were the elite: they would book the whole back row of lover's seats (2/9d) and their favourite film was *Goofie Learns to Fly*. www.pembrokestory.org.uk. William Yorke's (great grandson) book *William Haggar: Fairgound film-maker* (Accent Press, 2007). *Phantom Ride*, a theatre piece based on Haggar's films was performed at Chapter Arts Centre in Cardiff in 2008, so there is continuing interest in this pioneer of film-making.
9. The nameplate of the Haggars' tractor steam engine, which was used to haul the movable cinema and provide electricity, was erected above the entrance of the Pembroke cinema for many years: this was *The Maid of Cefn Ydfa*, the title of one his early film and stage successes. The traction engine had been sold to Johnny Butlin in 1914. *William Haggar: Fairground Film Maker, op. cit.*
10. I have a fine engraving of Pembroke Castle after Turner. These nineteenth century prints can be an extremely pleasing record of visits to Pembrokeshire. There are many, but especially

good are Carew Castle and Manorbier Castle. Look for Paul Sandby's renditions of Manorbier.
11. The architects for the subsequent flats were the Argents of Penally who I remember from my early days at Tenby Golf Club. See the section on Penally for more on them.
12. There are exhibitions in the present castle, including a video, tracing the history of the castle and its owners, as well as an exhibit dedicated to King Henry.
13. There are few decent places to eat, though in 2010 the Courtyard Deli Café in Trewent Court, reached through the passage next to florists on Main Street, has become a welcome addition.
14. See Edward Laws p 402. The Meyrick family were key to the development of PD.
15. One of the trusts which would be attacked by 'Rebecca and her daughters' ('Merched Beca') in the wide-spread protests of the 1840s. These began in Efailwen, near Clunderwen in 1839, just inside the Carmarthenshire county border.
16. See www.pbase.com/abwhitt/image/37332537 for images of this and other good photos of Pembrokeshire.
17. From 1969 to 1996 part of this building was used as the clubhouse for the South Pembrokeshire Golf Club, which is now based at Pennar and which has an oddly blue concrete clubhouse – you get good views of the Pembroke estuary and the Haven and thus the course is enjoyable, and cheap.
18. See www. pdst.co.uk – this also has an extract from the interview with Wing Commander Derek Martin, one of the few surviving Sunderland captains.
19. From 1957 for almost thirty years it was used as a local HQ by BP for their refining operations in the area. Chapel Bay Fort is to be developed as a war museum, opening in 2014.
20. From their website in 2010.
21. The ship was salvaged, re-named three times, and bought eventually by a Chinese company.
22. Fenton.
23. There's the predictable Arthur and Gawain stuff as well. Take it or leave it.
24. Published by Graffeg in 2009. Wilson says, "Freshwater East and its neighbours Barafundle and Broad Haven South represent a magical trinity of Pembrokeshire beaches."
25. The estate itself was less fortunate, being on the losing side in the Civil War and requisitioned in the Second World War. The Cawdors left long ago to return to Scotland and the mansion was eventually demolished in 1963. The Merrion MOD camp now occupies the location.
26. Pike, tench, perch and eels.
27. The National Trust website gives details of a six mile walk that takes in the ponds and the Stackpole Warren and Quay.
28. You are unlikely to turn further north than the eight-arch bridge, but this route would take you in another half mile or so to Stackpole Church at Stackpole Elidor. The painter David Tress (see Haverfordwest and elsewhere in this book) on one of his too infrequent painting trips south has a fine painting of this church.
29. Fenton includes an engraving 'at her Ladyship's expense' of Lady Cawdor's drawing of the scene. The house was full of art, including a full length portrait of Lord Cawdor by Sir Joshua Reynolds and of the Lady herself by Sir William Beechey.
30. Watch out for the comparatively rare Marsh Orchid – a pale purple, phallus blue-bell of a plant. Also, along the coast there is always the chance of spotting fulmars and choughs.
31. Barafundle is, incidentally, the title of a 1997 album by Gorky's Zygotic Mynci, a bilingual rock band.
32. There is a film planned for release in 2010 called *Barafundle Bay* which may increase visitor numbers. Let's keep this quiet... In 2006 *Country Life* magazine named it as the best picnic spot in the UK and in 2004 it was Best Beach in Britain by the *Good Holiday Guide*. I was tempted to leave Barafundle out of this book – it's too wonderful to share with so many people.
33. Included in his posthumous *Selected Poems* edited by John Ormond (Seren, 1989).

34. 'Barafundle Bay' from *Crossing Over* (Seren, 2007).
35. See *Arthur Giardelli: Conversations with Derek Shiel* (Seren, 2001). The congregation included members of the 56 Group Wales, the organisation of artists which Arthur helped to found in 1956 and of which, in 1998, he became President for Life. While writing this book I finally acquired one of Arthur's constructions 'Low Tide and Freshwater West' – a two foot by eighteen inch board on which he has placed shells, a slate and part of a watch. It is arguable that no-one in the UK was making such works when Arthur began in the 1950s. Time, the seasons and the significance of our living became for this artist essentially what was at stake on the beaches of Pembrokeshire. See also his connections with Amroth in the East section.
36. Estorick was to be Arthur's dealer later.
37. In my interview with him in 1994 he remembered that Kenneth Clark had lent him a copy of the *Divine Comedy* which Arthur was set to illustrate.
38. He later attended Morris's art school at Benton End in Suffolk – as did Maggie Hambling and Lucien Freud.
39. See also Herr Brawn in Tenby market.
40. See page 21 in *Welsh Painters Talking*.
41. Check their website or the free Pembrokeshire paper *Coast To Coast*.
42. When I passed my driving test in 1966 there was no roundabout in the county at which one could be tested.
43. Toby Driver's book (*op. cit.*) has excellent aerial photographs of the areas now restricted, including the medieval farms at Pricaston, Flimston and Westland. Castlemartin's name may refer to the Norman Martin de Tours. Flimston was featured in the *Hidden Histories* tv series on S4C and BBC Four in 2009. CADW are monitoring the erosion of this remarkable promontory fort. Check in your *Coast to Coast* for the days when guided visits to these sites can be booked through the National Parks Authority.
44. John Tripp in his Dylanic mode in 'Stackpole Quay', in *The Poetry of Pembrokeshire*.
45. There are interesting photographs of Stackpole Court in the National Trust booklet 'Stackpole and the Cawdors: Evolution of a Landscape' by Arabella Friesin. They underline the tragic loss of that building after the neglect and damage caused by the military occupation during the war. The Nazis couldn't have done worse.
46. This may well commemorate some fertility rite or folk custom. As with many other small villages Maiden Wells's war memorial with ten dead in the Great War, and three from the Second, is still a shocking proportion.
47. The centre is now set in forty eight hectares of land, including woodland and a lake. Lockley's book, illustrated by C.F. Tunnicliffe, became a Penguin in 1980 and thus gained a substantial readership. It has been out of print for a number of years, but can be bought from the usual sources on line. My copy was bought from the ever reliable Albie Smosarski's Cofion Bookshop in Tenby. The present centre director is Chris Millican.
48. When the RAF requisitioned the property in the war the Gaddums stayed on and occupied the basement for the duration.
49. One of the original pipelines to the refinery at Swansea passed within fifty yards of the Orielton estate. It was due in part to the spoilation of this part of the county that Lockley emigrated to new Zealand in 1970, where he died at the age of ninety-six.
50. They are mentioned by Giraldus Cambrensis.
51. David Howell quotes in 'Landed Society in Pembrokeshire, c.1680-1830' in *The Pembrokeshire Historian*, No 3, 1971.
52. For example, in the 1955/56 season over one thousand wildfowl were trapped, ringed and released. Peter Scott visited that year as part of his system of ringing decoys. Birds from Orielton were tracked as far as the Baltic and northern Russia. See FSC website Field Studies 7 (1991).
53. Lockley and his sons were especially brave in their handling of and care for bats: see

chapter 6 of Orielton. They also went into Wogan cave at Pembroke Castle to catch and ring bats.

54. There is another FSC in Dale. Dale Fort, a Napoleonic fort from 1856, has courses and residencies. It has strong links with Irish students.

55. See the Festivities Section.

56. Remember Gareth's (hopefully apocryphal) story of surfers between here and the MOD coastline for the Castlemartin Range being taken by Army off-shore inflatables and towed to dangerous distances from the shore to discourage them from trespassing again.

57. Included in my collection *Preparations. Poems 1974-79* (Gomer, 1980).

58. From 'Blackberries at Pwllcrochan' in *Heaven's Gate* (Seren, 2001).

> The rain chills my face and neck.
> It sweeps from the west, blearing the hard
> gleam of the massive pipes and tanks
> where Bummer George's wood has been sliced
> out of the land. The wet gusts carry
> the dull, metalled workings of the refinery.
>
> I start to pick the plump, washed, blackberries.
> In my cupped hands they have the weight
> of blown birds' eggs, and their seedy,
> sweet music plays in the mouth.

59. And no-one told me that there was a bit of Civil War history attached to the place: a troop of Parliamentarians had landed on the beach and were surrounded in the church by Poyer's men. There was some fighting, but a truce was agreed and the Roundheads sailed off again. I just remember cold evensongs with Uncle Ivor and the cousins and few others.

PLAYING THE COURSE

Tenby Golf Club is the oldest in Wales, it is confidently claimed; first formed in 1888. It is also one of the great pleasures of British golf and of a sporting visit to Pembrokeshire. The course runs the length of the South Beach and is, essentially, a burrows/links course with lots of sand and tough coastal grasses. I learned to play as a schoolboy here and am now a country member. The disadvantage to being a 'country member' is that you cannot vote on club issues (nor could any lady member until relatively recently) or enter competitions; the advantage of being a country member is that one can legitimately walk on at Penally and play a few holes of an evening; the other advantage is that you cannot enter most competitions or vote on club issues,.

Let me offer you my round at Tenby:

The First, *Danny Carew*, named after one of the finest players the club has produced, sets you the challenge not only of driving over the ridge of grasses to an unseen fairway, but also of doing so in full and close view of the clubhouse. It was not always the case. When I joined as a junior in 1962 the clubhouse was at ground level, next to where the final green is situated now and where the lower car park has its edge of protective trees. The original clubhouse was, in fact, former Great War huts from the Army. The present clubhouse was opened in 1966. There were still 'Artisan' members back in the 1960s, tradesmen who worked on the course and clubhouse to offset a portion of their membership fees. Tenby was a posh club, run by the professional classes and gentry, as was often the case in the early days of the sport. The club was formed in 1888 at Tenby Town Hall; Sir Charles Phillips and Mr Griffiths of Penally Court Farm agreed to allow golf on their land and nine holes were created. Richard Ormond, son of Arthur, the man who edited the centenary handbook for the club and a former editor of the *Tenby Observer*, is convinced that golf greatly pre-dates that official formation of the club: there is written evidence of the magistrate's court in town in the middle of the nineteenth century being suspended because the mayor and others wished to play golf.[1]

The first hole was played from the edge of the former quarry in dog-legged right around what is now the clubhouse's mound. So many cars were hit and cards torn up at the beginning of rounds.

That is now the practice area. Behind you, over your left shoulder was the art-deco-ish edifice of the South Beach Pavilion, a 1930s leisure complex for ballroom dancing, skating and cinema which the famous architect Clough Williams-Ellis, the builder of bizarre Portmeirion, described as "a six storey affair in shabby concrete".[2] In my growing days in the town we had a choice of two cinemas, though the Pavilion was a faded place and was demolished in the 1970s.

When you've finished, you walk to the second tee across the fenced footpath which takes Kiln Park holiday-makers over to the beach; a deal negotiated some thirty years back with the leisure group who own the huge site. It preserves the course and gives the site its *raison d'etre*. There are the remains of the large lime kilns to the west of the caravan site; another reminder of the importance of industry and mining to this area.

The second, *Tom Grant*, is a straightforward, undistinguished hole, though the target narrows to a green defended by two open-mouthed bunkers and a collar of thick grass. It's named after one of club's longest serving professionals. On days when they've moved the tee back to the competition placement alongside the first green in the lee of Black Rock the carry is sixty or seventy yards longer and the narrow fairway a more elusive target. Back in the 60s I remember Arthur Booker showing me his slow swing from that tee. Arthur was the man who encouraged me to knuckle down in the front row; who picked me as the Pembrokeshire Schoolboys hooker in the 1961/62 season; which focussed me at school. Arthur was a fine man, tall, handsome, firm, but mild-mannered, he seemed to create his own time in everything he did; one of the Few, he had flown Hurricanes in the war, so I suppose everything was gained time and unhurried after that; something I've rarely achieved. He swung steady and through the ball like a caress that day: middle of the fairway on the second.

The third is a gem. The *Dai Rees* hole which was included in Peter Allis's ideal British links compilation. Short – 382 yards – the narrow fairway snakes to the right and leads to a bottle-neck between two humps of long rough grass. Average golfers will lay up in this space, for only the single-figure player, the devil-may-care tripper or the fool will go for the green with their second. The green is a sloping saucer on a plateau guarded by a bunker on the left and no-man's land and the path to the fourth on the right. In my early playing days the hillock to the right of the valley was rough-bunkered, but it is no easier now that the sand has been grown over by wiry grasses. You need to drop the ball on a six feet square area to be anywhere near the pin. This is what links golf, British golf should be about. Forget the big hitters – Tiger Woods would not benefit from a bombshell drive; it's all about that second or third shot here. Anything missed on either side and you'll need Mickelson's feathered touch of loft to bring the ball down vertically. So, Woods with a seven iron off the tee and Mickelson to float one on: not much, is it? Unless Dr Mathias, captain of the club in the 1920s, caught you; it is said that he once ordered a man off the course for using an iron off the tee on a par four. It was ungentlemanly so to do, he said. The course is bigger than the player. This hole marks the association of the famous Welsh pro who played in eight Ryder Cups and led us to victory over the USDA in 1957. Dai Rees often played the course and was made an honorary member in 1967.[3]

The fourth, *The Bell*, is probably a bad golf hole. From the top tee, if you can pull your eyes from the view over the straits to Caldey, for this is the first hole to take you to the coast, you have to hit or carry a plateau which then dips down into the first of two valleys. Big hitters may roll down into the valley. But then you are faced by a ridge of grasses with the unseen promise of a green another fifty yards beyond; so where's the skill? Oh, do not forget to check the small green-shaped board at the side of the path from the tees; a blue peg tells you where today's flag is positioned; the pros would hate it, but they always have a caddy to measure out the yardage and line them up. Mere mortals take a wedge or nine iron and go slightly left of centre to let the slope pull you back to the true. Which is what I do one evening in June, to leave me ten feet from the hole (having lost my topped drive and dropped a second ball on the plateau to save walking back. A scurry of bobtailed rabbit as I clatter down the slope to the green, but at the edge of the burrows' gorse there are three young foxes, cubs the size and fluffy softness of young puppies.[4] Two retreat into the safety of the gorse cover, but the third grooms each paw in turn and watches me two putt out. I leave the green and, knowing there is no-one behind me, and caring to watch the young fox as I walk away, decide not to ring the old rusty bell that hangs on the path to the fifth tee to signal that the green is clear for the next golfers. Fox and rabbit, gorse and sand

and golfer: the locus genii.

The Fifth, *Swn y Mor.* Means 'the sound of the sea' in Welsh. Do the sensible thing – take an iron to the left of the great mound between you and the white house on the horizon and leave yourself a nine iron or so to the face-sloping green defended by its two fearsome bunkers.

Further instructions

It will surely be the end of a day –
early May on the cusp of spring and summer.
An evening refreshed by sun and wind
after rain has cleared the view across to Gower
and Pendine sands to the east,
Tenby clustered around the spike of St Mary's.

Best to take a line directly from the fifth tee
through that red-blinking buoy
to the white dome of the Caldey lighthouse.
You'll cross to the mid-point from buoy to shore
and have him idle the engine,
keeping the bow aimed at St Margaret's Island
to take the tide's run.
Then swing gently so that from the leeward
you can let spill what remains of me.

Watch the cormorant plotting parallel lines low
a foot or so it seems above the sea,
stitching his invisible net over
the clustered silver and blue of mackerel
frantic and fierce, above the pollock and bass;

This is the sea that David Jones,
at peace with the monks,
cut into wood as a bay of calm
beyond the grazing cows.

Around the fifth and thirteenth tees
the small fists of purple orchid
will have pushed through the heather
and the sharp and buttery gorse.

> Someone waiting to play might drift
> and turn to take in the view:
> see the smudge of a boat out fishing
> and that will quicken the heart.

You need no further instructions: do the sensible thing. With my ashes

The Sixth, *Lifter's Cottage* I last birdied on that rare fox June evening when the low sun was buttery over Penally. In truth, it's a mere wedge, even for a short, old Welshman. But you have to really loft one to land softly on a green that slopes away at the sides. It is not uncommon to play to the tenth green and find yourself joining people off the sixth who have carried over to the almost joined-at-the-hip tenth. And they'll be often putting from your green back on to the sixth – the safest ploy. And apologetic hunching of the shoulders.

The Seventh, *Railway*, has you teeing off right next to the railway line and what must have been a supervised crossing point for pedestrians. You can still walk off the course and over to Penally at this point. You'd need to be careful, but the trains are infrequent, as I've said. Your drive has to thread between the ubiquitous thick grass and gorse on the left and the marshy edges parallel to the railway line on the right.

The Eighth, *Penally Butts*, takes you a short walk to the new tee next to the gate for the Pembrokeshire Coast Path up to Giltar Point. One used to have to drive blindly over the second and western public footpath, but common sense and the litiginous nature of our society means that this is no longer feasible. Here you may find yourself scrutinised, or worse, by passers by. There is also the possibility of rapid automatic fire from the Penally butts army practice range to your right. The camp at Penally has been used by the British Army for over a century: regular soldiers, cadets and the Territorial Army are housed in what appear to be modernised Nissen huts and lorried over to the firing range. If you walk the Coast Path towards Giltar you look down on the range and can see the securely banked target area.[5] That path leads up to one of the most breath-taking views; as you walk look back at the stretch of the South Beach and the town; to the right the edge of Worm's Head on the Gower and then Caldey and St Margaret's like a whale and her calf in the ocean. On the metal map at the start of the path it indicates that there are practice trenches from the Great War on the cliffs. They are not easy to spot and it requires imagination to translate the soft hollows into mock-ups of the Western Front. "This handful of softened foxholes,/freshly turned earth;/a sheep curl out of the weather/where a man might lie and look up/for a pattern of cloud or stars."[6]

What must those young men have thought? After 1916 they would have known of the probable carnage they faced and the diminishing chances of them coming through, returning to their farms, shops and boats in Pembrokeshire.[7]

The Ninth, *Monk's Way*,

Now we are at the furthest point
and after this one half the round's done.

Hold now,
They've not played their seconds
and you've been a monster.

Though you've been getting a mighty length
that carry over the corner of beach
will stretch you.
From here
the South Sands runs a mile or so.
There's the island with its monks and perfume;
the last boats filling up.
The town is held like coloured paper
on the spike of St Mary's spire.

The spring rabbits are plump and tame,
You could reach down and stroke or strangle them.
These are the Burrows where the sea and all creatures
gnaw at what we have made.

Half way round:
that's the way home.
There can be no finer spot than this.

It's clear now; straight as you can.
Off you go.

The Tenth, *James Braid,* is named after the famous Open champion who designed the original nine hole course in 1902. It has a long carry to a narrow fairway and then the prospect of a bottle-neck gap for your second shot between grass mounds to an undulating green glimpsed only if you are squarely in the fairway. This is the busiest part of the course, where the tenth, thirteenth and sixth greens and two tees are bunched together, a sort of hub around which much of the course revolves. There may well be balls on the wrong tees and greens: blame it on tiredness and the strong prevailing westerly.

The Eleventh, *Giltar,* turns you back to the west and points you again at Giltar where in 1896 a young art student home from the Slade dived off into the war, misjudged the tide and almost scalped himself. Bandaged and shaken he occasioned much attention and adopted more bohemian dress and behaviour on his return to London. Augustus John rarely returned to the town of his birth, but owed much to that fated dive. Your second shot has to negotiate a valley before the rise to a small and difficult green. Anything other than straight will probably lead to a lost ball and much wasted time, because you do not get a good view of Caldey and the coast until you've played your next tee shot.

The Twelfth, *Y Ddau Gwm*, challenges you to cross the ddau gwm, or two small valleys, that protect the elevated green. As you walk the path to the green you begin to get that spectacular view again. The gorse of the dunes has been chopped in recent years, but that whole dune line would have been mined and barbed-wired in the Second World War; at one time there were trenches and foxholes manned by the Belgian Liberation Battalion. The South Beach would have made a good landing point for an invasion, though why would the Germans have risked that sea crossing? Remember the Spanish Armada.[8]

The Thirteenth, *Duneside*, has its tee next to the fifth. This is the only par four I have ever driven: one autumn evening with a strong wind backing from the south south west and a sweet thump. Ended up at the back of the steeply sloping green: took three putts. Better to take a steady iron to the left shoulder of the ridge and play up with a wedge to avoid two Scottish, wicked bunkers on the right front of the green.

At the beginning of the last century you'd have been at risk here from inexperienced marksmen. The army used the distance between St Catherine's Island and Giltar point for large-bore rifle practice. While you wait to drive take in that view and judge the distance for yourself. Did they use red flags to clear the beach of Edwardian bathers and walkers? If you played off the white tee at the ninth you'd have had at your back a low wall serving, apparently, no purpose. That was the position of the butts. How did they signal firing safety? Flags? Who would have wanted that job – over a mile away, flashes of gunfire, with the delay in the sound carrying against the westerly wind. And the dull thump of bullets against the banks and targets.

The Fourteenth, *Black Rock*, used to be the seventh and the way directly home. You play judiciously over the fifth green and have precedence over those playing that hole. I was asked to caddie a couple of times in the summer vacation of 1964 and earned a few bob towards my membership fee. The one I remember was a wealthy man, a director of the Lotus sports car company. On this hole his energy deserted him and his ill health could no longer be disguised. He asked me to play the remaining holes home for him: I suppose that, technically, I had broken the rules of amateur golf by doing so. It is a reachable par five with a narrow green nudging up to the Kiln Park path and the early shadows of Black Rock. I am old enough to remember playing off the rock, used very rarely now because of complaints from the cottage beneath it. What a prospect: the caravan park and railway line to your left; the first fairway to your right and a cluster of bunkers between. In the clubhouse is a photograph of Lloyd George posed with his hosts at the foot of the Rock. He played here when he was Chancellor of the Exchequer in 1908. The man who would lead us to victory in the war; did he hear the rattle of practice rifle-fire at the Penally butts when he played?[9]

The fourteenth is where I remember taking part in what must have been one of the strangest golfing occasions on this course or any other. Our deputy head Bill Davies had a daughter Eleanor who was an archer. He organised a match over several holes, including this one, between a handful of the school's golfers and the Tenby Archers – they had targets in front of or near our greens. Our drives went further of course, but they had larger targets once the green was reached. Was it then or later that I remember blonde, fresh Angela against the backdrop of the copse and Penally in the distance? Putting, I think. Where are all the young archers and golfers now?

The Fifteenth, *Fitchett's Copse*, is appropriately named after Ernie Fitchett who was the club professional (in post 1948-67) and who designed the three holes across the railway. Ernie was a warm and generous man; he was so encouraging to me when I joined. He came to Greenhill and gave free lessons. I was a working class lad and he put together a set of second-hand clubs for me – some with hickory shafts – to get me going. This is a tight and tricky par four with your drive hemmed in by the railway line and a great expanse of gorse and scrubby trees. Take an iron.

The Sixteenth, *Four Winds*, is named after the fine white house at the back of the greatly elevated green. Four Winds bought in the 1960s by our games mistress, Penny Hilling; one of the previous owners had been a West End theatre 'Angel', one of the financial backers of plays and musicals. There's no plaque on this hole, but this was the scene of my first (of only two) golf trophies. In 1965, just before leaving for university, I won the match-play Junior

Challenge Cup. I had a nervous six (or was it even seven?) to beat a man in his sixties by 3 and two. This was an open competition for any member of the Conies, or higher handicap, section. I had progressed to that point by beating my games teacher Denzil Thomas in the semi-final. Denzil, Llanelli, Neath and Wales, taught us to play hard and aggressively. When I joined the golf club a few years back as a country member I would see Denzil, motorised on his ride-on trolley, old and unwell, playing seven or nine holes until he could play no longer. One afternoon, after putting on the tenth I crossed him coming off the thirteenth green to his ride-on parked near the fourteenth tee. He looked at me hard as I extended my hand; as he shook it firmly his eyes lit up in recognition, "You're the 'ooker from Carmarthen," he said.

The Seventeenth, *View O'Caldey*, demands that you play from the edge of the Four Winds tennis court and, ignoring the Kiln Park caravans to your left, that you hit a sloping green set between trees and treacherous gorse. That gorse provided me with a steady supply of balls when I was a poor, guinea-a-year-schoolboy member. There is indeed a view of Caldey on the horizon as well as a side view of Black Rock and the promise of your final hole. In my last summer vacation at Greenhill School I got the job of painting the toilet blocks (the outsides) at Kiln Park site: I remember the paint being bright green.

The Eighteenth, *Charlie's Whiskers*, now has a wall that wasn't there when I played here first; it's protecting path walkers from the hooked shot. And the grassed ridge you play blindly over with your second shot was sand dunes in my learning days here. There's that photograph of David Lloyd George at the foot of Black Rock: he's wearing a suit and tie, which is how a gentleman should present himself on the course. He and his hosts would have been sitting close to the clubhouse, which was the quarryman's cottage and which had been bought four years before. After your second shot over the ridges you'll discover where you've landed. The pine trees and the modern clubhouse (functional, low-slung) are bound to be an anti-climax after the course. But you're probably glad, relieved, to have made it. Don't count the lost balls, the tight lies of the fairways, the unplayable, unforgiving grasses that collar the narrow fairways and greens. Carry home with you the views, the most unforgettable views in Welsh golf. Why 'Charlie's Whiskers'? Well, that indefatigable man Dr Mathias put in place the protective ridges to the right of the green.

The Nineteenth: shower, go in for a drink, but pause to look at the photographs lining the corridor from the changing rooms: David Lloyd George, Dai Rees, over a century's worth of captains and champions and teams. And don't miss on the board at the side of the snooker table – Junior Challenge Cup: 1965 T. Curtis.

Notes

1. *Tenby Golf Club – The First Hundred Years* (1988) was written and edited by John Mabe and Arthur Ormond: my teachers Arthur Booker and Bill Davies were also involved in its production.
2. There is a photo in John Tipton's *Fair and Fashionable Tenby.*
3. Dai Rees (1913-1983) was one of the outstanding British golfers of the mid-century. He came second to Arnold Palmer in the 1961 Open.
4. In 1906 the sale of rabbits caught on the course realised £35 and eleven shillings, a considerable sum in those days.
5. The army has had a close relationship with the club and the course in terms of land ownership and access. Soldiers (officers) were able to play the course during times of war as honorary members; though not on Sundays until after the Great War. In fact, the Rector of Tenby called a public meeting in the Market Hall to protest against the playing of golf on Sundays, a decision only reversed when returning soldiers added their voices to the argument.
6. From my poem 'The Trenches at Giltar' in *Crossing Over* (Seren, 2007).
7. See the piece on James Charles Thomas in the section on Rosemarket in the North.
8. Tipton has photographs of this in his book.
9. See 'The Captain's Diary' in my collection *Taken for Pearls* (Seren, 1993).

FESTIVITIES

In the last hour of the decade Margaret and I walk between the moon shadows of the railings, along past the museum and on the path around Castle Hill in Tenby. There is a full blue moon over Caldey Island and the Castle Sands are blue-yellow under this most clear and starry sky. It is so cold, below freezing, and the stretch across Carmarthen Bay is a basin of crisp, solid air all the way to Burry Port, the Gower and two forlorn lighthouses. Prince Albert's marble is like an ice sculpture, but there are warm noises at our backs from the town where Tudor Square, as of old, prepares itself for the new.

Walking back up Crackwell Street and around onto High Street we join the swelling crowd, boisterous and good natured: two Twenties Flappers, an Irish Leprechaun, men dressed as women, women dressed as men, the Blues Brothers, assorted ghouls, a hairy fairy. Men with cans, girls with almost nothing on teetering on impossible heels, accompanied by heels that time has wounded. Jimmy Achooo shoes.

This, or something akin to it, has been the case for centuries and Edward Laws reported "throngs of people parade the streets... to see the old year out... They sing

> Get up on New Year's morning
> The cocks are all a-crowing;
> And if you think you are too soon,
> Get up and look at the stars and moon;
> Get up 'tis New Year's morning."

I wonder how many of this lot will do that.

And at four minutes to midnight the fireworks start: they shower above Tenby House pub;[1] and then the two nets strung across the square are loosened and the balloons fall and float over the crowd. Shouts and cheers, but no-one sings; it hasn't been organised. We recognise Yanni, the owner of Caffe Vista, and shake his hand with New Year greetings. It all seems a bit lacking in focus, but we have not spent the evening fuelling in one of the pubs, so perhaps we are missing the essence. We drive the four miles back to Lydstep and settle down to the best bits from the Jools Holland Hootenany which we've Sky-recorded. That bit's the same as every other year, but my Mum has gone and where her armchair was there is now a

sofa bed for the grandchildren. In with the new.

On New Year's Day we opt for the NYDS at Saundersfoot.[2] The First Minister Rhodri Morgan is featured in the current *Tenby Observer* wearing the 2010 swim/rugby shirt: in previous years it's been Gareth Edwards, local rugby international Tom Shanklin and other sports stars.[3] *The Observer* piece implies that this NYDS will be one of his last functions before retiring at First Minister, but when we reach the beach and I ask one of the Swim marshalls he admits that Rhodri is not actually there. "It's just the photograph, see. He's giving his support."

Those who are present include a ghoul from the Rocky Horror Show, various bears, an unconvincing Elvis, cowboys, two butterflies and a collector with a large net, Darth Vader, the wheelchair fake and his hairy carer from Little Britain (and with them, of course, the Only Gay in the Village). Radio Pembrokeshire is there – 'live' – and there are five cheerleaders from the Llanelli Scarlets. The tide is a long way out and I wonder if all of them will make it into the water; though the sea is like a mill pond and the temperature is a good couple of degrees above freezing by their 11.30 am.

start. Last year there were over eleven hundred swimmers and £46,000 was raised for charity.

In the afternoon of the first day our son Gareth and daughter-in-law Madeleine and little Huw Arthur arrive. We decide to enjoy the sunniest of afternoons with a walk, down the path to Lydstep Headland but this time, for a change, we bear left down to the caravan site and along the beach to ascend the eastern cliff at the Haven. This is quite steep but Gareth has Huw perched across his chest in the Baby Bjorn and we make good progress, up past the dramatic blow hole and Frank's Shore beach. I remember Reg Smith telling me how he and the local boys would climb most of these local cliffs – no ropes, no fear – and collect gulls' eggs, sometimes to eat – 'too fishy by half' – and how they'd play 'blinkies' – lining up a row of eggs and then seeing how many they could smash, blindfolded, by hopping. And how soft Alan from the village, 'a bit touched', had swallowed fourteen eggs raw for a bet.

The sea is calm, the gulls perched or gone fishing and the sky as blue as it ever will be this year, surely. The sun is sinking over Lydstep Headland behind us to the west. There are bruised edges of cloud to the north, over the Preselis.

But as we turn inland from Valley Field Top to face the World War One trenches[4] on Giltar those clouds have dropped and sped towards us. The sky is now bizarrely split into two characters – blue and sunny and black and threatening. We are caught in flurries of snow and can see a screen of misty white rolling towards us. On the news last night there were three men lost in avalanches in Scotland. This is how it can happen – an afternoon stroll becomes a moderate coastal hike and then an unpleasantly cold and wet scramble down under the railway bridge to the Tenby-Pembroke road. I wave down a passing car (two young people from Manorbier) and am given a lift the two miles back to our house to collect my car, then return to collect the others. Back in Lydstep Baby Huw is well wrapped, but has seasonally rosy cheeks. We have come through: mulled wine and mince pies. Huw is on the carpet in front of the fire gurgling and full of milk.

A scattering for Doris and Huw

Four months to the day she died I walk on to the Headland
through the dark woods where it is muddy
and the cattle stand tired and sullen after days of rain.

Then along the path to the wide sky,
the rain having cleared the air,
bringing the colours of the cliffs and fields alive.

A smooth ebb tide in the Haven where the lights are coming on
and the gulls settling on the column of rock
at the mouth of the old limestone quarry below.

I move more slowly to the teetering edge of the Point
to face the end of the islands,
the last yellow of Sandtop Bay.

This is as far as your father and mother went with her ashes,
Madeleine plump with you and Gareth,
our big, muscled surfer, all passion and sadness,

standing on the very edge where I could not go
to shake his grandmother into the wind
over the limestone drop to the green sea.

This evening's held a quiet and lonely moment.
A kestrel rises from the cliff's face
and startles me. I shout twice Huw, Arthur! over the sea;

too many memories and not a prayer.
Then your name – Huw Arthur –
once more, as a whisper.

The next day the four of us (and wrapped up Huw) walk from Penally across the golf club and the length of the South Beach. There's a scattering of snow and glinting ice on the paths and the sixth and ninth greens are frozen. The course is closed. The strange phase of the moon which gave us the clarity and blueness of New Year's Eve and the clearness of the western sky a day later has drawn the tide out about as far as I've ever seen it. Sker Rock is high and mighty, and, beyond, the Woolhouse Rocks are clear, like a reefy island, where in January 1938 the *Fermanagh* out of Belfast went down in a hurricane force wind.[5] Today those treacherous rocks seem to float as on a lake, and it's almost as if you could walk around St Catherine's Island. We can't manage that, but Gareth and I do walk around the base of Castle Hill on the sands, underneath both new and old lifeboat stations, past the harbour entrance and over North Beach where the Goscar Rock is still like a Viking prow when the tide is out; the beach café where I worked one school summer holiday selling, with no success, chilled milk cartons to the castle-building families is winter-boarded. In that same building that summer John Uzzell Edwards was painting and showing his work – his semi-abstract gestural splashes and Celtic sweeps. I was thrilled to see original art, but perplexed by the difficulty of the work.

We cross to the icy steps and climb gingerly up to the gap-toothed space that was the Royal Gatehouse Hotel. We meet Margaret and Madeleine and baby Huw Arthur in Caffe Vista, wipe condensation from the window panes and look out across the flat and distant sea past Monkstone Point to Amroth. January the second: where on earth would you rather be?

On the next day, the first Sunday of the year, there has been arranged a point-to-point race meeting at Lydstep. The course is on the fields across the road to the north of Celtic Haven. Over the years we came a couple of times for the Easter Monday meet with my mother. There's the attraction of a flutter (harmless betting of shillings rather than pounds, or even guineas) and the tick-tack bookies' antics. Town folk can forget how large horses are: you have to admire these amateur riders and the risks they take, riding out to the edges of the fields and then returning to the shouts of the home straight.

As the *Tenby Observer* announces, "Permission from the landowners of the free draining sandy soil course has been granted to stage this exciting addition to the calendar, with the course's proximity to the coast a bonus in helping to survive any possible frost threats at this time of the year, thus making the meeting a definite target for local trainers and many from outside the area." But today, after the sub-zero conditions of the New Year weekend, the sandy soil is frozen and the meeting has been postponed; until January 10th, when we are not down here. It's another beautiful day so Margaret and I head out towards Pembroke and bear left through Hundleton and past the Speculation Inn towards Freshwater West.

The expanse of beach is unspoiled; unspoiled unless you happen along when a film crew is in occupation. In the summer of 2009, within weeks of each other, both Ridley Scott's *Robin Hood* and the inevitable block buster *Harry Potter and the Deathly Hallows* filmed at this location. The Harry Potter film reconstructed on the beach the Shell Cottage in which Harry, Ron and Hermione take shelter. It attracted many on-lookers, but not on the scale of the Ridley Scott enterprise which spent much longer at Freshwater West and employed hundreds of extras for its battle scenes – horses charging and boats capsized. Scott was 'blown away' by the location and its Atlantic lashing: "Why didn't I know about this place before?" Er, Ridley, it's west Wales; why would you know? And let's keep it to ourselves, eh?

Freshwater is long and flat and stunningly presents the sea westwards from its north, north west/south, south east angle.[6] We park at the Broomhill Burrows end and walk the length of the sands to the edge of the Furzenips, those acres of low rocks which divide Freshwater West from Frainslake Sands. Back in the summer these sands had more horses galloping than a decade of Lydstep point-to-point meetings. Russell Crowe (as Robin Hood) on a white charger was being pursued by what seemed to be hundreds of horsemen – Moors? the sheriff's men? One of the lesser known incidents, was that beach scene, from the annals of Sherwood Forest. But with Cate Blanchett to be saved from the wicked

Sheriff, who cares? It is widely reported than Crowe and the other actors ate at a local pub one evening and left a tip of £600. Feared by the rich, loved by the poor, Robin Hood, Robin Hood, Robin Hood.[7]

We watch the Irish Ferry move out of the Haven and up towards the open sea, her tall white sides becoming a darker stern. Then drive back through Castlemartin and Warren, past the MOD ranges and The Golden Plover which will always be known as Arthur Giardelli's house; and then I think that we might take in a detour to Pwllcrochan. But the afternoon is cooling and the narrowing roads are glinting ominously. I shall save up the nostalgia that will flood from Pwllcrochan for later in the year. There will be another time to circumvent the Texaco refinery that blots the landscape of my childhood and wind down from Wallaston Cross to what remains of the school, church and Old Rectory.[8] We swing back towards Pembroke and my head fills annoyingly with the Robin Hood song from the black and white tv series: handsome Richard Green each week sending his arrow straight and true into that Sherwood oak. Which is what my cousins and I tried to do in the woods around Pwllcrochan. And growing up and growing old means that you learn too much: that the Robin Hood series was written by a 'communist Jew' McCarthy-ed out of work in Hollywood and exiled in England.[9] And that the steep potato fields that were warm and fruitful in the earlies season and the eggs my cousins climbed and stretched for, blown and labelled to nestle in their cotton wool shoe boxes and the elder trees by the back door and the outlawed fields of Bummer George, would all be swallowed and squashed by the oil refinery.[10] And that, more often than not, it is the Sheriff, not Robin, who wins.

Notes

1. The house where Paxton lived and from which he developed the modern town.

2. There was the option of going across to Amroth for the world record attempt at the biggest Elvis look-alike NYDS with Roy Castle's widow officiating at the count. Tenby's Swim is traditionally on Boxing Day. Over the Christmas holiday other attractions include the Boxing Day South Pembrokeshire Hunt at Cresswell Quay and the charity swim at Tenby.

3. Sports achievers are now always called 'legends' in Wales. Probably a dozen caps is a prerequisite for this; or being old enough to have played when caps were not as cheap. Why not Rhodri Morgan, 'political legend'? The only celeb at the NYDS appeared to be someone called

Anna Ryder Richardson who has opened a zoo at St Florence, taking over Manor House Wildlife Park. She is, apparently, a former model and interior designer (tv shows). In 2009 she and her husband received an interest-free loan from Pembrokeshire Lottery to develop a night shelter for their expected white rhinos. No, honestly. See also the South section.

4. This handful of softened foxholes,
freshly turned earth;
a sheep curl out of the weather
where a man might lie and look up
for a pattern of clouds or stars.

from 'The Trenches at Giltar', *Crossing Over, op. cit.*

5. She was bound for Llanelli from Drogheda. The captain was lost and eight crew members were saved from the sinking steamer by the Tenby lifeboat. The RNLI crew were variously decorated for their actions. See *A Tenby Lifeboat Family* by Avis Nixon. In the same book Avis Nixon recalls an old Tenby New Year's Day custom of 'First Foot In'. In order to bring good luck and prosperity it was necessary for the first person to cross the threshold of a house on New Year's Day to be a dark-haired man; a service her father, Brixham fisherman Harry Rowse, performed for neighbours in Cresswell and Saint Mary's Streets. Woolhouse may refer to the impression that spume over the rocks resemble freshly carded wool – B.G. Charles, *The Placenames of Pembrokeshire* (National Library of Wales, 1992).

6. Quite a different day and season from one in which "the brute combers build the water-head/And grass girds up the dunes the shock washes." Roland Mathias 'Freshwater West Revisited' in *The Poetry of Pembrokeshire.*

7. The film had a cast of eight hundred and used one hundred and thirty horses. A fair bit of work for the locals, then.

8. Regent Oil (later Texaco) bought my uncle Ivor's Old Rectory for an enormous sum in 1959 (about what you'd pay for a BMW today). They never used the land and soon afterwards bulldozed the Old Rectory into the ground. See the previous section on Freshwater, Pwllcrochan etc. in West. See also my poem 'From Brunel Quay' in the North section.

9. This was Ring Lardner Jr., an Oscar-winning writer, and member of the 'Hollywood Ten'. His film scripts included: *Forever Amber, The Cincinnati Kid* and *M.A.S.H.* Lardner had helped to raise funds for the Republican cause in the Spanish Civil War, in which his brother served (the Abraham Lincoln Brigade) and was killed. Lardner – loved by the good.

10. Texaco apparently have a 'fluid catalytic cracker' facility at Rhoscrowther. This can refine the particular crude oil from Chad in west Africa – Doba crude. It is piped to the coast on the Bay of Guinea before being shipped to Pembrokeshire. Guinea is the corruptly-run, mineral-rich, poverty-stricken country to which Margaret and I send a monthly amount to support a young girl and her village. The Fern Hill-esque escapes to Pwllcrochan of my child-hood have been thus been linked by crude oil and sophisticated finance across half a century and two continents to Koko Poly and her childhood.

BIBLIOGRAPHY

Pembrokeshire: The Buildings of Wales Series, Pevsner Architectural Guides, Thomas Lloyd, Julian Orbach and Robert Scourfield, New Haven & London, 2004
Augustus John: A Biography, Michael Holroyd, Heinemann 1974 and later Penguin editions.
Pembrokeshire – The Forgotten Coalfield, M.R. Connop-Price, Ashbourne, Landmark Collections Library, 2004.
A Historical Tour Through Pembrokeshire, Richard Fenton, 1903 (Dyfed Council Cultural Services, 1994).
The Story of the Milford Haven Waterway, Sybil Edwards, Herefordshire, Logaston Press, 2009.
The Poetry of Pembrokeshire, Tony Curtis, Bridgend, Seren, 1989.
The Description of Pembrokeshire, George Owen of Henllys, ed,. Dillwyn Miles, Llandysul, Gomer Press, 1994.
Pembrokeshire: Historical Landscapes from the Air, Toby Driver, Royal Commission on the Ancient and Historical Monuments of Wales, Aberystwyth, 2007.
The Journey Through Wales and The Description of Wales, Gerald of Wales, tr. Lewis Thorpe. Harmondsworth: Penguin, 1978.
The History of Little England beyond Wales and the non-Kymric colony settled in Pembrokeshire, Edward Laws, 1888: The reprint edition 1995 by Cedric Chivers Ltd, Bristol for the publisher, Cultural Services Department, Cyngor Sir Dyfed County Council.
A Topographical Dictionary of Wales 1833, Samuel Lewis, London, 1833: available through the National Library of Wales website.

THE PHOTOGRAPHS

THE AUTHOR

Tony Curtis is Emeritus Professor of Poetry at the University of Glamorgan where he introduced Creative Writing in 1981; he ran this discipline as both an undergraduate and post-graduate subject for nearly thirty years. He was born in Carmarthen in 1946 and moved with his parents to Pembrokeshire in 1960. His grandmother's family had farmed in the county for generations and he had been visiting them through his childhood. He played rugby for Pembrokeshire Schoolboys and golf at Tenby before leaving for Swansea University. He and his family have taken over his mother's house in Lydstep and they stay there frequently.

He has written and edited over thirty books, including The Poetry of Pembrokeshire and has won a number of literary prizes, including a Gregory Award, The Cholmondeley Award, the Dylan Thomas Prize and the National Poetry Prize. He was elected as a Fellow of the Royal Literary Society in 2001 and was awarded a D.Litt. from the University of Glamorgan in 2004. His nine collections of poetry all include poems based in Pembrokeshire which deal with its landscape, characters and history. Tonycurtispoet.com

***

This book would not have been possible without the support of all those who were prepared to talk to me and share with me their Pembrokeshire; they are the substance of this book. Margaret, as always, has been the sharer of my journeys, my first reader.

This book is dedicated to those generations of Barrahs and Thomases, who are our roots in Pembrokeshire; to my parents Leslie and Doris Curtis, to Jim John and Reg Smyth who came most of the way and to our friends in Lydstep and Tenby who make every visit a homecoming. Also, to Gareth, Madeleine and Huw, Bronwen, Jon, Megan and Ellis, all of whom are growing to love the county as we do.

INDEX